TALMUD AND APOCRYPHA

A COMPARATIVE STUDY OF THE JEWISH ETHICAL TEACHING IN THE RABBINICAL AND NON-RABBINICAL SOURCES IN THE EARLY CENTURIES

BY

R. TRAVERS HERFORD, B.A., D.D.

Author of CHRISTIANITY IN TALMUD AND MIDRASH · PHARISAISM, ITS AIM AND ITS METHOD · THE PHARISEES · JUDAISM IN THE NEW TESTAMENT PERIOD · *Editor of* PIRKE ABOTH · *Contributor to* THE LEGACY OF ISRAEL ETC., ETC., ETC.

TALMUD AND APOCRYPHA

A COMPARATIVE STUDY OF THE JEWISH ETHICAL TEACHING IN THE RABBINICAL AND NON-RABBINICAL SOURCES IN THE EARLY CENTURIES

BY

R. TRAVERS HERFORD, B.A., D.D.

Author of CHRISTIANITY IN TALMUD AND MIDRASH · PHARISAISM, ITS AIM AND ITS METHOD · THE PHARISEES · JUDAISM IN THE NEW TESTAMENT PERIOD · *Editor of* PIRKE ABOTH · *Contributor to* THE LEGACY OF ISRAEL ETC., ETC., ETC.

KTAV PUBLISHING HOUSE, Inc.

NEW YORK

1971

FIRST PUBLISHED 1933.

SBN 87068-158-3

MANUFACTURED IN THE UNITED STATES OF AMERICA
LIBRARY OF CONGRESS CATALOG CARD NO. 72-150532

TABLE OF CONTENTS

BOOK I

BOOK II

THE DEVELOPMENT ALONG THE RABBINICAL LINE

TABLE OF CONTENTS

BOOK III
THE NON-RABBINICAL LITERATURE

DIVISION I—THE APOCRYPHA AND PSEUDEPIGRAPHA

DIVISION II—THE NEW TESTAMENT AND PHILO

TALMUD AND APOCRYPHA

A COMPARATIVE STUDY OF THE JEWISH ETHICAL TEACHING IN THE RABBINICAL AND NON-RABBINICAL SOURCES IN THE EARLY CENTURIES

BY

R. TRAVERS HERFORD, B.A., D.D.

Author of CHRISTIANITY IN TALMUD AND MIDRASH · PHARISAISM, ITS AIM AND ITS METHOD · THE PHARISEES · JUDAISM IN THE NEW TESTAMENT PERIOD · *Editor of* PIRKE ABOTH · *Contributor to* THE LEGACY OF ISRAEL ETC., ETC., ETC.

THE JEWISH ETHICAL TEACHING IN THE EARLY CENTURIES

Book I

Chapter I

INTRODUCTION

A DISTINGUISHED Jewish writer has laid stress on the fact that Judaism, as a body of thought, belief, and practice, is by no means simple, by no means uniform in its various representatives, that there are, in short, ' many Judaisms '. Certainly there are many different types of what is nevertheless rightly called Judaism; and if that name be, as it usually is, especially reserved for the religion of those who returned from the Captivity, and their descendants, then the pre-exilic religion is one more type, or even an assemblage of several types, of the religion of the people of Israel. From the far distant past the line can be traced, in the Old Testament Scriptures, of a continuous development of the Hebrew religious consciousness; and that literature contains the expression of many different aspects of Hebrew thought and belief. If the survey be extended so as to include not merely the literature of the Old Testament, but also the Apocrypha and Pseudepigrapha, together with the Talmud and the Midrash, one common characteristic is to be found in all the different types whose thoughts are expressed in those often widely dissimilar writings. It is true of them all to say that they draw no distinction between religion and morality, such as a philosopher would draw. And this is by no means a merely negative characteristic; it shows that to the early Hebrew, and no less to the later Jewish, mind religion was the right conduct of life in communion with and in the service of God. The whole of the literature above referred to contains teaching directed to the right conduct of life, and that teaching is always given as religious, not merely ethical. It is not that such teaching forms the whole contents of the literature in question; there are in it many and various elements which deal with other aspects of thought and belief and practice. The range of topics included in the several books extends from the early folk-lore of Genesis to the visions of Apocalyptic and

B

the minutiae of the Halachah, from the poetry of the Psalmists
and the winged words of the Prophets to the severity of the
Mishnah, and the secret lore of the Kabbalah. Some of these
various elements are present in one book or class of writings and
absent from others. But the element of combined religious and
ethical teaching runs through them all, more prominent in
some, less conspicuous in others, but never wholly absent. It
is this, called for convenience throughout the present book
Ethical Teaching, which will form the object of our study.
And, more particularly, the period over which that study will
be extended is one in which there is a very wide and clearly
marked difference in the literature which contains it. The
period chosen is that which begins with the return from the
Captivity, when the name Judaism is first properly applied to
the religion of Israel, and comes down at least so far as to
include the rise of Christianity. There is indeed no natural end
to the development of Judaism, which has lasted till the present
day and still continues. But the period named includes the
various Apocryphal writings, also the teaching of the followers
of Ezra who eventually became the Rabbis, also the Gospels
which contain all that is known of the teaching of Jesus, and
finally the writings of Philo. Ethical teaching, as above defined,
is found in all these, though in other respects the contrasts are
very marked, and forms the connecting link between them all.
  Merely to collect from these various sources the ethical teaching which they contain, and to show the general likeness
between the different portions, would hardly be worth the
trouble, though no doubt interesting. It is not merely the
ethical teaching but the associated matter which gives its
peculiar character to the literature in which it is found. On the
one hand the writings forming the Apocrypha and Pseudepigrapha contain a considerable amount of Apocalyptic
matter along with the more specifically ethical. And on the
other hand, the Rabbinical teaching, at first oral and afterwards collected and written down in the Talmud and the
Midrash, falls into the two divisions of Halachah and Haggadah
(terms which will be explained below); and while the Haggadah
contains a large amount of ethical teaching, the contrast is
very marked between Halachah and Apocalyptic, even though
the Halachah is fundamentally ethical.

[2]

Here then are two great bodies of teaching, the Apocryphal (and Apocalyptic) and the Rabbinical, sharply contrasted while yet both had their ultimate source in the Old Testament, and both were developed side by side with apparently little, if any, contact of one with the other.

Scholars who have dealt with the Jewish literature of the period have not failed to notice the clear distinction between these two bodies of teaching, and have usually tended to exalt one by comparison with the other. Christian scholars have extolled the Apocryphal writings as being representative of the ancient free prophetic spirit, the ' true child of prophecy ', to use the words of the late Dr. Charles, who was in his time the foremost exponent of the Apocrypha. And they have contrasted it with the legalistic character of the Rabbinical teaching, which they apparently regard as the opposite of the prophetic spirit. Jewish scholars, on the other hand, have quite naturally placed a high value on the Rabbinical teaching, and paid but little attention to the Apocryphal literature. They have always maintained that the real essence of Judaism is expressed in the Rabbinical literature, and that the Apocryphal literature is by comparison of very small importance.

It is the purpose of this book to study the relation of both these literatures to each other, to show how, and if possible why, both were developed from one common source, although they followed lines which diverged so widely from each other. My aim is not to offer a final opinion upon the comparative merits of the two literatures, but to show them side by side, and in some degree to account for the differences between them, in order that the student who knows the Apocrypha may learn what was the real intention of the Rabbinical literature which he has been accustomed to regard as hard and narrow, and that the student of Rabbinics may learn wherein the real value of the Apocryphal literature consisted, at all events to its readers.

Both these literatures are undeniably products of Judaism and it is as such alone that they will be considered here. But part of the antagonism to which the study of these literatures has given rise is due to the fact that the Apocryphal literature has a much more direct bearing upon the rise of Christianity than could be claimed for the Rabbinical. Its study is therefore highly important for the light which it can throw upon Christian origins. It is true that Christian origins, and especially the teaching of Jesus, cannot be understood without a knowledge of the Rabbinical teaching; but it is beyond dispute that the spirit of the Apocryphal literature was much more in accordance with early Christian teaching than the spirit of the Rabbinical literature could be or ever was. Yet this, after all, is a side issue—or rather a minor issue—in the present connexion. Even supposing Christianity had never appeared at all, the Apocryphal literature would still be there, an indisputable product of Jewish writers, and therefore a proper object of study quite apart from any influence it might afterwards exert. It ought to be studied exclusively on its own merits, as being the form which certain Jewish writers chose to give to their thoughts concerning the matters on which they wrote.

The present work is intended to be a contribution to the study of the Judaism of the early centuries, of a kind differing from those of previous scholars in that it will seek to present side by side the two main types of teaching and to show each of them as being a natural development of the older teaching contained in the Old Testament Scriptures. For this purpose an account will be given of the teaching of the early Scribes who followed the lead of Ezra, which was finally written down in the Talmud and the cognate literature. This will be followed by a survey of the Apocryphal literature, not in such detail as to give a minute account of each book, but sufficiently full to allow of an estimate of its value as containing ethical and Apocalyptic teaching.

The Rabbinical literature will come first because, as oral teaching, it is older than the Apocryphal books, although the written form of it is later. It will be necessary to inquire into the purpose and method of this teaching and the means of its transmission, all the more because it is not contained in any contemporaneous literature. The part played by the oral teaching of the Scribes is seldom recognised, perhaps seldom known, by those who draw their conclusions mainly from the written and easily accessible documents of the Apocrypha and Pseudepigrapha. In this connexion the influence of the Synagogue is of very great importance; and this influence, also, is seldom if ever duly recognised by those who have written on the Judaism of the period with which this book is concerned. That the history of this period is often obscure, is a disadvantage which must be admitted; but, for the purpose of this book, that fact is of so much the less importance because what forms its subject matter is, on the one hand, a body of teaching whose main principles and chief contents are perfectly well known, and, on the other hand, a series of books actually written and extant. It may not be possible, for instance, to say precisely when and why the author of the Testaments of the Twelve Patriarchs wrote his book; but the book is there, and its contents can be studied by any one who will read. And so of all the others.

All the teaching, oral and written, which will come under review, dates from a time subsequent to the return from the Captivity; much of it, indeed, from a time when the Old Testament Canon was substantially complete. It will therefore be well to begin our study by a review of the Old Testament as the primary, if not the only, source of the later teaching to be found in the Jewish ethical literature.

Chapter II

THE OLD TESTAMENT AS THE MAIN SOURCE OF THE LATER ETHICAL TEACHING

THE Hebrew Scriptures are divided, in Jewish usage, into three groups known by the names of Torah, Nebiim, and Kethubim, usually translated the Law*, the Prophets, and the Hagiographa (literally the Writings). This threefold division appears as early as the Prologue to the book of Ben Sira (Sirach, Ecclesiasticus), whose date is usually placed at 132 B.C. or thereabouts. This does not imply that all the Writings, other than the Torah and the Prophetical books, which eventually formed the third division of Holy Scripture, were so regarded in the time of Ben Sira's grandson, or were even in existence. It merely shows that in his time there were *some* books which were so regarded. For the collection of the first two groups fairly probable and definite dates can be assigned. The Torah received its final form probably in or not long after the time of Ezra—say, about 400 B.C. The Prophetical books (including the historical books other than Chronicles) may have been collected and finally arranged, say, about 250 B.C. Whether there was ever a definite collection of the Hagiographa into a closed group, and, if so, when that was made, there is, so far as I am aware, no evidence to show. There was, certainly, in the Rabbinical schools of the first century A.D. a sort of recognition of the accomplished fact, after debate concerning one or two books (Song of Songs and Ecclesiastes), but nothing which could be described as a definite closing of the Canon of Scripture. The book of Ezekiel was the subject of discussion on the same occasion, but the Canon of the Prophets had long been closed, and there was no intention of reopening it. (See the Mishnah, Jad. iii. 5.)

* The word 'Torah' will be used throughout this book, untranslated. It does not, and never did, mean 'Law'. It means, and always has meant, 'Teaching'. But, as Torah is a word of fundamental importance in the study of Judaism, in any of the many phases of that religion, the convenient and also the only correct practice is to use always the word 'Torah', and never, except for special reasons duly explained, to render it by the word 'Law'.

[7]

When, therefore, it is said that the Hebrew Scriptures formed the main source of the later Jewish ethical teaching, it has to be borne in mind that its several component parts did not acquire their authority at one and the same time, and that it was not finally recognised as a complete body of Holy Scripture in its present form, until perhaps the beginning of the Christian era. But canonisation is one thing, existence of the several books is another. The Prophetical books, or the more or less fragmentary material which they now contain, were in existence before they were collected and canonised; much of that material obviously dates from before the Captivity, and was brought back with them by the returning exiles. Ezra must have been well acquainted with most of it. So, also, the traditional ascription of the Psalms to David and of Proverbs to Solomon makes it probable that some of the Psalms and some of the Proverbs were known at the time of the return. What we call the historical books (excluding Chronicles) must have been in existence at that time, substantially in their present form, known to the priests and the learned, though not (so far as appears) definitely canonised till long after the return. If this be true, then it follows that the later parts of the Hebrew Scriptures (whichever these may be) were written under the influence of the earlier parts, and drew from those earlier parts as their main source; they do not stand on the same footing of original authority, they are not so many independent sources of teaching, ethical or any other. It was only when the Canon of Scripture was finally recognised as closed that the same equal authority was ascribed to all its parts, and the complete body of sacred writings became the primary source of all the later teaching. And even when this stage was reached, the significance of the threefold division still remained. The Torah ranked above all the rest of Scripture in the veneration felt towards it, partly because of its greater age as being in common acceptance the Torah of Moses, and partly because, through the influence of Ezra and Nehemiah, the heads of the people in solemn assembly (Neh. viii-ix) had sworn to observe it. Whether Ezra had read (Neh. viii. 2) only the Priestly Code, and not the Pentateuch, matters little, because the allegiance which was sworn to what he did read was extended to the complete Pentateuch, as the Torah, when the final collection was made. In Jewish tradition,

[8]

the binding oath recorded in Neh. ix. 38 has always been held to apply to the Torah as a whole, without the remotest suggestion that it had ever been restricted to one part only. Of course, Jewish tradition knew nothing of the modern theory of the composite structure of the Pentateuch.

(A) THE TORAH

First and foremost, then, in the Hebrew Scriptures the Torah stands as the primary though not the only source of the later Jewish ethical teaching, as indeed it was the primary though not the only source of everything else in the Judaism of post-biblical times. The name Torah was applied in the first instance to the teaching contained in the Five Books ascribed to Moses, and the books themselves when collected and canonised were naturally known by that name. The meaning of the word Torah was greatly extended in later times, as will be shown when we come to deal with the development of Judaism along the line of the Scribes, the Pharisees, and the Rabbis; but it did not lose and has never lost its primary connexion with the Pentateuch, even down to the present day.

The Torah, as a body of Scripture, served as a source, and even the main source, of ethical teaching because it contained what had been handed down from the far distant past as being the most precious treasure of Israel. Whether Moses himself had written it all, or whether it had grown to its final form only by successive stages and through the labours of many men, it still embodied the most sacred record of what had been done, thought, believed, and lived for in the centuries of Israel's past. Though the record closed with the death of Moses, that only served to enhance the veneration which was felt towards it, and does not alter the fact that the Torah as a whole, when it was finally canonised, was regarded as the embodiment of what Israel, or rather Judaism, then stood for. If it had been felt to be out of keeping with the religious ideas of Ezra and his contemporaries, there was no reason why they should have pledged themselves to accept it, as they so enthusiastically did.

The Torah, as a written document, is not laid out on the lines of a text-book, whether of ethical teaching or of anything else. It contains a great variety of matter, all of which could be made the subject of study but none of which is treated in the

[9]

manner that would be required for such study. The main line of the story, so to speak, is the origin and rise of the people of Israel, from the creation of the world to the death of Moses. The main thought, to which all leads up, is that Moses received from God and delivered to Israel the revelation which henceforth was to set Israel apart from all the other nations of the world. The divine teaching, Torah, then given to Moses was contained partly in the positive and negative commands—' thou shalt ' and ' thou shalt not '—but also in everything else which the Pentateuch contains, as being that which God ordered him to write down. Some of it, e.g. the story of creation, was imparted to him as being beyond the range of his own knowledge. Some of it, which might not seem to be of any special importance, he wrote because God thought fit that it should go into the record. Something like this was the way in which the Torah was regarded by those who first possessed it as a whole. What they had was all divine teaching; and they had to make out for themselves what it taught, upon this subject or upon that, as occasion might require.

In regard to ethical teaching the Torah contained that in abundance, both in direct precepts and in the indirect form of narrative, song, or legend. A modern reader is well aware of the fact that the contents of the Torah represent very different ethical levels, and he explains this by saying that the ethical consciousness of Israel developed towards an ever higher ideal from a comparatively low beginning. But an ancient reader, in the time of Ezra let us say (and for long afterwards), had no such idea. To him what was written in the Torah was there because God willed that it should be there. It was all equally sacred, and, so far as it was precept, was all equally binding. Nevertheless, in practice, the lower ethical elements, as they may be called, did not carry the same weight as did the higher. The ethical consciousness of Israel did rise in the course of centuries, as is shown by the whole of the Old Testament; and those who led the way in the upward march of Judaism to the great height which it attained, laid little or no stress on the ethics of the earlier time which they had outgrown. Doubtless God, in his wisdom, had taught these things, but he had taught other and greater and higher things, and it was these greater things which contained the essence of his revelation. Among these 'greater things' the Ten Commandments stand pre-eminent, as laying down for all time the foundation of the Jewish ethical teaching. They exactly illustrate what in the Jewish mind ethics has always meant, viz. the right conduct of life as a true service of God. They are in the form of divine commands indicating what shall and what shall not be done by those who would serve God aright—in the first instance, 'the people whom he had chosen for his own inheritance'. The occasion on which they were proclaimed, the giving of the Torah on Sinai, is described in such a way as to impress the mind of the reader with a deep and lasting sense of the tremendous importance of what was then done; and that impression has never been effaced from the Jewish mind through all succeeding centuries. In the Ten Commandments is implied the relation of the worshipper to God, and also some of the main lines of man's true relation to his fellow man—not specifically Jewish, but universal.

Along with the Ten Commandments must be mentioned the great declaration (Deut. vi. 4-7), 'Hear, O Israel, the Lord our God, the Lord is one; and thou shalt love the Lord thy God with all thine heart and with all thy soul and with all thy might', etc. That passage, known from its first word as the Shema, sounds the keynote of all Judaism, and has been its watchword through all the centuries of its existence. It is contained in Deuteronomy, and that book in its ethical teaching may be said to amplify the central thought of the Shema.

The Ten Commandments and the Shema are singled out for special mention because they are fundamental in Judaism as perhaps nothing else has been which is found in the Torah, unless it be the great text, Lev. xix. 2, 'Ye shall be holy, for I the Lord your God am holy'.

But there is no need to collect and classify all the ethical teaching therein contained. The point at present is this, that the Torah, as a whole, served as a primary source of ethical teaching because it contained such teaching in abundance, venerable through age and invested with divine authority; and that since some of its contents were ethically higher than others, though in theory all were equally divine, the advancing ethical consciousness of those who developed Judaism laid the

chief stress on the higher elements. The Torah, as the primary
source of ethical teaching, offered all that it contained to all
who studied it, and they naturally drew from it that to which
their own ethical consciousness responded.

(B) THE PROPHETICAL BOOKS (Nebiim)

In Jewish usage the Prophetical books included those bearing
the names of Joshua, Judges, Samuel, and Kings, along with
those ascribed to some prophet by name. The reason for this
inclusion, which at first sight seems rather arbitrary, was
perhaps the fact that the historical books were valued not as
history pure and simple, but as history recorded from the
ethical, i.e. the prophetical, point of view. In the form in
which they have come down they show on every page the
marks of editorial approval or disapproval, according to the
standard of a time much later than that of the events recorded.
And the standard is that of men who had learned from the
great prophets and had studied Deuteronomy. If the history
contained in these books had been treated simply as history,
the record would have been very different. As it was treated,
the object in view was to show the history as a record of the
divine dealings with Israel and Israel's response thereto. In
a word, the history was told from the prophetic point of view
by men who, if not themselves prophets, were entirely at one
with the prophets in their outlook and their ideals. If this had
not been the case, it is open to question whether any record of
the history of Israel would have survived. When, therefore, the
time came at which it was felt to be desirable to collect together
all the Prophetical writings, it was a true instinct which led
the men responsible for that collection to include in it the books
Joshua—Kings, and to call them as they did the Earlier
Prophets* (Nebiim ha-rishonim).

The date when the collection of the Prophetical books was
made was certainly much later than that of the final completion
of the Torah. Apart from slight editorial touches, the Torah had
acquired substantially its present form by about 400 B.C. The

---

* This is the usual title in the Hebrew Bible. Whether the name is as early
as the collection of the Prophetical writings and was used by the collectors,
I do not know. But the name clearly indicates what was felt to be the real
reason for the inclusion of the books in question.

Prophetical books may have been collected perhaps about 250 B.C. The questions arise, why were they collected at all? And, if collected, why not at the same time as the Torah? Perhaps the first question is needless. So great a body of religious teaching, much of it the work of men who had stood in the very front rank of Israel's leaders, could not be ignored or neglected. It was teaching by men who had spoken by direct divine commission, who said that the word of the Lord had come to them personally—'Thus saith the Lord'. Those who had so spoken, or written, had had a powerful influence in shaping the course of their people's history; and, whether or not in their own time they had been listened to, their words remained as the guide of Israel's aspirations and the rebuke of his sins. The lesson which they taught, mostly before the Exile (though not wholly), was driven home by that severe discipline into the minds of those who had the deepest concern for the future of Israel as bound to the service of God. Men like Ezekiel, himself a prophet and an exile, had begun to learn that lesson; and Ezra, with those who followed his lead, took the first decisive steps towards putting in practice what that lesson had taught. When the Torah was completed and canonised, by Ezra or under his influence, the abundant witness of the Prophets was his strongest support, because he intended, by means of the Torah, to secure that actual personal service of God, in all the acts of a righteous and holy life, which the Prophets had urged upon an unheeding people. By the labours of Ezra the Torah was established as the supreme authority for the Jewish people, the record of the full and complete revelation which God had made to Moses, and by him delivered to Israel. There could be no question of setting up, alongside of the Torah, another and, in some sense, a rival body of Scripture. The Prophets were on any computation comparatively recent; Moses belonged to the far-off past, and the Torah attributed to him had a prestige which no writing of more recent days could emulate. The desirability of making a final collection of the Prophetical books would only then begin to be felt when the fact came to be recognised that prophecy had ceased, ' there is no more any prophet'. And that fact would only become apparent by lapse of time, as men noticed how long it was since any prophet, even a very minor one, had appeared.

[13]

It was then possible to survey the whole body of Prophetical literature as it had come down, and give to it its final form. Some of it needed but little arrangement, being in the form of a book by a known author. But much of it was composite, the work of the original author having been enlarged by subsequent additions, made through a long period of time, as can be seen in the books bearing the names of Isaiah and Jeremiah. No doubt most of this work of enlargement had been already done before the final collection was made, and what then remained to do was to set the mark of approval, so to speak, upon the entire collection as a whole.

When this was done the Prophetical books were thereby recognised as a body of Holy Scripture; but it does not follow, and it was not to be expected, that this second collection was placed on an equal level with the Torah. That was never done in Jewish tradition. When once the Torah had been made the supreme authority, there obviously could not be a second supreme authority beside it. The Prophets had their own place, as messengers of the divine will, and revealers of his nature; and those who exalted the Torah were the very last who would depreciate the Prophets. But what they chiefly regarded in the Prophets was the teaching they gave, and not the 'great freedom of speech' which they used in giving it. The contrast between the prophetic freedom and the constraint of the Torah, is one which does not appear to have been present to the minds of the men who set up the Canon of the Prophets and gave it a second place only beside the Torah.

As a source for the later ethical teaching of Judaism, the Prophetical literature is rich and abundant. Whatever else the Prophets were, they were witnesses for righteousness and denouncers of sin in a people who ought to have served God as a holy people: 'Ye shall be holy for I am holy'. And full use was made of the Prophetical books in the development of the later ethical teaching. But they contained also an element which became of very great importance long after the Canon of the Prophets was closed, and which gave rise to the whole body of Apocalyptic literature. This is only noted here, and will be discussed at length when we come to deal with the Apocalyptic books. It could not be left without mention in any estimate of the Prophetical literature as a source of later teaching. There is no need to survey all the contents of the Prophetical books from the ethical point of view. The close connexion of the later teaching with the earlier will be seen when we come to discuss that later teaching.

(c) THE HAGIOGRAPHA (Kethubim)

In this division are included all the remaining books of the Canon, of whatever kind they might be. There is amongst them no such unity of form and contents as in the case of the Torah and the Prophetical books. The former was all Torah from beginning to end, and the latter were all Prophetical, or regarded as such. It was therefore a comparatively simple matter to collect and edit them. But nothing of that kind was possible in regard to other writings which for one reason or another might be deemed worthy to be regarded as Holy Scripture. Indeed, until the collection had been finally made and approved, whenever and however that came about, it was not possible to speak of *the* other books. All that could be said was that there were *some* other books. When we go through the list of those which now form the third division, the Writings, we see that they show great variety in their contents and in the probable date of their composition. First in importance is the Book of Psalms, then the books usually by modern scholars grouped as the Wisdom books, Proverbs, Job, Ecclesiastes; then the group known in Jewish usage as the five Megilloth, Ruth, Lamentations, Canticles, Esther (and Ecclesiastes); then Daniel; then the Historical books, Ezra, Nehemiah, Chronicles. There is no unity amongst these, either of time or purpose, which would serve as the reason for including, say, Esther, Job, and Daniel in one collection. All that can be said with safety is that after the Canon of the Prophets was closed, there were some books in existence, and other books appeared later, which, on various grounds (nowhere specified), were thought to be of special religious value, and therefore worthy to be placed in a class apart. There must have been a time when a line was drawn— or, rather, was admitted to have been drawn—between those which were recognised as being in that class and those which were not. Ecclesiastes was included and Ben Sira was left out; but Daniel was younger than both of them, and that book was included. That there was ever a deliberate choice and collection

[15]

made of the books now known as the Hagiographa has not been shown. More probably, those who were responsible for the final arrangement of the third division of the Canon were confronted with the fact that some books had already an established position and could not be left out, whether in themselves suitable or not. It would be interesting to know precisely why Esther, Canticles, and Ecclesiastes were admitted, or rather allowed to remain, in a collection which included Job and the Psalms, and were thereby ranked as Holy Scripture along with the Torah and the Prophets. When this position had been finally attained, the whole body of Scripture served as the source of later ethical teaching; but, even before that time, the line of development of that teaching was being marked by some of the writings which came eventually to form the third division. The Psalms may be said to represent on the whole the influence of the Prophets in poetical forms. The Wisdom books, though not wholly independent of the Prophets, indicate a source quite other than the Prophetic teaching. Indeed, it would hardly be known, from a study of Job and especially Ecclesiastes, that there had ever been any Prophets. The historical work now separated into the books of Ezra, Nehemiah, and Chronicles shows, in its whole structure and purpose, the influence of Torah as the accepted religious authority. Of the five Megilloth, Lamentations is evidently prophetical; Ruth, Canticles, and Esther probably owed their inclusion in the Canon to their popularity, whatever the reason for that may have been in each case. And the same may be true of Daniel, appearing as it did just at the outbreak of the Maccabean Revolt. With its appeal to the heroic spirit in defence of the ancient religion, and its new note of Apocalyptic promise, it must have been, if the phrase be allowed, the book of the year, and may well have been given a place in the Canon by reason of the impression which it made. And Daniel was clearly a result directly of the Torah, and no less directly of the Prophets, while striking out a new line of development. Such then, in general, was the material finally collected in the third division of the Canon, and thereby made to form part of the scriptural source of the later teaching, ethical and other. What further seems needful to be said will follow under the heads of the several books.

(1) THE PSALMS

The Book of Psalms contains, as may be reasonably supposed, all the devotional poetry extant when the final collection was made; certainly all that was deemed worthy of a place in the Canon. The collection must have been completed at a comparatively late date, if it includes Maccabean Psalms. But the problem of assigning dates to individual Psalms is so far insoluble that no general agreement has been reached; and even in regard to groups of Psalms forming the various minor collections in the whole book, only the most general conclusions have any weight. Arguments based on differences of language, style, and thought are of very little value even for fixing the date of the group, let alone of the particular Psalm. Because the collector of a group would naturally include in it pieces of varying age and character, for reasons which satisfied himself. And a poet writing in one age might quite well reproduce the style and thought of an earlier poet. It is safe to say that Ps. xix. 7-14 and Ps. cxix could not have been written before the Torah had been made supreme by Ezra; but they may belong to a time when the Pharisees were becoming a distinct spiritual force. Ps. cxxxvii appears to have been written by a poet in exile, out of his own experience; but it could quite well have been written by a much later poet putting himself in the place of one of the captives in Babylon. The Psalms contain no single historical allusion which can be relied on with certainty as shown by any general agreement. Any number of plausible, and some brilliant, suggestions have been made. Perhaps some of them have hit on the truth, but there is, so far, no means of proving their success in doing so.

And yet the Psalms can hardly be left, so to speak, floating in the air without any apparent connexion with the history of the people in whose midst they were written. They are traditionally ascribed to David, but the number of those which could on any reasonable possibility be made to fit in with the circumstances of the life of David, his character and the range of his thought, is extremely small. There may be Psalms of David, but there is no agreement as to which they are. On the other hand, the so-called Psalms of Solomon, written in or about the middle of the last century B.C., were not included in the Psalter, though apparently quite as suitable as some that are. By that time, and perhaps considerably earlier, the Book of Psalms was closed. The titles attached to many of the Psalms are by all scholars regarded as historically worthless as indications of authorship. But they are by no means worthless if taken as indications of the source from which the several Psalms were drawn. The most promising starting-point for the inquiry into the origin of the Psalter is the evidence of the Book of Chronicles. As every scholar knows, the Chronicler reproduces in his narrative the ideas and institutions of his own time, which was perhaps the beginning or middle of the third century B.C. He ascribes to David and his ' chief musicians ' the musical arrangements of the Temple, which only means that Psalms were sung in the Temple in the time of the Chronicler, and that he assumed without hesitation that so it must have been in David's time. He makes David sing (1 Chron. xvi. 8-36) a Psalm which is put together from portions of three Psalms now in the Psalter; which would seem to show that in the Chronicler's time the whole Psalter was regarded as the work of David. Otherwise, the hymn sung by David on the occasion just mentioned would surely have been taken from one of those attributed to David in their title. When a Psalm has a title such as ' For the Chief Musician, after the manner of Jeduthun. A Psalm of David' (Ps. lxii), the word 'for' and the word 'of' are the same in Hebrew, viz. *le*. If it implies that David composed the Psalm, it equally implies that the chief musician composed it, which seems impossible. Now Jeduthun, Asaph, and Heman are mentioned by the Chronicler (1 Chron. xv. 19) as among the chief leaders of the singers, and were presumably heads of guilds entrusted with the Temple music, whether or not they were themselves living in the Chronicler's time. The assumption lies ready to hand that each of these Temple guilds had its own collection of Psalms, and that when a Psalm is described as being ' for ' or ' of ' (*le*) so and so, the meaning is only that it was from a collection associated with that name. The chief musician might well have had his collection, and analogy would suggest that there was a collection of Psalms attributed to David. We thus get to the probable existence of several collections of Psalms in use when the final arrangement of the Psalter was made. But it is evident that any one collection may have contained pieces of very different age and on very different

[18]

subjects, and no conclusion can safely be drawn from the contents of any one Psalm as to its age or authorship except within very wide limits. It is quite possible that somewhere in the Psalter are Psalms which David actually composed. It is no less possible that much later Psalms were attributed to him. The only facts that clearly emerge from the study of the origin of the Psalter seem to the present writer to be that the final selection was made at a time when the Temple singing was a long established and highly organised institution, that there was, in the possession of those responsible for the singing, a mass of material consisting of Psalms, or portions of Psalms, of various ages, and that it is now beyond the power of any criticism to sort these out chronologically.

Considered as a source of Ethical Teaching the Psalter is richer in such material than might perhaps be expected. A Psalm is primarily a religious lyric, whose main object is to express emotion rather than to teach morality. The emotion is awakened in the mind of the Psalmist by the thought of his relation to God, and part of that relation is the service which he owes to God. There is room, therefore, for reflections on the conditions of that service, the frame of mind, the disposition of heart, the qualities and virtues appropriate to such service. Such Psalms as Ps. xv, xxiv. 4, 5, xxxiv. 11-15, and especially the two Torah Psalms xix. 7-14 and cxix were evidently written from this point of view. And it is a natural step from the portrayal of the ‘ righteous ’, the man who serves God and is approved by him, to the portrayal of the ‘ wicked ’, the man who in every particular is displeasing to God. Both descriptions, as is natural in lyric verse, are charged with emotion; and the emotion aroused in the poet’s mind by the thought of the wicked passes at times into violent hatred, expressed in the most open manner, as in Ps. cxxxix. 21, 22, and practically the whole of Ps. cix. When the Psalter, as part of Holy Scripture, served as a source of later Ethical Teaching, this element played its part along with the nobler emotions, and left its traces in some of the later literature. If the fierce passion expressed in some of the Apocalyptic books needed a sanction from Scripture, the Psalter could provide what was wanted. To modern readers this element is the least worthy among all that the Psalter contains, but considering it from the point of view of the influence which the Psalter exercised upon later Jewish thought and teaching, it cannot be overlooked. The explanation of its presence in the Jewish mind and its expression in the Psalter, is a problem of psychology and does not concern us here.

(2) THE PROVERBS

The book bearing this title belongs to a class of which no representative has as yet been examined. The other books usually reckoned along with it are Job and Ecclesiastes, and the three are grouped together under the head of the Wisdom literature, on account of the great stress laid upon wisdom, its excellence and the duty of acquiring it. This is especially the case with Proverbs, but may fairly be extended to the other two books. In Proverbs the whole book deals with wisdom under one or another of its aspects. In Job the main subject is a theological problem, while wisdom is a side issue; and in Ecclesiastes the author seems to be more interested in cynical pessimism as a form of wisdom than in wisdom as such. More will be said in regard to Job and Ecclesiastes when we come to deal separately with those books. In regard to the book of Proverbs, the question at once arises why was it included in the Canon of Scripture? And why was it placed in the third division?

The question why Proverbs was included in the Canon at all is suggested by the fact that there is hardly anything in its contents which is specifically Jewish. The same is true of Job and Ecclesiastes, and may thus be called a characteristic of the Wisdom literature as a whole. There is no obvious connexion —perhaps no connexion at all—between the three canonical representatives of that literature and either Torah or Prophecy. The Wisdom literature would seem to be an independent growth. Of the three examples (the only three in the Canon of Scripture), Proverbs alone affords any indication of the existence of what might be called a school of writers; and the most that can be said of Proverbs is that it is evidently made up of collections from different sources. That Solomon was the author of the whole is impossible, and rests upon nothing more than the assertion (1 Kings iv. 32) that Solomon 'spake three thousand proverbs'. Whether any of these is now included in the canonical book there are no means of deciding. The whole tone of the book is very unlike what might be expected in a work by Solomon. But, apart from the general tone of the book, there is hardly any indication which would point to the age, let alone the authorship, of the several aphorisms which it contains. As in the case of the Psalms, but with more evident truth, pieces of very different age may have been included in one collection, and we cannot tell what reason induced the collector to include one and exclude another, nor why he arranged them in the order in which they now stand. A late writer, or collector, might imitate the thought and style of an earlier time for reasons of his own. To speak of interpolations, as some critics do, seems only to show that the critic, if he had himself written the book or made the collection, would have arranged the contents differently. Possibly the intention of the writer or collector is not now represented by the existing text; but it is impossible to prove that this is the case, still less that he *must* have written so-and-so. Hardly more can be said of the origin of Proverbs than that it contains aphorisms of unknown date and authorship, presumably gathered through many years by men whose mental activity ran on other lines than those of Torah or Prophecy. Even this is perhaps too much to say, because in the later Judaism the collection and construction of aphorisms was associated with the most zealous devotion to Torah. The tractate of the Mishnah known as Aboth (*Pirké Aboth*) is the most conspicuous instance of this fact. Proverbs differs widely from Aboth, and yet the existence of the later book and the veneration which has always been felt towards it may help to explain the inclusion of Proverbs in the Canon of Scripture. For the central thought of Proverbs is wisdom, and the central thought, not only of Aboth but of the Talmudic literature generally, is also wisdom, expressed in terms of Torah and summed up in the phrase ' The fear of the Lord is the beginning of wisdom . . .'. This occurs in Proverbs ix. 10, and may not have meant the same to the author of the aphorism in Proverbs as it meant to the Talmudic Rabbis. Now, not only the teachers who created the Mishnah, but their forerunners at least as early as the second century B.C. called themselves and each other by the name of the Wise. This is shown in Aboth i. 4, in the saying of José b. Joezer of Zeredah: ' Let thy house be a place of meeting for the Wise ', etc. This teacher was living *c.* 200–160 B.C. (See my *Pirké Aboth,* p. 25.) He used the term as a familiar expression needing no explanation. Those who thus called themselves, and were called, the Wise were the men who followed the lead of Ezra and became the early Sopherim (Scribes); and it was they who finally collected and arranged the Scriptures of the Hebrew Canon. When therefore a body of men, engaged on that task, found, in the literature with which they had to deal, a collection, or several collections, of aphorisms by Wise men of an older time they would have a natural inducement to include these in the Canon, even though the contents of those collections were not markedly Jewish. The natural inducement would be the fact that the subject matter was wisdom, to whose appeal no one claiming to be Wise could be indifferent. In this way I believe is most easily to be explained the fact of the inclusion of Proverbs and the other Wisdom books in the Canon.

That they should be placed in the third group follows at once from the fact that the Canon of Torah and that of the Prophets were already closed; and even if they had not been, the Wisdom books could not possibly be considered as Torah or Prophecy. There was no other place for them than the miscellaneous group whose members were gradually receiving canonical recognition. There is nothing to show when Proverbs was finally edited and canonised; but it can hardly have been earlier than 200 B.C., and may well have been much later.

The Wisdom literature, as a part of the Canon, served very naturally as a source of the later Ethical Teaching, being itself a compendium of such teaching. Yet it is perhaps of more importance as the forerunner of the book of Ben Sira and of the Aboth, than as containing specific maxims which influenced later teachers. The note which is sounded in Proverbs was echoed in the two later books just named, and has never for long been silent in the Judaism of the succeeding centuries.

It will be convenient to add what seems needful about the other two representatives of the Wisdom literature which were admitted to the Canon, viz. Job and Ecclesiastes.

(3) JOB

When the term 'Wisdom literature' is used, it should be borne in mind that it is only a modern epithet applied to the three canonical books already named. It does not imply that there was a school of thought or a body of writers whose activity extended over a considerable number of years, and of whose works the three books in question are now the only survivors. The collection, and perhaps the construction, of aphorisms was congenial to the Jewish mind, as it was to that of other Eastern peoples, and probably no age was entirely lacking in men whose tastes lay in that direction. But Job is far other than a collection of aphorisms; and to rank Job with Proverbs, as another product of a 'school' of Wisdom writers, is to be misled by a name. Job stands by itself, and its author was surely not the product of any ' school '. When the poem was written, and by whom, are questions upon which no agreement has been reached, or seems likely ever to be reached. It is one of the supreme creations of Hebrew genius, with no rival and no successor.

By its inclusion in the Canon, the poem of Job took its place as part of the collective source of the later ethical teaching. Why it was included cannot be decided with any certainty. For it is even less Jewish than Proverbs, and has no obvious connexion with either Torah or Prophecy. Moreover, though the subject is one of profound interest, and the treatment of it a direct challenge to a theory of retribution which had been almost universally held, it is by no means certain that the poem received the attention which it might be supposed would have been paid to it, if its greatness had been recognised. The patience of Job passed into a proverb (cp. Ep. Jac. v. 11), but nothing is said of the boldness which challenged the Almighty and disputed the justice of his ways. If those who finally arranged the Canon had felt themselves free to examine every book on its merits, or to judge it by the standard of what they themselves would consider essential in a book worthy to rank as Holy Scripture, it is conceivable that they would have rejected Job. But we may fairly suppose that they found this book already in the literature with which they had to deal, a book of unknown age, of which indeed Moses came to be suggested as the author (b. B. Bathr. 14*b*), and too important to be excluded. The undercurrent of reference to wisdom would provide sufficient ground for admitting a book which certainly did not deal with wisdom on conventional lines. Those who admitted

Job into the Canon may have had a becoming sense of the grandeur of the poem; but, in the influence which the poem exerted upon the later ethical teaching, a recognition of that grandeur is not conspicuous. From this point of view, it is the whole book as it is read now in the Hebrew text which is of importance. No account need be taken here of the various attempts to show that the poem is really a composite work, ranging from theories which exclude the Elihu speeches and the descriptions of Behemoth and Leviathan, to others which reduce the book to a mass of interpolations and accretions forced upon a barely intelligible text. Fortunately, those who were responsible for the formation of the Canon were not troubled by critical questions, and gave to posterity all the Job they knew, perhaps not fully recognising what they did.

(4) ECCLESIASTES (Koheleth)

If it is a matter of some surprise that Job was included in the Canon, the surprise is much greater in the case of the extraordinary book known as Ecclesiastes. Not only is there here, as in Job, hardly any specifically Jewish element, the whole tone of the book is alien from the fundamental optimism of Judaism in all its higher forms of expression. Even if the author were only the 'gentle cynic' which some have seen in him, he would be out of the main line, indeed out of any line of Judaism otherwise known. He stands by himself, as completely as the author of Job; and if that poem marks the highest point attained by Hebrew genius, it would be hard to find a writer who touched a lower level, in respect of the nobler qualities of the Jewish mind, than the author of Ecclesiastes. It is not for nothing that the motto of his book is 'Vanity of vanities, all is vanity'. There is no more perplexing, and even provoking, book in the Hebrew Scriptures, and generations of scholars have wrestled with the problems it presents. Even so early as the first century A.D. objection was taken to its inclusion in the Canon (see above, p. 7), and that objection was raised by men who followed in the succession of the earlier teachers who had arranged the Canon and included Ecclesiastes in it. The thing had been done, and was not likely to be undone; but there were at least some who wished that it had not been done.

Why was it done? How did it come about that this book, so

alien in its thought from the main principles of Judaism as expressed in Torah and Prophecy, to which may now be added the Psalms and Proverbs and Job, should be given a place along with them in the Canon? The book purports to be the work of Solomon, under the enigmatic name of Koheleth (i. 1), and the presumption lies ready to hand that the book was taken into the Canon as a genuine work of the wise king. This may have been the case; but, if it had been, it would hardly have been necessary for the author to explain that Koheleth was a wise man (xii. 9). Wisdom was part of the traditional character of Solomon, and the words in xii. 9 may well be the explanation by the author of his identification of Koheleth with Solomon.

That the book really was written by Solomon is not now maintained by any competent scholar. The thought and the language alike make such a view untenable. It is generally held to belong to a very late period in Jewish history, probably the Grecian period, although no precise date can be fixed. It had therefore no glamour of unknown antiquity to support its claim to inclusion in the Canon. When it first appeared, no doubt, the ascription to Solomon would provide some such glamour. And yet the so-called Psalms of Solomon were not admitted into the Canon, in spite of their name. The key to the riddle of Koheleth, at all events one of the riddles, is to be found probably in the Epilogue, xii. 9-14. Some scholars have held that the Epilogue is not by the writer of the rest of the book, but by an editor, and that his intention was to give a sort of certificate to justify the recognition of a book so unusual in its contents, and, in some of its teaching, so little in accord with the principles of Judaism. But the language of the Epilogue does not differ appreciably from that of the main body of the book, being marked by the same or similar harsh constructions and unusual words. An editor, especially if he were recommending the book for recognition, could have written better Hebrew, being presumably one of the later Sopherim. The present writer holds that the Epilogue was written by the same man who wrote the preceding chapters. Then why did he write the Epilogue? Why did he cease to use the first person—'I, Koheleth, was king ', etc.—and in xii. 9 begin to use the third person—'Moreover Koheleth was wise ', etc.? The meaning of this change would seem to be that the author, in the body of the book, presented the views of a man such as Koheleth describes himself to be, not as wholly agreeing with them (hence the occasional inconsistencies), but as containing much that was deserving of study. In other words he presented, in somewhat disjointed form, a series of reflections upon life from the point of view of a man who had had a bitter experience, in order to show the kind of wisdom which he had learned in the course of it. He gave to his lay-figure the name Koheleth, for reasons which have never been satisfactorily explained, and virtually identified him with Solomon. In this case, the book would be a work of imagination, in which the writer clothed his own thoughts in a slight and easily penetrable disguise. Yet, if he was only presenting his own thoughts, why should he add, in the Epilogue, what seems like a correction of some of his own statements, a readjustment of the balance which had been rather seriously disturbed in earlier passages of the book? Why should he not have written the whole so as to be consistent with itself?

An alternative possibility is that the writer had really found a body of teaching by some reputed wise man, and that he reproduced this in his own words not in those of the original sage; that he indicated this otherwise unknown teacher by the cryptic name Koheleth, with the hint that he was Solomon. This would account for the consistency of language throughout the book, including the Epilogue; and would also explain why, in the Epilogue, he thought it well to add a caution to the reader lest he should be misled by some of the things which his ' Koheleth ' had said. It is a further and very attractive variant of this theory that (as suggested by Margoliouth, J. Enc., *s.v.* Ecclesiastes) the work of the wise man in question was written not in Hebrew, but in some other language, and that the writer whose words form the Hebrew text translated the book of the foreign sage. This would, or might, account for some of the harsh phrases to be found in the Hebrew, the translator finding a difficulty in reproducing the words of his original or even in some cases failing to understand them. And this might throw some faint light on the name Koheleth. Instead of twisting doubtful meanings out of the word regarded as Hebrew, is it not possible that Koheleth represents the name of the teacher or the title of his book *in the original*; in other words, that it is some non-Hebrew name reproduced as nearly as might be in a Hebrew form?

The present writer inclines strongly to this last view. If it is correct, then the book which is now read as Koheleth was not in itself part of Jewish literature at all, not even of the Wisdom literature. It was brought into that literature by the (supposed) translator, who saw in it a very striking and remarkable work, which those who studied wisdom ought by no means to neglect. It was thus its close connexion with the pursuit of wisdom which probably brought it within the range of those who had already included in the Canon books of wisdom such as Proverbs and Job, and inclined them favourably towards Koheleth in spite of its very un-Jewish tone. For good or for evil Koheleth was included in the Canon, and thus was in a position to exert an influence upon later ethical teaching.

This brings us to the end of the Wisdom literature now included in the Canon. With one very notable exception, the remaining books so included are of only slight importance for the special purpose of the present book, viz. the development of the later Jewish ethical teaching from its main source in the Hebrew Scriptures. The remaining books, with the exception of Daniel, are Ruth, Esther, Lamentations, Canticles, Ezra, Nehemiah, Chronicles. The last three are historical. The first four (forming, along with Ecclesiastes the group called the five Megilloth) are miscellaneous pieces, interesting in themselves but not connected by any underlying unity, ethical or any other. They were included in the Canon presumably for reasons applying separately in each case, but which need not be discussed here. We turn, therefore, to the one book marked above as an exception, whose importance for the study of the later Jewish teaching cannot be denied, viz. the book of Daniel.

(5) DANIEL

According to the view now almost universally held, the book of Daniel belongs to the period of the Maccabean Revolt, or more particularly to the period of persecution immediately before the Revolt. It is thus one of the latest, perhaps the very latest, book in the Canon; and, while it is not possible to assign a definite date at which the Canon of the Hagiographa was closed, if it ever was intentionally closed, the fact remains that the book of Ben Sira, earlier than Daniel, was left out of the Canon although by its contents it might seem well deserving of inclusion. There must have been some strong reason for admitting Daniel.

The book bearing his name is marked off from all the other Canonical Scriptures by its form and contents. It contains history, but only in a series of vivid stories plainly intended to teach a definite lesson. It relates a series of visions in which the course of future events is disclosed or explained to Daniel; but the difference is very noticeable between the narration of these visions and the utterances of the Prophets in the older time. The book could not be classed with the Prophetical literature, if only because the Canon of the Prophets was closed; and the historical element, so far as it was history, was plainly regarded by the author as of less importance than the visionary element. The book is, of course, the first known instance of the Apocalyptic type of literature, of the books which convey their teaching through the medium of visions or oracles purporting to disclose the hidden future. Daniel is the first of many Apocalyptic works, some of which will be studied in later chapters of this book. If Daniel had not been included in the Canon, the Hebrew Scriptures would, in one very important respect, have failed to serve as the main source of the later Jewish ethical teaching. Daniel provides the link which connects the whole of the Apocalyptic literature with the Old Testament, and thus enables a real relationship and a common ancestry to be established for descendants so unlike each other as Halachah and Apocalypse. Daniel is itself a product of the already existing Canon. Not only do the stories in the earlier chapters bear witness to a time when the authority of the Torah was owned as supreme; the visions are clearly the result of studying the Prophets, as indeed the writer indicates (ix. 2). And the later Apocalyptic books could be traced back to the Prophetic writings in much the same way even if Daniel had not been written; but it would then have been less easy to show the relationship between the two divergent types of teaching mentioned above, which it is the main purpose of the present work to elucidate.

Daniel appeared at the time when Antiochus Epiphanes was

persecuting those of his Jewish subjects who would not abandon their Judaism in favour of his Hellenism. It was a time of severe trial and determined resistance, when passions were deeply stirred, and when courage was the courage almost of despair. The message of Daniel was that the end of oppression was near; men in olden times had defied a heathen tyrant; the most powerful kingdoms, the most cruel oppressors, had been proved helpless before the God of Israel; and so it would be in this last oppression. What the reception of Daniel actually was, on its first appearance, can only be guessed; but it can hardly be doubted that such a book at such a time would give a powerful encouragement to those who were in so desperate a strait, and it may even have been, as it were, the match which set fire to the train of revolt. A book which spoke so strongly to the hearts of the faithful among the people, and which answered so completely to their needs at that time could not be ignored or criticised, even if anyone had wished to do so. It won its place as Holy Scripture and its inclusion in the Canon not, we may suppose, by any definite decision on the part of those who were responsible for the Canon, but, so to speak, by acclamation. Nothing, of course, could be done at the moment. In the first stages of revolt no one was thinking about the definition of the Canon of Scripture. But afterwards, when victory had been achieved and the short period of prosperity under the Hasmonean princes had begun, no one could forget the message of Daniel or deny for a moment that the book of mysterious visions and stirring narratives was indeed Holy Scripture. However the actual facts may have been, it is certain that Daniel found and kept his place in the Canon from that time forth.

Daniel is the only avowedly Apocalyptic book in the Canon, and the question will come up for consideration in a later chapter: Why were the other Apocalyptic books amongst the Apocrypha and Pseudepigrapha excluded? These later books contain ethical teaching along with the Apocalyptic matter, in varying proportion, while Daniel contains no ethical teaching except what is implied in the narratives of the earlier chapters. The ethical teaching of the post-biblical period, which will form our main study, is mainly based on the Hebrew Scriptures, but the connexion is with other books than

Daniel. That serves to connect the Apocalyptic element in the later teaching with its source in the Old Testament.

We have now surveyed the Hebrew Scriptures considered as the main if not the sole source of the later teaching, and are in a position to study the various use which was made of those Scriptures by men who had at their disposal the Old Testament in its completed form. No attempt has been made to draw out from each book those especially ethical elements which it was able to supply. That will be more conveniently done when the various types of the later ethical teaching come under review. What has been secured so far is the starting-point for the development of that teaching along the diverging lines of Halachah and Apocalypse, with ethics as the element which they shared in common. To the study of that development we may now proceed.

Book II

THE DEVELOPMENT ALONG THE RABBINICAL LINE

CHAPTER I

EZRA

IF the teachers who produced the later ethical teaching had waited until they held in their hands the complete body of the Canonical Scriptures, the record of the centuries between the return from the Exile and the beginning of the Christian era would have been a blank page. As we have seen, the formation of the Canon was a gradual process; and the earlier portions were made use of for purposes of study and instruction long before the latest portions were added. Moreover, before that time was reached some writings were in existence which were never included in the Canon at all, viz. the earlier of those known as the Apocrypha and Pseudepigrapha. The study of the post-biblical ethical teaching must therefore begin at an earlier date than the closing of the Canon, and earlier than that of the oldest of the Apocryphal books. The book of Ben Sira is commonly dated at about 180 B.C., a date which is later by two centuries or more than that of the closing of the Canon of the Torah. Those two centuries were by no means empty in respect of ethical teaching, being indeed the period in which the principles were laid down which regulated the development of Judaism along the Rabbinical line. What Judaism became under the leadership of the Sopherim and the later Rabbis, was the result of what was done and taught in those two centuries, irrespective of what might or did come afterwards.

It is therefore of the greatest importance to ascertain so far as possible the course of development of Jewish teaching during those centuries, the ideas which underlay it, and the forms in which those ideas found expression; all the more because in the very scanty treatment usually deemed sufficient for the subject, the significance of those ideas and the meaning of those forms are seldom understood. And yet, for the real comprehension of Judaism in any of its later types, the knowledge of what was being taught and practised during those centuries is indispensable. Now the line of succession, so to speak, which comes down through the Sopherim and the Rabbis had its starting-point, beyond any question, in Ezra. And while it is not to be supposed, and is here certainly not suggested, that Ezra was the only man of his time who left his mark upon its thought, or that his contemporaries were unanimous in following the lead which he gave, yet no one else gave so strong a lead or had such an unbroken succession of followers who worked on his lines and developed his principles. Moreover, his work had for its direct result the ethical teaching which eventually found its literary expression in the Talmud and the Midrashim. That result was not, so to speak, a by-product of his main work; it was rather the indispensable complement of what was no doubt the more conspicuous element in that work. It is therefore strictly in accordance with the main purpose of the present book to inquire closely into the nature and significance of the work of Ezra, or, more simply, to find answers to the questions: Who was Ezra? and what did he really do?

If the existence of Ezra, as a historical personage, depended wholly on what is contained in the books bearing the names of Ezra and Nehemiah, there might be something to be said for the view put forward by destructive critics that he was nothing more than a creation of the Chronicler's inventive faculty. Such an assertion has indeed been made, by Torrey, in his Ezra studies, but it has not met with general acceptance. Less extreme critics have admitted, on the evidence of the Canonical books, that Ezra was a real person, and that he had something to do with that change in the character of the Jewish religion which took place at or about the close of the fifth century B.C. Some scholars have placed his date after that of Nehemiah, 445-4 B.C., separating the two men by well-nigh half a century. The changes have been rung on all the possibilities. Yet reading the existing books with careful attention, the present writer does not feel obliged to dissent from what has been the prevailing opinion, viz. that Ezra came up from Babylon in 457, on a mission to Jerusalem, and that he only succeeded in his purpose, whatever that was, when he received the powerful help of Nehemiah, who came as governor in 445, having been expressly appointed to that office by the Persian king. Together they carried out a reform, of which the most momentous incident was a solemn undertaking to walk according to the Torah, an undertaking made on behalf of the whole people by their leading men, who signed their names to the document containing the promise (Neh. x).

But the statements in the two Canonical books are not the only evidence for the real existence of Ezra. The Rabbinical tradition, though it evidently possessed very few details about him, regarded him as in some sense the second founder of Judaism. Thus it is said (b. Succ. 20a): 'For in the beginning, when Torah was forgotten of Israel, Ezra went up from Babel and founded it'. And again (b. Sanh. 21b): 'Ezra was worthy that the Torah should have been given through him to Israel, if it had not been that Moses preceded him'. Moreover, that the Rabbinic exaltation of Ezra was not based merely upon the Scriptural record is shown by the fact that several ordinances were attributed to him (b. B. Kamma 82b, cp. j. Meg. 75a), of which no trace is found in the Canonical books. Whether these ordinances were in fact issued by Ezra may be open to question; but there was no need to attribute them to him unless he had already taken an important place in the tradition. That there should have been a real tradition, orally transmitted and reaching back as far as Ezra, is in no way impossible.

Ezra, then, went up from Babylon upon a mission to Jerusalem, and he did so by royal warrant. At least, the book gives (Ez. vii. 11-26) the text of a sort of 'firman' purporting to be from the Persian king, whereby he was authorised to establish 'the law of thy God which is in thine hand' (ib. 15) and to 'appoint magistrates and judges which may judge all the people that are beyond the river, all such as know the laws of thy God; and teach ye him that knoweth them not. And whosoever will not do the law of thy God and the law of the king, let judgment be executed upon him with all diligence' (vv. 25-26). Meyer (*Ensteh. d. Judentums*, pp. 60-70) strongly maintains the authenticity of this document, and the present writer accepts his judgment. The object stated in the royal warrant to Ezra corresponds very closely with what Ezra actually, though not immediately, accomplished, viz. the establishment of the Torah as the constitution of the community in Judea. At the same time it may be allowed that Ezra perhaps did not contemplate that object from the same point of view as that of the Persian king; and, in any case, in what he did accomplish, he apparently made no use of the extensive authority conferred upon him, and succeeded by persuasion instead of by the very ample powers with which he was entrusted.

In the beginning of the chapter (Ezra vii), in which Ezra first appears, there is given a short summary of the purpose of his mission, not in the words of the royal warrant, but of the compiler of the memoirs of Ezra now incorporated, or excerpted, in the canonical book. We read (vii. 6): ' This Ezra went up from Babylon; and he was a ready scribe in the Torah of Moses which the Lord the God of Israel had given '; and (v. 10): ' For Ezra had set his heart to " interpret " the Torah of the Lord, and to do and to teach in Israel statute and judgment'. From these passages it is evident that in the opinion of the writer, whoever he was, the main purpose of Ezra had for its object the Torah, and more especially the task of making known its contents and teaching the statutes and judgments which formed a large part of those contents. The word usually translated ' seek ' (v. 10) is ' darash ' (*lidrosh*), and when applied to Torah it can only mean ' interpret ', in accordance with the common usage of the word in the later literature. To ' seek ' Torah makes no sense, if only because Ezra did not need to ' seek ' what was already ' in his hand ' (v. 15) and what he was taking with him to Jerusalem. To interpret the Torah was a necessary part of that process of teaching which he went there to begin. He is called a Sopher, and more particularly a ' ready ' Sopher, which implies that he had something to do with a book, in this case, of course, the book of the Torah, and that he was expert in his calling, whatever that was. Even supposing, which does not seem very likely, that his calling was merely to write copies of the book, that would still show that the book was his main concern. But it can hardly be supposed that the Persian king would choose a mere copying clerk for a mission which was of such importance as to need a royal warrant and the very extensive powers which were conferred in it. Ezra was quite evidently the agent for the establishment of the Torah, and the fitting agent because he was an expert in his knowledge of it. He had ' set his heart ' to expound it, and ' to do and to teach in Israel statute and judgment '.

This view of what Ezra set out to do and actually did, exactly

[34]

fits in with the subsequent development of Judaism by the labours of the Sopherim, which would otherwise be left without explanation. And it does not fit in with the usual view of Ezra's work, which is that his main concern was with the Temple and the priesthood. For that view it may be claimed that he is called ' priest ' as well as ' Sopher ', and that the book which he brought with him was either the Priestly Code or contained that as its only novelty. Assuming that it was only the Priestly Code, and therefore of special interest to the priesthood, still it was for the Temple staff to put it into operation. There was already a Temple and a High Priest and a staff of subordinates, and they were quite competent to do all that was necessary. Ezra, no doubt, was very desirous that the Temple and its whole system should be put on a proper footing, and the royal warrant made special mention of the house of God, the sacrifices to be offered, and ' whatsoever shall be needful for the house of thy God ' (v. 20). But all these things were covered by the establishment of the Torah; if that were made the controlling authority, the requirements of the Temple would be met along with many other matters for which the Torah gave directions. It is nowhere said that Ezra himself took any part in reorganis-ing the Temple system. It may indeed well be doubted whether the High Priest and his associates would have put up with the intrusion of an outsider, even though a priest, into the affairs of the Temple. It was quite another matter if Ezra merely pro-vided the opportunity and brought the necessary authority to carry out what the Priestly Code required. When Ezra had secured the ratification of the Torah by the solemn consent of the governor and the heads of the people (Neh. x), the priests could do all the rest, so far as the Temple system was concerned.

The view that Ezra's interest and activity were mainly con-cerned with the Temple and the priesthood seems to be based on the assumption that there was really nothing else for him to do, and that Judaism, in his time and down to the Christian era, was a religion whose whole meaning was summed up in Temple and priesthood. This is very far from being the case, as will be shown presently. No doubt the Temple, as long as it stood, was the most conspicuous institution connected with the Jewish religion—and it was held worthy of all the veneration and devotion which could be shown to it. Also, it was the only

[35]

institution which attracted the attention of Gentiles, so that it might well seem to be all that there really was in Judaism. But there were movements of thought in Judaism, all through the centuries from Ezra onwards, which were not primarily connected with the Temple, and which produced results such as the Temple never produced and was not in a position to produce. It is the omission to take account of this side of Judaism which, perhaps from ignorance of it, has led most scholars to regard the work of Ezra as having been restricted to the minor issue of the Temple and the priesthood. Judaism was no more and no less a priestly religion after his time than it had been before; and Judaism, since his time, was by no means an exclusively priestly religion, whatever it had been before. It may be a paradox, but there is a good deal of truth in the assertion that what saved Judaism from becoming a purely priestly religion was precisely the work of Ezra.

The Rabbinical saying about Ezra quoted above (p. 33), that when the Torah was forgotten Ezra went up from Babel and founded it, shows a true insight into the real significance of his work. The Torah had indeed been given by Moses, or rather given to Moses and by him declared to Israel. But Israel had not paid due heed to it, had indeed lived as though the Torah had never been given. This is what the saying means that ' the Torah was forgotten of Israel'. And the statement that the Torah was in this sense forgotten is the conclusion drawn from the lesson of the Exile. Before that national disaster there had been plenty of teaching, guidance, advice, warning, and threat, enough to have kept Israel walking in the right way, if only he had taken heed to obey. The Exile was a punishment for national transgression (see especially Ez. ix. 7), a punishment which the prophets had foreseen but which they were powerless to prevent. All their eloquence, all their lofty teaching, had fallen upon deaf ears, so far as the people in general were concerned, and nothing except the sharp lesson of the Exile could bring them to their senses.

Ezra, following the lead of Ezekiel, saw that what was needed for the future, if Israel was to have a future, was that the people must obey the teaching already divinely given, and obey it with a deliberate intention which they had never shown before. They must do so not merely as a community, but as individual members of that community. There was Torah in plenty, and Israel's first and supreme duty was to make that Torah for the future the guide of his life. To place the Torah in the position of supreme authority in Judaism, and to win the people to the recognition and acceptance of that supreme authority was what Ezra set out to do, and what to a considerable degree he actually did. Indeed, his object was fully attained, though not in his own time. The acceptance of the Torah was secured in the great assembly when the covenant was signed (Neh. x); but it was long before the authority then recognised in theory was unanimously accepted in practice. Nevertheless, Ezra had established the supremacy of the Torah *de jure*; and what he did was not undone, nor ever has been undone from that day to this. And this is what was meant in the Talmudic saying, already quoted, that Ezra 'founded' the Torah after it had been forgotten.

The acceptance of the Torah expressed in a covenant signed by all the heads of the people was not secured by Ezra until after the lapse of several years. According to the statement of the canonical books of Ezra and Nehemiah, there was an interval of some twelve or thirteen years between the arrival of Ezra in Jerusalem and that of Nehemiah as governor of the Jewish community. What Ezra did during those years by way of accomplishing his mission is not stated. But it is clear that he did not use the authority with which he was armed by the royal warrant to enforce the acceptance of the Torah as 'the law of God and the law of the king' (Ez. vii. 26), and in so refraining he surely showed wisdom and statesmanship. What he desired was a voluntary acceptance of the Torah; and he may well have spent the twelve years before Nehemiah came in quiet efforts of persuasion, explanation, and argument. Perhaps he might not have succeeded in the end without the help of Nehemiah, for the final decisive act of ratification was not secured until that very energetic and zealous colleague appeared on the scene. Nehemiah was entirely at one with Ezra in his devotion to the Torah, to judge from the tone of his memoirs contained in the book which bears his name. It is true that he does not mention Ezra by name, except in the account of the dedication of the walls (Neh. xii. 36), a verse which has been pronounced to be an interpolation after the easy manner of critics of the text. But he certainly was the means of securing Ezra's main object, the ratification of the Torah. In the list of signatures to the Covenant (Neh. x. 1-28), that of Nehemiah comes first, as governor; and it is again significant that no appeal is made to his own authority as the representative of the Persian king or to that conferred by Ezra's royal warrant. The Covenant was the voluntary act of the people expressed through the leading men, and Nehemiah was by his position first amongst them. Why Ezra himself did not sign is not explained, but the absence of his name in no way discredits the fact. After all, it is quite conceivable that he regarded the Covenant as the act of those to whom he had been sent, to which, therefore, his own signature was not required. However it may have been, he had got what he wanted, the Covenant had been signed, the Torah had been established.

This was beyond any question the real object of Ezra's mission, the key to that reformation of the Jewish religion whereby it acquired the character indicated ever since by the name Judaism. Whatever else is recorded of him or attributed to him had its source in the one central idea of the supremacy of the Torah. Not much else, indeed, is related of him, and nothing of equal importance. But it is useful to note how even this little falls into line with the main idea. Thus it is told at some length (Ez. ix-x) how, on his arrival in Jerusalem, he was greatly distressed on account of the mixed marriages between Jewish men and non-Jewish women. This was, of course, a violation of the older law as laid down in Deuteronomy (vii. 3), therefore quite independent of Ezra. Mixed marriages might and probably did take place before the Exile, in spite of Deuteronomy; and the reason why they became a conspicuous feature in the community after the return was presumably that there were more men than women amongst the returned settlers, and that the shortage of Jewish women was made up from non-Jewish sources. It is not said that Jewish women married non-Jewish men. Ezra must have made some suggestion for dealing with this problem. It is stated (Ez. x. 2) that ' Shechaniah . . . one of the sons of Elam, answered and said unto Ezra We have trespassed against our God and have married strange women of the peoples of the land. Now therefore let us make a covenant with our God to put away all the wives and such as are born of them, according to the counsel of my lord, and of those that tremble at the commandment of our God. And let it be done according to the Torah. Arise, for the matter belongeth unto thee, and we are with thee. Be strong and act'. From this it is evident that there were already in Jerusalem men who were prepared to support Ezra in whatever he might do to root out the evil of the mixed marriages, and who were in agreement with his main policy of establishing the Torah. For the proposal of Shechaniah was 'let it be done according to the Torah'. The real ground of objection to the mixed marriages was that these were forbidden by the Torah, and that there could be no question of a community pledged to walk according to the Torah if that community was not purged from the admixture of Gentile blood. The mixed marriages showed that there was a considerable danger that the Jewish community would in time lose its identity and become assimilated to the population in whose midst it lived. It has been well remarked by G. F. Moore (*Judaism*, i, 19 f.) that there was nothing particularly Jewish in this policy of preserving the purity of religion by the prohibition of mixed marriages. It was no mark of narrow bigotry on the part of Ezra and those with whom he worked. It was a means of ensuring the possibility of a community which should carry out the task committed to it from of old, of being the chosen witness of God to the world (cp. Isa. xlii. 6). And it must be remembered that after the return from the Exile the only bond of union which the Jews possessed, other than that of blood, was their religion. They no longer had a political status as subjects of an independent kingdom. If their religion was not preserved, Jews as Jews would cease to exist. And if the religion was to be preserved, the strain of Jewish blood must be kept free from Gentile admixture.

It has been argued that if Ezra did anything at all in the matter of the mixed marriages, he must have done so at a later date than the second administration of Nehemiah, and this argument furnishes one of the supports for the theory that Ezra lived at a considerably later period than Nehemiah. The argument turns on the improbability of two attempts to deal with the mixed marriages. If Ezra had secured the dissolution of the marriages, why should Nehemiah have trouble over the same subject, as he says he did? (Neh. xiii. 25.) But it may

[39]

equally be asked: Why, if Nehemiah took action in the forcible manner which he describes, was it necessary for Ezra (assuming him to be of later date) to do the same over again? There is no necessity, at all events on this ground, to date Ezra later than Nehemiah, as there is no contradiction between the two statements. A policy so severe as the dissolution of the mixed marriages must certainly have met with much opposition, or, at the very least, much unwillingness on the part of many who were called upon to comply with its requirements. And it is not in the least wonderful that Nehemiah, in his second administration, should find attempts being made to break away from the agreement by renewal of the practice against which it had been directed. This is indeed only a particular case of what happened in regard to the fundamental question of the establishment of the Torah. In spite of the fact that the solemn ratification of the covenant had committed the whole community, including all the leading men, to the observance of the Torah, it is clear that there were those, perhaps a considerable number, who were not keen on Ezra's policy and were ready to take opportunities of evading its strict demands. This is shown by what Nehemiah relates (Neh. xiii) of various abuses which had crept in during his absence from Jerusalem, in the interval between his first and his second administration. It is indeed only what was naturally to be expected.

If then we try to form some idea of the position in the community after Ezra had accomplished his main purpose, we shall probably not be far wrong if we suppose that he had a considerable body of supporters, but not the whole community on his side. Everyone, of course, acknowledged in word the authority of the Torah, but not everyone shared the intense conviction of Ezra which had established that authority. Thus it is worthy of note that Eliashib, the High Priest, did not sign the Covenant, an omission which could hardly be accidental. If the Chronicler had invented the whole story, he would scarcely have made such a blunder as to leave out the High Priest. Moreover, if Ezra's main object had been, as usually supposed, to exalt the Temple and the priesthood, the least that the High Priest and his staff could do would have been to give Ezra the most hearty support. But if Ezra had come to set up the authority of the Torah as supreme, that was, or might become, a means of lessening the authority of the High Priest and of the priesthood generally. For they had been, from time immemorial, the source of whatever religious teaching, Torah, had been given. It would not be at all wonderful if the High Priest felt some uneasiness at what Ezra was doing, and did not welcome what he could not prevent. It was the High Priest Eliashib whose laxity made trouble during the second administration of Nehemiah (Neh. xiii. 4).

The supporters of Ezra in establishing the Torah included, as we have seen, many of the leading men of the community; but other co-operation was necessary if the authority of the Torah was to be maintained as an active controlling factor in Jewish life. There must be men who were willing and also competent to *teach* what was enjoined in the Torah, explain its provisions, and bring them to bear upon cases of uncertainty which might arise. The need for such exposition was expressly mentioned in the description of Ezra's original purpose, ' to interpret the Torah of the Lord and to do and to teach in Israel statute and judgment ' (Ez. vii. 10). When he solemnly read the Torah to the people, it is said (Neh. vii. 7) that certain men whose names are given, ' and the Levites caused the people to understand the Torah . . . and they read in the book, in the Torah of God, distinctly ' (or, perhaps, ' with an interpretation ', as in R.V. margin), ' and they gave the sense so that they understood the reading '. Whatever this refers to, whether translation of the Hebrew into Aramaic or explanation of what was read, the intention clearly was to *teach*, and not merely to *read*, in order that what was read might be understood and acted upon. The work of Ezra, therefore, needed the co-operation of men who could teach the Torah, being qualified to do so by their own study of its contents. It is not said that Ezra himself trained and appointed such teachers; but he can hardly have failed to do so, for the work of interpreting the Torah which was certainly carried on from an early period after his time was entirely such as his work required, and there is nothing to make it unlikely that he himself began it. The men who carried on the work after his time and on his lines were the Sopherim, and we must now inquire into the nature of their activities and the results to which those activities led.

[41]

CHAPTER II

THE SOPHERIM

ALTHOUGH the words Sopher and Sopherim are usually, and rightly, rendered by 'Scribe' and 'Scribes', and are found in use during periods of time long after that of Ezra, yet they are applied to his immediate followers in a special sense. It is recognised that those who were thus called Sopherim belonged to a group whose existence came to an end, the succession of teachers who bore the name was not prolonged after a certain time. When various institutions or usages are ascribed to the Sopherim, the reference is to the successors of Ezra, and not to the scribes in general. The well-known phrase *tikkunē Sopherim*, denoting certain corrections made in the text of the Hebrew Scriptures, means that those corrections were made in the particular period after Ezra and by the men who carried on his work. It does not mean that corrections in the text could be or were made by this or that scribe at any subsequent period.

The Sopherim, in this special sense, were the men who made it their business to teach and interpret the Torah in order to make its authority effective, and thus carry out the intention of Ezra. To realise that intention it was necessary that the contents of the Torah should be made known as widely as possible, the meaning of its statements and precepts understood, and directions given for carrying the precepts into effect. Merely to proclaim the supremacy of the Torah, or even to secure its ratification by the people, as Ezra had done, would have been of no use unless the success so far achieved had been followed up. Those who followed it up were the Sopherim, *par excellence*, and the name indicates that they were concerned with a book, i.e. the *Sepher Torah*. Whatever needed to be done in relation to that book it was especially their business to do, whether it were to write copies of the text or to teach and explain the contents or to apply its teaching to practical cases on which a decision was necessary. To call them jurists or doctors of the law is misleading, if only because Torah is not Law; and the use of either term places the facts of Judaism in a false light.

[43]

Those who are called in the New Testament 'lawyers' or 'doctors of the law' were not lawyers in any sense in which that word would be naturally understood; they were simply teachers of Torah, with whatever that might imply.

The Jewish tradition, which knows of the Sopherim as the successors of Ezra, mentions an institution apparently belonging to much about the same time, to which the name the Great Synagogue is attached. To this body are ascribed various ordinances and regulations affecting the religious life of the community, and it was supposed to have continued in existence for a considerable time. Simeon the Just (probably the earlier of the two bearing the same name), who died 270 B.C., is said to have been one of the last members of the Great Synagogue (Aboth i. 2). The Great Synagogue, therefore, if it were a real body, lasted some 170 years after the time of Ezra. Kuenen showed long ago that the conception of the Great Synagogue was based on the assembly described in Neh. x, which ratified the Torah; and he drew the conclusion that the Great Synagogue as a continuing and continuous body never existed. That conclusion is only tenable in the sense that the particular body assembled by Nehemiah for that special occasion did not meet again. It would, indeed, have been impossible to make such an assembly permanent. But an assembly of some kind there must have been, in the sense of a body of persons entrusted with the task of carrying out and carrying on the work which Ezra had begun, doing, in fact, precisely what the Sopherim were believed to have done. The tradition about the Great Synagogue and that about the Sopherim are only two forms of one tradition; they do not cancel, but rather confirm each other. They point to the existence of a teaching body, with power to regulate the religious life of the community on the lines of conformity to the Torah, and they indicate that this teaching body continued to function until the death of Simeon the Just. That these two traditions refer to the same institution or body of persons is proved by the statement in Tanḥuma (*Beshallaḥ*, p. 87*b*, ed. Lublin, 1879), referring to the *tikkunē Sopherim* mentioned above: 'For the men of the Great Synagogue read these verses otherwise; and therefore they were called Sopherim, because they counted all the letters in the Torah and interpreted it'. That is to say, the Sopherim and the men of the

Great Synagogue are identified in the most explicit manner, and what follows from this identification is that the Sopherim who succeeded Ezra as teachers and interpreters of the Torah, regulators of the religious life of the community in accordance with its principles, maintained some sort of corporate existence until the death of Simeon the Just, about 270 B.C. Some form of government, or rather of managing the religious affairs of the community, there must have been, as a mere matter of practical necessity. Jewish tradition points to such a body in what it says about the Sopherim and the Great Synagogue, and it gives no hint of any other governing body. The conclusion seems reasonable that there really was a governing body, of the kind indicated, during the period which is defined by the date 270 B.C.

During most of the period thus marked out the little community in Judea was under the rule of the Persian kings, and only passed under Greek supremacy in 332 B.C. by the victories of Alexander the Great. The Persian rulers, living far from Judea, seldom interfered with the internal affairs of their Jewish subjects, and were content to leave their public business in the hands of the governor of the province. If the royal taxes were paid, and order maintained, the Jews might organise their own life as a community in the way that seemed best to them. They had but little contact with other nations, and no political independence. They were mainly concerned with meeting the simple requirements of their communal life in accordance with the Torah. For this purpose the Sopherim, forming as it would seem a sort of council, were sufficient. And it is in harmony with this view of their function that tradition ascribed to the Sopherim, or the Great Synagogue, the first beginnings of a liturgy of public prayer, and some not clearly defined activity in connexion with the collection and arrangement of the Scriptures. If, as is probable, the institution of the Synagogue began during this period to assume something of the form familiar in later times, it is quite certain that the Sopherim would have a considerable share in its organisation. Indeed, it is quite possible, and even likely, that the idea of the Synagogue, brought back from Babylon by the returning exiles, owed its successful adaptation to the conditions of Judea to the fostering care of the Sopherim. More will be said of the Synagogue presently.

[45]

The change from Persian to Greek rule made a great difference in the condition of the Jewish subjects who passed from the one to the other. It was no longer possible for them to live in quiet seclusion as on the whole a religious community, because, under Greek rulers, whether their capital was Alexandria or Antioch, the characteristic ideas and practices of the Greek culture began to make themselves felt far more powerfully and far more intimately than had ever been the case with Persian ideas and practices. And not only so, but Judea, as part of Palestine, lying between Syria and Egypt, was coveted by both; and the wars between them made the former peaceful life of the Jewish community impossible.

We are probably not far wrong in supposing that the decline of the Sopherim began when the disturbing influence of the new Greek culture first made itself felt, and when the turmoil of war made it difficult for them to meet in Council as they had formerly done. Simeon the Just, the High Priest of his time, and apparently president of the Council, had sufficient authority to keep them together; but when he died in 270 the organisation, such as it had become, fell to pieces, and the period of the Sopherim came to an end. 'Simeon the Just was of the survivors of the Great Synagogue' (Aboth i. 2).

We must now inquire more particularly into the kind of teaching given by the Sopherim and the part which they played in developing the tradition which long afterwards found literary expression in the Talmud and the collected Midrashim. The contents of these collections are of various dates, and no doubt much belongs to the early centuries of the common era. But some parts are much older, and, what is of more importance, the principles which regulated the form and substance of those contents date from the time of the Sopherim. The Mishnah was not finally codified until *circa* A.D. 210, and the Talmud much later. But the Mishnah began to grow about 170 B.C.; and that, without which there would not and could not have been any Mishnah at all, was the work of the Sopherim.

This indispensable ground principle which resulted eventually in the whole of the Talmud and Midrash literature was the duty of interpretation of the Torah. It was a duty because the Torah had been divinely given for the guidance and instruction of Israel; and obviously the intention with which the Torah had been given would have been frustrated if those to whom and for whom it was given did not learn what was taught in it, and do what it enjoined. For the Torah had been deliberately accepted on behalf of the whole people by its leading men, and accepted with a solemn promise to walk in accordance with it. So far as it went, it was henceforth the supreme religious authority for the community. The meaning, therefore, of what was contained in it must be explained so that the people might clearly understand what it really was to which they had pledged themselves, fuller directions must be given for the performance of acts as to which the Torah gave few or no details, cases must be decided for which the Torah made apparently no provision; and, even where no explanation was needed of simple and direct statements or positive teaching, there was need that such positive teaching should be brought home to the mind and heart of the people. To interpret and teach the Torah was the main work of the Sopherim.

The form in which that teaching was given was a sort of running commentary on the text, in which the particular lesson or precept which the teacher desired to give was connected with a particular passage of Scripture, and the two always taught together. This is what is meant by Midrash—or, rather, this form of exposition is called the Midrash form, as distinguished from the Mishnah form in which the precept was given without reference to any passage of Scripture. The Mishnah form was not used by the Sopherim; they used only the Midrash form, which, however, was never abandoned even when the Mishnah form came into use. The Midrash form was supposed to be that in which Moses had originally taught the Torah, and to use that form was called ' teaching after the manner of Moses'. Leaving Moses out of the question, it is much more likely that the Midrash form was ' after the manner of Ezra'. For it fairly describes what he and his assistants did when he read the Torah, and he and they ' read in the book, in the Torah of God distinctly ' (or, with an interpretation) ' and they gave the sense and caused them to understand the reading ' (Neh. viii. 8). Whether, on that occasion, or even on the following days on which the Torah was publicly read, there would have been time to add the exposition to the reading of the text, may well be doubted; but, with subsequent leisure, those who made it their business to teach the Torah would naturally adopt such a method. There was indeed no other which they could have adopted. If the people were to be taught at all, it would have to be by oral instruction in some more or less public manner. Doubtless, instruction could be and was given to private inquirers who went to consult the priests, the recognised sources of religious information; but such a method was only individual, and its results upon the people as a whole could only be very partial. And that the people as a whole were taught, and somewhat thoroughly taught, is shown by the subsequent history, particularly in the Maccabean revolt against Hellenism. More will be said of this later.

The Sopherim, then, taught the Torah in the form of Midrash; and it is not known, as it is not probable, that the teaching which they thus gave varied to any noticeable extent during the whole period of their activity. We are not left wholly in the dark as to the method of their ' exposition '. The Mishnah, although most of its contents are much later than the period with which we are at present concerned, has incorporated a few fragments of far earlier date, which are pronounced by competent authorities (see Frankel, *Darké ha-Mishnah*, pp. 5-6, and Weiss, *Dor Dor*, i, p. 69) to be from the time of the Sopherim. One such passage is found in M. Sotah, viii. 1, 2, and is worth translating as a specimen, almost the only one to be found, of the exposition of Torah by the Sopherim. It runs as follows: 'The battle-priest, when he spoke to the people, used to speak to them in the holy tongue, as it is said (Deut. xx. 2) " and it shall be when ye are come nigh unto the battle, that the priest shall approach ", this is the battle priest, " and shall speak to the people " in the holy tongue, " and shall say unto them, Hear, O Israel ", etc. [ye approach this day unto battle against your enemies]. "Against your enemies" and not against your brethren. Not Judah against Simeon, and not Simeon against Benjamin, so that if ye fell by their hands they would have mercy on you, as it is said (2 Chron. xxviii. 15) "and the men which were expressed by name rose up and took the captives, and all that were naked amongst them they clothed out of the spoil, and they clothed them and shod them and gave them to eat and drink and anointed them and carried on asses all that stumbled, and brought them to Jericho the city

of palms to their brethren and they returned to Samaria ".
" Against your enemies " ye are going, so that if ye fall by their
hand they will not have mercy on you. " Let not your heart
faint, fear not, nor tremble," etc. "Let not your heart faint "
because of the neighing of horses and the clashing of swords.
" Fear not " because of the striking of the shields and the (?)
clamour of the warriors. " Nor tremble " at the sound of horns,
" neither be ye terrified " at the sounds of war-cry. " For the
Lord your God is he that goeth with you." These come with the
means of victory of flesh and blood; ye come with the means of
victory of the All-present. The Philistines came with the means
of victory of Goliath. And what was his end? In the end he
fell and they fell with him. The children of Ammon came with
the means of victory of Shobek. What was his end? In the end he
fell by the sword and they fell with him. But ye, ye are not so;
for " the Lord your God is he that goeth with you, to fight for
you ", etc. This is the camp of the Ark. " And the officers shall
speak to the people, saying, What man is there that hath built
a new house and hath not dedicated it, let him go and return
to his house ", etc. Alike if he has built a house for hay, a house
for cattle, a house for wood, a house for treasures; alike whether
he builds, or buys or inherits, or it is given to him as a gift.
" And what man is there who has planted a vineyard and has
not yet made it free for use? " etc. Alike if he plants the vineyard, or plants five trees for eating, and even of five different
sorts. Alike if he plants, if he drains, if he props, if he buys, if he
inherits, if it is given to him as a gift. " And what man is there
who has betrothed a wife," etc. Alike if he have betrothed a
virgin or a widow, or even one who is waiting [for levirate
marriage]. And even if he hear that his brother [whose widow
he is to marry] has died in the battle, he turns back and goes
away. All these hear the words of the priest from the ranks of
battle, and turn back, and provide water and food and mend
the roads.'

The above passage is not at all in the usual style of the Mishnah, where the actual words of Scripture texts are very rarely
given in connexion with the declaration of the decision
(halachah) which it is the main business of the Mishnah to
make. The whole process of interpretation and definition
tended to become more and not less elaborate as time went on;

E

and a method so simple as that shown in the above passage was quite out of date in the age when the main structure of the Mishnah was put into shape. It is true that no conclusive proof can be given that it really is from the period of the Sopherim; but if it is not, then they must have used a method of interpretation even more simple, and it is hard to imagine a simpler method if there was to be any interpretation at all. Also it must be admitted that if the passage belongs to the period of the Sopherim, it must date from the very end of that period, because the text, 2 Chron. xxviii. 15, is quoted, and that book is believed to have been written somewhere about 300 B.C., only thirty years or so before the end of the Sopheric period. Nevertheless, the passage may be fairly taken to represent the general method of the Sopherim in their interpretation, which cannot have altered greatly if at the end of the period the method was still so simple. The first important change was made when the Mishnah-form was introduced (see above, p. 47, and below, p. 66), and that was an innovation in 170 B.C. or thereabouts when José b. Joezer of Zeredah was the first to make use of it. (See Lauterbach, *Midrash and Mishnah*, the whole essay, and especially p. 29 ff.)

The passage above quoted shows how the Sopherim interpreted the Torah on its preceptive side, by way of defining more closely the scope of the commandments given in the text. The distinction between the preceptive and the non-preceptive portions of the Torah is fundamental in that type of Judaism which is represented by the Sopherim, their later successors the Tannaim, and the Talmud and Midrashim generally. Interpretation of the Torah had for its purpose the elucidation of its meaning on both of these sides; and the two forms of interpretation, and more particularly the results obtained by interpretation along both those lines, were indicated by special names—on the preceptive side by Halachah, on the non-preceptive side by Haggadah. There is no positive evidence to show when these two famous words were first introduced; but it is probable that both date from the period of the Sopherim, from a time at all events earlier than the introduction of the Mishnah form. Because, since the Mishnah form consisted in teaching the practical course of action apart from its scriptural basis (if it had any), there must have been some means of referring to the practice to be defined, and that is precisely what the word Halachah served to make possible. The Mishnah form consisted in teaching the Halachah without its scriptural basis. The Sopherim must have had the idea of what is connoted by the word Halachah, and they may quite well have had the word. It is probable that the word Haggadah was originally wider in its scope than its later use would indicate*, and was applied to every statement of the meaning of Torah. The word means simply ' declaration ', ' announcement '; and the teacher, giving his view of the meaning of a passage, would say ' the Torah *declares* ' so-and-so, whether it were preceptive or non-preceptive teaching which he was explaining. Later, when the term halachah was applied especially to the interpretation of the preceptive side of Torah, the other term, haggadah, was restricted to the interpretation of the non-preceptive side. And this is the real meaning of haggadah in all its later developments, with only this qualification that haggadah is made to include the whole of Scripture, and not merely the Torah, as its subject matter. Still, the Torah was fundamental; and the interpretation of what it contained, whether in the form of halachah or haggadah, only used the rest of Scripture for the purpose of developing and illustrating what was rooted in the Torah.

The development of halachah and haggadah into the vast body of teaching collected in the Talmud and the Midrashim belongs to a later time than that of the Sopherim, and cannot be considered here. But it is of great importance to observe that the principles on which that development was based underlie all the work of the Sopherim, and really go back to Ezra. The Torah, as he left it, was the supreme authority in the religious life of the community, as has already been shown. It was a declaration of the will of God, and also the record of what he had been pleased to make known concerning himself, his ways, his dealings with mankind and kindred subjects. It was the duty of those to whom the Torah had been given, especially after they had solemnly bound themselves to its observance, to make the kind of response which the nature of the case required. If God commanded that they should do this or that, then the first thing required was to *do* the will of God thus declared to

* On the meaning of Haggadah, see Bacher, *Terminologie*, i, 33.

[51]

them. Nothing ought to come before this duty. Nothing else ought to be considered as the essential of true religion, and in the type of religion with which we are at present concerned, which was developed along the line from Ezra to the Talmud, nothing else ever was considered as the essential of the true religion. Many other things might be, and were, important, but nothing else could be *the one essential*, to take precedence over everything else. To *do* anything is an exercise of will, and is an expression of the personality of a living soul. It is the means by which a man, so to speak, makes his mark upon the sum total of things around him. To *do* is to make a change in the previous order, to bring about what had not been, virtually to create it. From this point of view, to *do* is more than to *be* or to *know* or to *believe*. Because these latter are possible for a man without his going beyond the enclosure of his own self. In *doing* he goes beyond it, brings some direct influence to bear upon the persons or things around him, so that they become other than they were before. To do the will of God is to give in the service of God the most that he can give, and that is the conscious act of his own will, whereby he intentionally sets himself in harmony with God. It is not enough merely to *know* the will of God or to *believe* in it, or in God whose will it is. Before all else he must *do* it.

Whether reflections of this kind were present to the minds of Ezra and his successors I am not prepared to say. But they certainly had a deep insight into the meaning of the personal act, as an expression of will. The reason why they laid such immense stress on *doing* the will of God was perhaps only this: That the Torah was given to all and not to some; and while not everyone could *know* or *believe* or *be*, everyone could *do* what was commanded to be done, and thereby prove his real allegiance to God, make a definite expression of his will to serve God.

Now the Torah contains many precepts, some of them precise, some of them indefinite. In regard to the clear and straightforward precepts the only thing was to do them, and there was nothing more to be said. In regard to the others, if the meaning was uncertain, it must be made clear, if it was indefinite it must be defined, so that obedience to the command might be given with deliberate intention and full understanding. If God had made known his will in the Torah, there must be some exactly right way of carrying out what was there enjoined; and if the right way was not known, it must be sought until it was found. When it was found it must be stated, for the future guidance of all who were in a position to act upon that particular command, whatever it was.

Now the halachah was intended to define the obligation in regard to the several precepts of the Torah. It was a declaration on the part of responsible teachers that in a given case *this*, and not *that*, was the right way of performing the act commanded. Halachah was a rule of right conduct, a direction to a man how under such and such circumstances he should '*walk* (halach) in the ways of the Lord'. And, from its simplest beginning in the teaching of the Sopherim, as seen in the passage quoted above, down to its latest elaboration in the Talmud, halachah has always meant just that. But the halachah was only a direction how to fulfil a given command; it was still left to the man concerned to *do* the act required. That was his personal service of God in the case before him, and unless he did the act with the intention of serving God thereby, his act was worthless, even though he had followed the direction of the halachah in doing it. The *opus operatum*, as it was called in another connexion, had no validity in Judaism. Doubtless, in practice, there were many lapses from the severe austerity of the theory; but the theory was as above described, that the conscious and intentional serving of God in every act where God had declared his will, was 'the whole duty of man'.

It was therefore almost a matter of course that the interpretation of the Torah should lay the chief stress upon the halachah, because to *do* the will of God was essential and was within the competence of everyone. But it was no less a matter of course that the haggadah, the interpretation of the non-preceptive side, should be developed side by side with the halachah. Because the non-preceptive portions of the Torah were just as truly divine teaching as the preceptive, and it was just as much a duty to learn what was so taught. But there was this difference between them, that the haggadah was not defined in precise terms as the halachah was, it was given not as a rule but as a suggestion, an illustration, an explanation; it was directed not to the will but to the understanding and the imagination.

[53]

And this explains why the ethical teaching of the Rabbis, following the Sopherim, was given mainly in the form of haggadah. The duty of showing kindness, pity, love, etc., is certainly part of what God requires from man; but these are general, not special; they can be expressed in unnumbered ways, and could never be fixed by any definition. No halachah of sympathy or goodwill, of friendly help or neighbourly kindness was ever possible, or ever contemplated. All such duties are left undefined, ' committed to the heart,' as the later Rabbis expressed it (b. B. Mez. 58b), and left to the spontaneous feeling of the moment which called for them. But, though undefined, they could be made the subject of teaching which should hold up examples taken from life or from the Scriptures, draw out the motives and lay stress upon the finer qualities of actions done from these motives. For this purpose haggadah was the proper means of expression, and was very largely used. The halachah was an enactment: ' *This* is the right way of fulfilling such and such a commandment'. The haggadah was a declaration that ' *this* ' was among the possible meanings of what God had caused to be recorded in the Torah. Halachah carried with it an obligation laid upon all who accepted the system which produced halachah; haggadah implied no obligation to receive the explanation offered as being the only right one. There could be only one valid and binding halachah in regard to the same commandment at the same time. There could be many haggadahs upon one and the same text of Scripture, and of these one might contradict another. ' God could say many things at once,' as it was remarked in later times. The consequence of this is that uniformity of doctrinal belief was never made an essential in Judaism, of this or any other type. There were indeed certain limits beyond which a Jew could not go and still remain a Jew, e.g. the belief in the Unity of God; but within those limits belief was free, and there never has been in Judaism any declaration of belief holding the same position as the Creed holds in the Christian religion. Those who first defined the terms halachah and haggadah lived long before the age when a creed was first formulated; and the reason why they attached an obligation to the halachah and none to the haggadah was based on the very obvious distinction that a man can only *do* one thing at once, while he can behold several aspects of truth at once. When he has before him the duty of fulfilling a command he can do *this* or *that* or the other, but not all three at once. The halachah directs him to do *this* and not *that* or the other, because *this* is the right way, and there cannot be more than one right way. When, on the other hand, he studies a text of Scripture (not involving a command), the haggadah tells him 'It means this, and it means that, and it means the other, and it may mean much else besides '; and he is not required to decide which is the only right meaning, but is left full of wonder at the divine wisdom which can say so much in so few words.

The reader will perhaps be asking himself what has become of the ethical teaching which was to be the subject of the present book, and of which since the introductory chapter little or nothing has been said? Why all this discussion of halachah and haggadah? The reason is that the system of interpretation of Torah, begun by Ezra and carried on by the Sopherim, was the framework within which was contained the ethical teaching they had to give, the form into which they cast it. It will appear later on that the substance of what they taught in regard to ethical subjects was to a large extent the same as that which was taught by men, Ben Sira for example, who did not use the method of halachah and haggadah. This is only to be expected, because the subject matter of all the ethical teaching was contained in the Scriptures, which were the common possession of all. What is characteristic of the Sopherim and their successors who developed the Talmud, is not their ethical teaching as distinguished from that of men of other types of mind, but the method in which they dealt with the subject which was common to all. The ethical teaching, in substance though not in form, is the connecting link between the Rabbinical and the non-Rabbinical types of Judaism, between that which worked out the dual concept of halachah and haggadah, and that which found congenial expression for its thoughts in Apocalyptic visions and the problems of mystic numbers. So far as the Sopherim are concerned, their ethical teaching can hardly have amounted to more than a simple exposition of what they found in Scripture. The passage quoted above, though its purpose is in the main halachic and not, strictly speaking, haggadic, yet shows how a very simple explanatory address (for this the passage quoted undoubtedly was originally) could be made

[55]

the means of teaching whatever the teacher had to impart, ethical or otherwise. It would not be safe to quote passages from the later Midrash to illustrate what the Sopherim taught, of an ethical character; but nevertheless, if the comparison could be made, it is not probable that any great difference would be disclosed between the earlier and the later teaching. On some points, no doubt, the Rabbinical Ethic advanced to concepts not found in Scripture; but in the main the Scriptural Ethic is the basis of the Rabbinic Ethic, and the difference is chiefly in the variety of presentation, the quantity not the quality of the results produced by directing the imagination of devout minds to the contemplation of sacred themes. When we come to study the book of Ben Sira, we shall find that his ethical teaching was closely akin to that of Scripture. The Sopherim were earlier than he; and though he was not one of them in the technical sense, yet he and they had much the same object in view as far as their ethical teaching was concerned, and we may reasonably infer that they were at least as much as he in accord with the ethical teaching contained in Scripture.

But we have not yet done with the Sopherim. We have yet to consider how they imparted their teaching. Their task, as successors of Ezra, was to *teach the people*, to make them acquainted with the Torah, so that they might walk in accordance with it. Their interpretation of Torah was a means to an end, viz. to train up a people who should in every point fulfil the Torah. How then did the Sopherim discharge this part of their task?

The only possible way of reaching the people, whether as a whole or in groups or individually, was by oral address. There was no question of writing books and circulating them. The people to be taught were just those who would be least able to read, and least likely to read if there had been any books. The Sopherim no doubt multiplied copies of the Torah, but the only persons likely to possess a copy were those whose duty it was to teach it. And it is a pure assumption that they all possessed copies. When the work of the teachers in later times is studied in the Talmud and Midrash it is found to be exclusively oral, by way of debate in the schools or discourse in the Synagogue; and there is not the faintest trace of any earlier practice of written instruction afterwards superseded by oral teaching. We may be quite sure that the Sopherim had no other means of instruction than the spoken word.

It is clear that, whatever means they used, they were able to make a very considerable impression on the people, and to bring under the influence of their teaching a large proportion of the community. The proof of this is the fact that when the Maccabean Revolt broke out, the rallying cry was defence of the *Torah*. 'Whoso is zealous for the Torah . . . let him come forth after me' (1 Macc. ii. 27). No doubt other motives contributed to the action of those who revolted with Mattathias and his sons; but zeal for the Torah was the only one which found utterance in a 'slogan', if the modern term may be allowed. The Maccabean Revolt broke out about a hundred years after the period of the Sopherim had come to an end, and it might be argued that it was during those hundred years that the people had learned the zeal for Torah which inspired the Revolt. But of those hundred years about eighty, from 270 B.C. to 196 B.C., were a period of anarchy, during which there were no recognised official teachers of Torah. The Sopherim had ceased to function and the Sanhedrin had not begun. (See Lauterbach, *Midrash and Mishnah*, p. 40 ff.) The absence of any but occasional teaching would tend to weaken the hold which the Torah had upon the people; and the fact that it was as strong as the Revolt proved it to be, shows how well the Sopherim had done their work, how deep and lasting was the impression they had made upon the popular mind.

We are obliged to conclude that they found, or made, some opportunity for instructing the people regularly, continuously, and in large numbers, so as in time to reach them all. The community was not large; but, even in the time of Ezra and Nehemiah, the towns and villages round about Jerusalem contained a considerable proportion of the total population. These could not all come into Jerusalem, even at the three great festivals; and if only those occasions were used, as they certainly were used, for instructing the people, still they only amounted to a few days in the year, leaving the rest a blank. Now one of the ordinances ascribed to Ezra (b. B. Kamma, 82*a*, *b*) was to the effect that the Torah should be read in the villages on the second and fifth days of the week, in addition to the Sabbath, those being the days on which the people of the several neighbourhoods came in to the villages to market. It is not impossible that Ezra himself actually made this ordinance; but, if he did not, it surely belongs to the Sopherim, or the men of the Great Synagogue. Here clearly is the opportunity which they needed for their popular instruction in Torah. When Ezra himself read the Torah (Neh. viii. 8) the reading had been accompanied by explanation, expressly for the purpose of causing the people to understand what was read. It was merely following his example if the reading of the Torah twice in the week beside the Sabbath were also accompanied by explanation for the same purpose. If this was done each week, in all the towns and villages—and, of course, in Jerusalem itself—the whole community would be reached, even if there were some who did not attend to hear the Torah read. And if this was kept up more or less regularly during the period of the Sopherim, and not wholly discontinued during the years of anarchy which followed, and revived under the Sanhedrin, then the Maccabean Revolt is, in its most important aspect, fully explained. Without such preparation by the public teaching of Torah, the Revolt would be unintelligible.

It is very tempting in this connexion to think of the Synagogue as the institution exactly fitted for the work of the Sopherim, and possibly created by them for the purpose. Undoubtedly in later times the Synagogue did serve this purpose, and serve it very well. But to assert that the Synagogue as known in later times existed already in the age of the Sopherim is to assume more than is warranted. The most that can be safely said is that there were in the time of the Sopherim weekly gatherings at which the Torah was publicly read and taught, and that from these weekly gatherings was gradually developed the Synagogue as it was afterwards known. The Synagogue was not primarily a house of prayer, and it has never in all its history been exclusively set apart for worship. It was, and is, primarily a place where the Torah is brought home to the hearts and minds of those who meet there, and where they learn to react to it in such ways as the occasion may require. The Synagogue certainly became an institution of the greatest importance in the later history of Judaism; but, so far as the Sopherim are concerned, all that is needed for the explanation

[58]

of their work as teachers of Torah to the people is secured by the assumption of weekly meetings as above described.

The Sopherim were probably priests, as Ezra himself had been. This was only natural, because it had been for ages the function of priests, and none others, to give what religious instruction was given; and when Ezra began his work of teaching Torah to the people, the priests were practically the only persons to whom he could turn for assistance in carrying it out. Levites, it is true, are mentioned in the description of the first public reading (Neh. viii. 9), and it is probable that many Levites took part in the work as carried on by the Sopherim. But they would do so presumably under the supervision of the priests. What was to be taught, particularly the halachah, must have been decided by the Council, because agreement amongst the responsible teachers was necessary if there was to be any halachah at all. The members of the Council were *the* Sopherim, *par excellence*; but after they had decided the teaching to be given, it still had to be made known among the people in the public assemblies, and Levites as well as priests of lower rank could well discharge this duty. Neither priests nor Levites were required to live always in Jerusalem; some would be found in every town and village, and only their occasional term of duty in the Temple would call them away. They were thus the natural agents and assistants of the Sopherim on the Council, for their special work.

Some light is thrown upon the Sopherim by a passage in the Mishnah (Aboth i. 1), where it is reported of the men of the Great Synagogue: 'These said three things: Be deliberate in judging, and raise up many disciples, and make a hedge for the Torah'. The men of the Great Synagogue are the Sopherim, as shown above (p. 44). The words attributed to them are obviously only suitable to a body of persons, they would be quite out of place if spoken to, or by, an individual. They would seem to be a sort of motto for the Sopherim, indicating their aim and method, the principles on which they acted. Deliberation in judgment was clearly necessary in the case of a council who had to make decisions, whether in fixing the halachah or in applying its results in particular cases, and whose members necessarily acted as judges of whatever courts of law there were. To make many disciples means, in any case, instruct as many persons as possible; but the reference is probably to the training of men who should themselves become Sopherim and so carry on their work. It hardly refers to the teaching given to the people, because ' disciple ' is not a word that would be naturally used of chance listeners in a crowd. Evidently the Sopherim must have made provision for training successors to themselves, if their work was to be carried on. To make a hedge for the Torah indicates that their care lest the Torah should be disobeyed led them to set up precautionary bounds which would have to be overstepped before the Torah itself was reached to its harm. It does not mean ' make the Torah into a hedge ', as some have supposed.

These three sayings are certainly very old, and may well date back to the days of the Sopherim. Whether they were a declaration officially made by them, or a sort of summary of their policy made by a later teacher, the author of them was well acquainted with their work. If the passage quoted above (pp. 48-9) from the Mishnah dates from the time of the Sopherim, it is equally possible that these sayings should have come down from the same period, perhaps from the closing years of the period, as the quoted passage did.

Finally, we may close this chapter on the Sopherim with the words attributed (Aboth i. 2) to Simeon the Just, who was one of the last members of that Council known as the Great Synagogue. ' He used to say: Upon three things the world standeth; upon Torah, upon the Service and upon the showing of kindnesses.' I may be allowed to quote from my edition of Aboth, p. 22: ' Torah signifies divine revelation, either the fact of communion between God and man or the wisdom so imparted. Though to Israel alone the Torah was given, yet Israel in this was representative of humanity. Intercourse between God and man is fundamental, and without it human life above the merely animal stage would be impossible. The "Service" is the service in the Temple regarded as the worship of God in the manner appointed by him. If one special element in the service be intended, that may be the sacrifices, as a symbol of obedience to the divine commands, or the priesthood as the appointed agency for performing the service. . . . Deeds of kindness denote unselfish beneficence in the fullest measure, to cover any good that one person can do to another. The " three

[60]

things " which are thus declared to be fundamental in human life are found to be Revelation, obedience to God, and brotherly love. It is possible, however, that the second term " the service " was intended to symbolise worship as a fundamental in human life, including in its meaning both obedience to the divine precepts and the functions of consecrated ministers. The saying is only true when thus generalised; but it would be hard to say how much of that more general meaning was present to the mind of Simeon when he uttered it.'

CHAPTER III

THE UNWRITTEN TORAH

THE period of the Sopherim, or the Great Synagogue, came to an end with the death of Simeon the Just, 270 B.C. But their work, as teachers of Torah, did not pass away, and the principles which they laid down, as above described, were carried further by a later succession of teachers who eventually became the Rabbis, and whose monument is the Talmud. The duty of teaching the people to know the Torah and to live in accordance with it, continued to be in their hands, as it had been in those of the Sopherim; and the difference between the Sopherim and their later successors was one of method, not of principle. To interpret the Torah was, and always remained, the object in view; but the later teachers developed methods of interpretation unknown to the Sopherim, and probably did so from a deeper understanding of the real significance of their work than the Sopherim had ever possessed. It will therefore be necessary to study these further developments along what for brevity I have called the Rabbinical line, so that we may understand the forms in which the teachers of that line gave their instruction, and may be able to form some estimate of the contents of that teaching, especially on the ethical side. Without some explanation such as is here indicated, it would not be safe to use the evidence of the Talmud and the Midrashim, as finally written down, for the purpose of illustrating what was taught in the period with which we are at present concerned. There is this difference between the teaching given on the Rabbinical line and that which is contained in the books of the Apocrypha and Pseudepigrapha, that the Rabbinical teaching was given in the form of halachah and haggadah, in accordance with a definite purpose of interpreting the Torah, and based upon a definite conception of what the Torah was and for what end it had been given. The instruction on these lines was the result of the labours of many generations of teachers, all directed to a common end. The teaching of the Apocryphal and Pseudepigraphic books, on the contrary, was the teaching of the individual

[63]

writers of those books, allowing for the fact that in the case of some of the books, e.g. Enoch, several writers of different dates have been at work. And only the fact that the Apocryphal and other books were written, while the Rabbinical teaching was oral, and not written down till long afterwards, gives a fictitious advantage to the former, as if in some way they were more authentic than the latter. The oral teaching, both by reason of the length of time during which it was systematically given and the minute care taken to make it effective for its purpose, was a far more important factor in the religious history of the Jewish people than the occasional appearance of this or that book, however striking and however excellent. I go on, therefore, to trace briefly the course of development of the oral teaching after the period of the Sopherim, so as to link it on to the Rabbis of the Talmud.

It has been shown by Lauterbach (*Midrash and Mishnah*, p. 40 ff.) that the transition from Persian to Greek rule had a powerful and lasting influence upon the life of the Jewish community. One of its immediate effects was to produce a state of anarchy in regard to the religious life of the people, through the decline and final disappearance of the Sopherim, as a collective body. Their Council ceased to function; and though it is hardly likely that every single Sopher died at the time, yet such as remained were only private individuals, having no authority except what might depend on their learning and personal character. There was no central body which could keep control of the religious life of the Jewish community or give the needful guidance. Politically, the country was the bone of contention between the Greek kingdoms of Egypt and Syria, and during the confusion of war the organisation of peaceful life had to do the best it could. This period of anarchy came to an end in or about 196 B.C., when the Sanhedrin was established to be the great Council of the Jewish people. In the interval since the Sopherim had ceased to function there may have been some attempt to keep up the weekly meetings for the reading of the Torah, and occasional teaching given by one or other of those who remembered and handed on the tradition of the Sopherim. But, in the absence of authoritative guidance, the people had gone their own way; new customs had found a place amongst old religious usages, and no halachah defined them, new ideas had been formed under the influence of the Hellenism which had permeated the land for more than a century, and there had been no one to point out the danger which thereby threatened the religious life of the people. It therefore became one of the most pressing necessities of the time to restore order in this confusion, and take steps to revive in some form what the Sopherim had carried on for so long. In the absence of direct evidence, it is impossible to say exactly what was done, but certainly something was done; for a teaching body of some kind began to function in the early years of the Sanhedrin, and developed into the Rabbinical schools of a later age without a break. The names of successive teachers, in pairs (zugoth), are mentioned in the Mishnah (Aboth i. 3-12; Peah ii. 6); and the first pair, José b. Joezer of Zeredah and José b. Johanan of Jerusalem, were certainly living in the early years of the Sanhedrin. Probably they were members of it, though not the president and vice-president as the Mishnah represents them. They would presumably be the leaders, in the Sanhedrin, of those who were concerned to defend the Torah against the influence of Hellenism, and to maintain its authority amongst the people. They were certainly in some position which enabled them to give directions, because two ordinances made by them are mentioned (b. Shabb. 14*b*); and it seems reasonable to suppose that those who formed what may be called the Torah party acted in concert, either as a group in the Sanhedrin or as a private council of their own, or perhaps both. What exactly was their relation to the Sanhedrin it is not possible to say, and for the present purpose does not greatly matter. The point is that in some form the leaders of the Torah party took up the interrupted work of the Sopherim, and carried it on, both as theoretical students of Torah and practical teachers of the people. On the practical side, they must have continued the old method of oral instruction at weekly meetings as the chief means of making the Torah effective; and in so doing they were gradually shaping the Synagogue into the form in which it became known later on.

But on the theoretical side, the study and interpretation of the Torah, they did not merely repeat what the Sopherim had taught; they introduced, perhaps hardly realising what they did, an innovation which became of vast importance for the

F   [65]

later Judaism. In appearance it was hardly more than a technicality of discussion; in reality it involved a new conception of what the Torah essentially was, and it made possible the continual advance and development through the centuries of the religion which was founded on the Torah. It affected the quality (and incidentally the quantity) of all the teaching which was given in the form of interpretation of Torah, especially on the side of halachah, but also on that of haggadah.

Mention has been made above of the Midrash-form, as contrasted with the Mishnah-form (see above, pp. 47 and 50). The innovation at present to be considered was the introduction of the Mishnah-form. The characteristic of the Mishnah-form is that it states the halachah without any Scripture text to serve as its basis; it merely declares that the halachah is so and so, and the importance of its adoption, along with the Midrash-form which was never abandoned, lies in the fact that it made possible the release of the halachah from the letter of Scripture, sometimes even cutting the connexion altogether. Lauterbach, in the essay already several times referred to, has shown very strong reasons for believing that the first teacher who used the Mishnah-form was José b. Joezer of Zeredah mentioned above, and that he did so as a means of dealing with the difficult situation set up during the period of anarchy after the cessation of the Sopherim. The difficulty was to find a sanction in the Torah for the new customs and practices which had established themselves in the community, at all events such as involved religious acts, which would have been the subject of a halachah in the more orderly time of the Sopherim, and which ought to be the subject of a halachah now, if only some means could be found of ascertaining it. In the case of many of these usages the old method of interpreting the text would be sufficient to give the sanction of the Torah to the act in question; but in other cases no interpretation of the text was regarded as a valid ground of the halachah, while yet there was agreement as to what the halachah ought to be. Or, to put it less technically, some new practice of a religious nature was deemed worthy of approval in itself, was such as to make it highly desirable to recognise it as a proper practice for Jews; but the authority of the Torah was the only authority admitted in Jewish religious life since the time of Ezra, and unless the new usage could be

[66]

brought under the sanction of the Torah, it could make no claim to be accepted, still less declared to be binding. How then could that sanction be given to it so that it might become the subject of a valid halachah? The answer which was found to that question was virtually this: That the practice in question (whatever it may have been) was evidently a right and good one for Jews to follow; and the fact that they had followed it for an unknown length of time, so that it was now established, might be taken to indicate that there really was a tradition enjoining that practice although there was not a word about it in the written text of the Torah. If this was so, then this tradition must have a certain authority of its own; and, since there could not be two supreme authorities, it followed that the Torah contained more than was set forth in the written text. In other words there must be, and must always have been, an Unwritten Torah alongside of the written one, not as its rival nor even as its commentary, but so that the two together, written and unwritten, constituted *the* Torah as it essentially was. To the Sopherim, as to Ezra himself, the Torah had been the written text of the Pentateuch, and the interpretation of it had taken the course of simple explanation in Midrash-form as shown above. José b. Joezer was apparently the first to arrive at the idea that the Torah contained more than the written word, that there was Torah which never had been written, and which, therefore, was none the less valid though no written text contained or confirmed it. The Mishnah records (Edu. viii. 4) three halachahs which were declared by him, and apparently in the end accepted, but which evidently met with some objection and gave occasion to his colleagues to call him 'Joseph the Permitter'. This was because by his halachahs, or by his method of obtaining them, he was able to declare that to be allowable which till then had not been allowable, since no interpretation of the written text had been found which would justify his conclusion. What he apparently did was to give up the attempt to interpret the text and to postulate a tradition, an unwritten Torah, alongside of it. (See Lauterbach, who devotes the greater part of his essay, *Midrash and Mishnah*, to the discussion of these halachahs of José.)

It was not unnatural that there should be much hesitation in adopting this new method of declaring the halachah, involving as it did a new conception of the real nature of the Torah. Certainly it would solve the problems which were the immediate occasion for its being proposed; but if it were adopted it would lead to conclusions far more important than the immediate occasion needed. What it amounted to was this, that the Torah was no longer confined to the written text with its interpretation, but was contained in a tradition of equal authority; and, further, that no one except the recognised and qualified teachers could say what the tradition contained; what, in a given case, was the practice to be followed according to the Torah, what was the halachah. In the last resort, the declaration of the contents of the unwritten Torah depended on the *ipse dixit* of the teacher, though it could only become halachah if it was adopted by his colleagues, with the result, of course, of greatly enhancing the authority of the teachers, at all events over those who accepted the theory. The lead which José b. Joezer had given was followed, but only gradually; and though the theory of the Unwritten Torah was finally accepted and worked out to its furthest consequences, as seen in the Talmud, yet those who most firmly maintained it were quite aware of the weakness of its foundation. They knew that it cut the connexion between halachah and the written Torah, and they knew that in appearance, at all events, it gave the teachers free scope to teach what they thought fit. Lauterbach has pointed out (*op. cit.*, p. 88) that the Rabbis were rather shy of discussing the basis of their theory, because it would give an opening to their opponents. And, in fact, it was precisely on this question that the Sadducees and the Pharisees were fundamentally divided. The Pharisees maintained the authority of the Unwritten Torah and the Sadducees denied it. (See the present writer's *Pharisees*, p. 64 f. and *passim*.)

But in spite of the weakness of its foundation, or rather its liability to be misrepresented, those who advocated the theory of the Unwritten Torah clung firmly to it, and were fully justified by the results which followed its adoption. The difference which it made was this: That it transformed the Torah from being only a written document already ancient and in danger of becoming obsolete into a continuous revelation keeping pace with the ages, and it threw upon the teachers the responsibility of giving, as Torah, that which in their own mind and conscience was the highest, truest, and best. Of the written Torah the *litera scripta manet*; but as time went on it became more and more difficult to fulfil its precepts to the letter, and the text was overloaded with interpretations (midrash), and supplemented more and more frequently by ordinances (gezēroth) of the priests, directions given for this or that occasion and for which it was never claimed that they were Torah. It was mainly in the Temple and by the priests that the written Torah could still be literally obeyed and its precepts fulfilled. The religious life of the people tended to become more and more dissociated from the written Torah; and if the process had gone on, Judaism as the religion of Torah would actually have become what it never did become, but what many people imagine that it did, a purely priestly religion, a mere affair of ritual and sacrifices. From such a fate Judaism was saved by the magnificent conception of the Unwritten Torah, and by the faithful devotion of those who worked out that conception, and who steadfastly adhered to the higher and avoided the lower interpretation of which it was capable. They recaptured the idea of religion as the service of the living God, present now as he always had been present to his people, revealing himself now as he had revealed himself to the prophets, and speaking not alone in the words of an ancient text, but in words which came from the heart and conscience of men who felt his hand laid upon them to ' guide them into all truth '.

A contrast is often drawn between the Rabbis and the Prophets (see *Pharisees*, p. 135 f.), very much to the praise of the latter and the disparagement of the former. The contrast, such as there is, appears only on the surface. The Prophets declared the word of the Lord as it came to them, they claimed his authority for what they said, and they said it without regard to any of the powers that be. The Rabbis, it is alleged, were tied to what had been said by ' them of old ', what had been handed down; and the point is brought out clearly in the famous words: ' He spake as one having authority, and not as their scribes ' (Matt. vii. 29). The writer of that Gospel had not got to the root of the matter, nor have they who like to compare the free prophetic spirit, which they find in the Christian religion, with the constrained utterance which they suppose to be characteristic of Judaism. The truth, in this as in so much

[69]

else, is only found by those who go below the surface. And the truth in the present case, or at least a closer approximation to the truth than is expressed in the merely plausible contrast noted above, is that the conception of the Unwritten Torah is the reproduction of Prophecy, the same in spirit though differing in form. Not indeed that every aspect of Prophecy was reproduced in the Unwritten Torah. The element of prediction was not included, and it should be noted that it was just this element of prediction which was taken up and made use of by the writers of the Apocalyptic books. It is possible that this was the reason or one reason why the Apocalyptic books were never recognised by the teachers of the Rabbinical line, and never included in the Canon. More will be said on this point when we come, in a later chapter, to deal with the Apocalyptic literature.

It is of Prophecy as the teaching of righteousness by divine command that the Unwritten Torah was the reproduction. Teachers of righteousness the prophets had certainly been; and it was, as we have seen, the object of Ezra and those who returned with him from Babylon to take to heart the lesson of the Exile and to make effective the teaching of the prophets, the neglect of which had been the prime cause of the national disaster. Ezra and the Sopherim had done this through the establishment of the Torah and the practical application of its teaching (which, in their view, included that of the prophets) by the method of interpretation. There was no opposition whatever between the teaching of the prophets and the method of Ezra and the Sopherim. The theory of the Unwritten Torah only carried farther what they had begun, in regard to the prophets and not merely in regard to the Torah. For the later theory reproduced another element in Prophecy in addition to the teaching of righteousness; and this further element was, though it may seem strange to say it, the prophetic freedom of utterance. The theory of the Unwritten Torah implied, as has been shown above, that those who declared its teaching and determined the halachah in accordance therewith did so on the authority of their own reason and conscience, and not by seeking their authority in the written text. The prophet spoke in the name of the Lord: ' The word of the Lord came to me, saying ', and so on. What does this mean, in the last resort, except that the prophet spoke out of his own reason and conscience, these being the only known means by which God declares his will to men? That, in the case of the prophets, their conviction that God really spoke to them was vivid and overwhelming goes without saying. But they could give no guarantee of the truth of what they declared beyond their own passionate sincerity. Men believed them, and most rightly believed them, through the force of their personality; but if that was not felt, there was no other proof that could be given. Men who under other circumstances and in other times have declared what their reason assured them was true, and their conscience compelled them to own as right, and who have sometimes suffered a martyr's death rather than deny it, are not indeed usually called prophets; but none the less they spoke at the bidding of God, and every brave and true and sincere man and woman, in all ages and countries, has done the same. We distinguish between prophet, martyr and ordinary faithful man or woman, because of differences in the manner and the circumstance in which they ' testified of what they knew '; but the character of the inward act is essentially the same in every case, implicit acceptance of what is owned to be of divine authority.

Now those who developed the conception of the Unwritten Torah, and consistently acted on it, while they certainly made no claim in so many words to speak in the name of the Lord, nevertheless did essentially what the prophets had done; they declared as true and right what their reason and conscience compelled them to own as the highest. That they gave their teaching forth in the form of halachah and haggadah, and not in the form of prophetic oracles, is a difference of method, not of essence. That difference was the obvious result of translating Prophecy into the terms of Torah, and it was a necessary result; but that difference does not affect the fundamental identity of the authority in each case. How far these ideas were consciously present to the minds of those who developed the conception of the Unwritten Torah it is not easy to say. But it is certain that they regarded themselves as the successors of the prophets, and that not merely in fact but by right. They took note of the fact that Prophecy had ceased. Whatever that might mean, the fact was undeniable. But they were aware that they and their predecessors, the Sopherim, not only followed the prophets in time, but had done, and were doing, a work very closely akin to that of the prophets, a work whose object was to realise in practice what the prophets had preached, and preached apparently in vain, to judge by the results. There is a curious saying in the Talmud (b. B. Bath. 12a), ' Prophecy was taken from the Prophets and was given to the Wise,' to which is added the remark: ' and it has not been taken from these'. That saying was the utterance of a Rabbi of the third century A.D., long after the period with which we are concerned; but it was assumed as an axiom in a discussion which certain still later Rabbis held concerning it. The discussion turned upon the question How was it possible that a saying should be uttered by one eminent man and again in a later age by another? The solution would seem to be that it was due to that which had been taken from the prophets and given to the Wise. And the difference between a prophet and a wise man was that the former gave no reason for what he said, while the latter gave a reason, his understanding being enlightened, so as to comprehend what he uttered. The prophet was like a blind man. The relevance of this passage to the subject at present under discussion is that the Rabbis felt that they had, no less but even more than the prophets, divine authority for what they taught, and that this was given to them after the time when the prophets had ceased to function. It was a way of expressing the belief that the revelation did not cease with the extinction of prophecy.

And the same belief underlies another remarkable passage in the Talmud (b. Erub. 13b) where it is said that for three years the House of Hillel and the House of Shammai were divided, each claiming that the halachah was according to its own view. At the end of three years ' a Bath Qol [voice from heaven] went forth, [saying] These and those have the words of the living God; but the halachah is according to the House of Hillel'. The particular controversy does not here concern us, nor the decision in favour of the House of Hillel; but it is significant that the teaching of the two Houses is declared to be ' the words of the living God ', and that this declaration applies to the two opposite views equally. The Rabbis of both Houses were engaged in defining the halachah, and in that task they were trying, in Kepler's phrase, 'to think God's thoughts after him,' and believed that God helped them to do so. That this is the meaning may be further shown by a passage in the Midrash, Pesikta d. R. Cahana, p. 152*a* (edition of Buber), where it is said that when certain sages met together to determine the halachah, ' God left the assembly above and came down and made small his Shechinah below ' (i.e. adapted it to earthly conditions). ' And why all this? So that if they went wrong in any thing, the Holy One, blessed be He, would enlighten their minds [faces] in the halachah and this is that which is written (Ps. lxxxix. 15), '' They shall walk [jĕhăllēchūn], O Lord, in the light of thy countenance ''.'

These passages may be enough to show that in the conception of the Unwritten Torah was implied the belief in the continuous progressive revelation of God, and that his authority was made known in the reason and conscience of those who sought to know his will, and not only in the written text of the Torah. And even there, only to the enlightened mind which sought to find the true meaning and was not content with the mere letter. This is what the Psalmist meant when he said (Ps. cxix. 18): ' Open thou mine eyes, that I may behold wondrous things out of thy Torah'. The conception of the Unwritten Torah is the key to all the subsequent development of Judaism along the Rabbinical line; indeed, without it there could hardly have been any development. What it did was to make possible an ethical advance in the teaching given, not merely by putting a higher construction on older teaching of less ethical worth, but by actually annulling an express command in the written Torah and replacing it by a halachah in accordance with a higher moral standard. This was done in regard to the famous law ' An eye for an eye ', etc. (Exod. xxi. 24-5), which was commuted to a money fine (M. B. Kamma viii. 1). So in many other instances. The whole tendency was to re-shape the halachah in accordance with the higher moral standard of those who from age to age were entrusted with the responsibility of fixing and declaring it. Not that there was any sudden change in this respect consequent on the adoption of the theory of the Unwritten Torah or the recognition of its validity. But a change there was, however gradual; and what it meant was that, under new conditions and in a form wholly unknown to the prophets, that which had enabled the prophets to declare the word of the Lord was again making itself felt in the minds of the later teachers. ' Prophecy was taken from the Prophets and given to the Wise; and from these it was not taken away.'

CHAPTER IV

THE REVOLT AGAINST HELLENISM

IN the preceding chapters we have seen what was done with the Torah by Ezra and his successors the Sopherim and the later teachers. The principles were laid down which defined the position of the Torah as the supreme authority in religion, and the methods by which that authority was made effective for the actual guidance of those who were pledged to live under it. Neither the principles nor the methods were accepted by the whole of the Jewish community until long after the time of Ezra; not indeed until after the final destruction of the national existence by the defeat of Bar Cocheba (A.D. 135) had left the upholders of this view of Torah without other than individual opponents. But even in the time of José b. Joezer and the first exponents of the Unwritten Torah, there is clear evidence that the work of Ezra and the Sopherim had produced a deep impression upon a large section of the community, an impression which was never afterwards effaced. To show this is necessary, because it is the proof of the importance of what was done by the teachers of Torah, not only by Ezra and the Sopherim but by all the teachers of the Rabbinical line down to the closing of the Talmud—to go no further. This work, being in the form of oral teaching, cannot be illustrated by contemporary evidence as to its subject matter until a date near that of the Christian era; but, from what has already been said, the nature of it is clear, and its importance for the knowledge of the religious life of the Jewish community is obvious.

The work of the teachers on the Rabbinical line, after Ezra, was put to a severe test by the Revolt against Hellenism with which the name of the Maccabeans is for ever associated. In the present section we shall study that Revolt, not in its general historical bearings, but as a factor powerfully influencing the status of the Torah in the regard of the Jewish community at the time and afterwards. Hellenism is the name given to the general influence of the Greek culture in all its many forms which spread over all the countries affected by the conquests of Alexander the Great. His vast empire was divided after his death in 323 B.C. amongst the most powerful of his generals, who established themselves as kings in their respective territories. But, whether the government was that of Ptolemy in Egypt or Seleucus in Syria, the culture was Greek, in language, manners and customs, trade, commerce, literature, art, religion; yet, although Greek, by no means of the quality it had possessed in the great days of its Attic brilliance. No doubt that quality was still there for those who could appreciate it; Plato could still be read, and the great library in Alexandria would not have been founded unless there had been some real sense of what Greek thought and literature had been at the height of their power. But Egyptians and Syrians remained Egyptians and Syrians; and the Greek culture which they adopted was of the kind which they could most readily assimilate. It was a culture which gave much freedom of action, both for good and for evil, provided much opportunity for enjoyment of the good things of life, and imposed little or no restraint upon conduct. The religion of Egypt or Syria could easily come to terms with the Greek religion, such as it was. Greek art was in demand as a means of adorning the new cities which rapidly sprang up. Greek athletics and public games gave a new interest to life, and were eagerly taken up. Everywhere the Greek culture brought, as it would seem, fresh air and sunlight brilliance and gaiety, wherever it came. Also, it brought vice and corruption, having no apparent moral standard, or none which any authority was able to apply or thought of applying. A light-hearted, easy-going manner of life was characteristic of Hellenism; and though it called forth heroes to assail it, it never produced any in its defence.

The Jewish community, ever since it had been settled in its small territory after the return from the Captivity, had lived continuously in the midst or the near neighbourhood of Gentiles, idolators of various sorts, and its members had kept themselves to themselves. The ' false worship ', as they would regard it, of their Gentile neighbours had no attractions for them, nor had the general manner of life of those from whom they looked upon themselves as a people set apart. And on the whole no one interfered with them. The Persian government, whose subjects they were, let them do as they pleased, so long as they obeyed its laws and paid the taxes it imposed.

But it was a very different thing when with the change from Persian to Greek rule Hellenism made its influence felt, and came pouring like a flood into a country which had known nothing of it. There was no escape from that influence. It was present everywhere, in the street and the market, in the everyday life and all the phases of social intercourse. Moreover, the source and centre from which it went forth was no longer the far distant capital of the Persian Empire, but Alexandria or Antioch, as the case might be, the seat of a ruler who was in a position to take much closer notice of his subjects than had been the case before. The Jews were, of all people then living, the least likely to adopt with ease the Greek culture; all their previous experience had been of a kind which in no way prepared them for it. Yet the very novelty of it, the variety of new interest and pleasure which it offered, could not fail to make it attractive. And attractive it certainly proved to be. Not many, perhaps, were able or inclined to study Greek philosophy or read the works of the great poets and dramatists; but the beauty of sculpture and architecture made appeal to every seeing eye, and even the severest disapprover could not escape the sight of them. Moreover, the Greek language acted as a powerful means of increasing the influence of Hellenism. For it was now a matter of necessity to learn Greek, as the common language of trade and business and social intercourse generally, not specially in Judea, but in practically all the countries of what is now called the near East. In the old days of the Persian supremacy there had been no need to learn the Persian language, unless on the part of the few persons directly connected with the office of the governor. The Jewish people spoke Aramaic, and the learned men spoke Hebrew in addition. So, of course, they continued to do, but they could not any longer carry on their daily life without some knowledge of Greek; and, speaking and hearing Greek, they naturally became acquainted with the ideas which lay behind the language.

It is safe to say that no one, high or low, who was living in Judea in the period which includes the whole of the third and the beginning of the second century B.C., wholly escaped the influence of Hellenism, but its effects were not equally marked in all classes. Some received it eagerly, others were more or less indifferent, and some were definitely hostile. Those who were most ready to adopt the new culture were, naturally, such as by birth or wealth enjoyed the privileges of the court and the favour of the king, since it was the policy of the government to Hellenise the subjects in every possible way. To this class belonged many of the chief priests, that is, the members of the great priestly families though not always the High Priest himself. Their interests centred in the Temple, but even they did not venture to Hellenise the ancient order of its services. That was only done by direct command of Antiochus Epiphanes, who caused an altar to be built in honour of Zeus Olympios on the great altar of the Temple, and offered swine upon it. Even he made no pretence of adapting the old use; he frankly abolished it. Until that act of violence had been committed, the Temple and its services remained as a barrier in the way of Hellenism. But though they refrained from attempts to Hellenise it, the chief priests and their associates in the wealthy and powerful families were foremost amongst the supporters of the new culture, and themselves adopted the new fashions.

At the opposite extreme were those who on principle disapproved of Hellenism in every form, and would not compromise in their opposition to it. Who and how many they were before the Revolt began, it is impossible to say; and after the Revolt had begun they were merged in the general body of the insurgents. But some resolute opponents there must have been, and they would probably be found amongst the most strict and severe members of the Torah party. Whether they would have been heard of if the Revolt had not broken out may be doubted. As for the great mass of the community, there must have been many degrees of inclination and disinclination towards Hellenism; and it is quite conceivable that if Antiochus Epiphanes had refrained from violent measures, had been content to go very slowly and, above all, had not thrown down a direct challenge to the Jewish religion, Hellenism might after all have prevailed and made the people of Judea like one of 'the peoples round about'.

The actual outbreak of the Revolt only took place after a period of severe persecution. A royal decree had been issued which forbade in the most explicit terms the practice of the Jewish religion, especially circumcision and the observance of the Sabbath; books of the Torah, when found, were torn or disfigured, and the owners put to death. Jews were required to eat swine's flesh, and to sacrifice after the Greek manner. In short, everything was done that could offend Jewish sensibility and outrage Jewish reverence for their religion. Antiochus had no doubt begun by supposing that it would be easy to make his Jewish subjects conform to his Hellenising policy; for indeed the first step had been taken by leading men in Jerusalem who asked the king for permission to introduce various Greek institutions into the capital city. He gave the permission, and naturally relied on the support of a powerful party in Jerusalem. When he found that opposition was offered, instead of the ready compliance which he expected, he resorted to violence in order not merely to compel obedience, but to make an end of that religion which stood in the way of his will. That anyone, let alone a whole people, should be ready to face torture and death rather than abandon their religion would be, to a man of his character, inconceivable. In that age, indeed, such a thing was without parallel. Religion as it was understood among the nations of antiquity was never taken so seriously that anyone would die for it. When, therefore, this wholly unexpected opposition was shown by the Jews, who to the number of hundreds suffered death and barbarous cruelty rather than be false to their religion, the king's fiercest rage was turned against the stubborn race, and a deadly strife was begun which could only end with the defeat of one or the other of the opposing forces.

The signal of revolt, after a period of passive resistance, was given by the priest Mattathias, of Modin, who, when called upon by the king's officers to offer sacrifice and thus to set an example to the people of the place, not only refused but killed another Jew who was coming forward to sacrifice, and then killed the king's officer. Whereupon, with his five sons, and all who dared to throw in their lot with him, he fled to the hills, and the guerilla war began in which his son Judas (Maccabæus) was the first and most famous leader. The course of events from the outbreak of revolt to the final attainment of national independence may be read in the history books, and does not concern us here. It is of more immediate importance to study the nature of the resistance to Antiochus, its ground, and the manner of its expression.

When Mattathias refused to obey the royal edict and defied the king, he said (1 Macc. ii. 27): 'Let every one that is zealous for the Torah and that would maintain the covenant come forth after me'. The appeal to rise in defence of the Torah was sufficient to rally to his support those who in increasing numbers fought under the leadership of Judas, Jonathan and Simon, and who must in the end have included by far the greater part of the Jewish people. It is significant that the Torah, and not the Temple, was made the watchword of the Revolt. For it was only a short while before that the Temple had been desecrated by the erection of the altar above mentioned (1 Macc. i. 54), an act which must have made every Jew shudder as Mattathias himself did (1 Macc. ii. 6-14). Nevertheless, the Torah and not the Temple was the ground of appeal; and so far as appears no other cry was raised during the whole course of the struggle.

Doubtless, other motives besides zeal for the Torah came in to help to secure the final victory, and they had a share in the fruits of that victory. But from first to last the struggle was between Hellenism on the one side and the Torah on the other; and the final result was that Hellenism was routed and the Torah left supreme, more or less acknowledged by everyone and openly challenged by no one.

Mattathias was a priest, but not one of the chief priests in Jerusalem. He dwelt in Modin, and it was as a townsman of that place that he did what he did. In other words, the Revolt had its origin and its support not in Jerusalem, but in the country amongst the rank and file of the people. The leading men in Jerusalem, or many of them, were notoriously Hellenisers, and would never have dreamed of rebellion for the Torah or anything else that was Jewish. They do not appear to have protested against the desecration of the Temple. The strength of the opposition to Hellenism, which broke out in the Revolt, evidently lay in the common people; and the fact that the call to rise in defence of the Torah met with so general and so eager a response shows that the common people must have learned in some way to look upon the Torah as containing the very essence of their religion. If their religion had been, as it is often supposed to have been, a purely priestly matter, centring in the

Temple and its ritual and directed by priests to that object, then the Temple and not the Torah would have been the obvious battle-cry, and it is quite conceivable that there might have been no revolt at all. There was a revolt, and the Temple considered as the symbol of the popular religion affords no explanation of it.

The explanation lies ready to hand in the work of the teachers of Torah described in the preceding sections. Ezra had begun it, the Sopherim had carried it on, and the later teachers had revived it after the period of anarchy caused by the change from Persian to Greek rule. Thus for at least 250 years there had been more or less regular teaching of the people concerning the Torah and their obligations under it. The weekly meetings at which the Torah was read dated perhaps from the time of Ezra, and there is no reason to suppose that they were ever discontinued, as it is certain that they developed into the synagogues of later times.* Such meetings were held as opportunity offered, and no one was obliged to attend them. We may fairly suppose that they only gradually increased in number so as to become customary institutions in the towns and villages, and probably at no time were they attended by the whole population of the place where they were held. Nevertheless, the influence of such centres of religious instruction, planted right in the midst of the people and carrying on a very definite work, must have been very considerable, and it would only grow stronger as time went on. This religious instruction was

* In Ps. lxxiv. 8 it is said: 'They have burned up all the "mōādē-ēl" in the land'. The words *moade-el* are rendered both in A.V. and R.V. by 'Synagogues of God'. The words mean literally, as in R.V. margin, 'places of assembly of God,' and they are not the name which was given to synagogues in times when the Synagogue was a well-known institution. To translate *moadim* by 'synagogues' is to assume that the Synagogue was a regular institution in the time of the Psalmist, which may very well have been the period of persecution just before the Maccabean Revolt. It is more accurate to translate, as in R.V. margin, ' places of assembly '; and if that is done, there need be no difficulty in referring the word to those regular meetings for the study of Torah which are mentioned in the text, and ascribed to Ezra and the Sopherim. These certainly developed into the Synagogue of later times, and it is only a question of how far the development had proceeded at the time of the Maccabean Revolt. Note that the *moade-el*, whatever they were, were connected with a building, which could be burned, also that there were a number of them: ' *all* the " *moade-el* " in the land '.

G

given by men who had a quite definite object in view, viz. to teach the Torah to the people, as Ezra had shown the way. And it does not appear that any other effort was made to bring religion to bear on the lives of the people. The Temple was useless for this purpose; all its influence was confined to those who could personally be present at its services, apart from the general prestige which it enjoyed as the one visible sanctuary of the national religion. Those who controlled the Temple never did anything beyond its precincts for the religious training of the people. Apart from the priests, a man like Ben Sira might give instruction to any who would attend his lectures, but he says nothing of any wider scope for his work. The Torah teachers, it would seem, had the field to themselves; and they had carried on their work for 250 years when the revolt against Hellenism came to show how thoroughly that work had been done. They had driven home the lesson of the Torah, what it was, what it meant, what it required, and what it held up as the true end of life; and when the call came, it was in defence of the Torah that the people rose in arms. ' Let every one that is zealous for the Torah and that would maintain the covenant come forth after me ' (1 Macc. ii. 27).

It is only natural to suppose that those who had been instructed in the Torah were not all alike in the response which they made when the persecution put their loyalty to the test. It is said (*ib*. i. 53): ' Many of the people joined themselves unto them, [the officials of Antiochus] those who had forsaken the Torah; these did evil in the land, and caused Israel to hide in all manner of hiding places'. The deserters were men who had been trained under the Torah, to some extent, otherwise they could not have forsaken it. How many they were is not stated; but of those who resisted and suffered death before the revolt began, the number must have been considerable, ' and with whomsoever was found a book of the covenant, and if he was (found) consenting to the Torah, such an one was, according to the king's sentence, condemned to death. Thus did they in their might to the Israelites who were found month by month in their cities ' (*ib*. i. 57, 58). Note that this went on ' month by month '. When Mattathias gave the signal of revolt, there were already others in other places who were only waiting for it. ' At that time many who were seeking righteousness and

[82]

judgment went down to the wilderness to abide there, they and their sons and their wives and their cattle, for misfortunes were multiplied upon them ' (*ib.* ii. 29, 30). The particular band here referred to were treacherously slain, because they would not fight on the Sabbath, even in their own defence. They were not of the number of those with Mattathias in Modin; he only heard of their fate afterwards. But the incident shows how the despair which led to revolt was present up and down the country. A more definite indication is furnished by the statement: ' Then were gathered unto them [Mattathias and his followers] a company of the Hasidim, mighty men of Israel who willingly offered themselves for the Torah, every one of them ' (*ib.* ii. 42). The Hasidim are here referred to as already known by name. They were the extreme devotees of the Torah, taking its obligations in the most serious and determined manner; and the fact that they were known by a special name marks a certain distinction between them and the rank and file of the people. It is not said that Mattathias or any of his followers were themselves Hasidim, but the fact proves that devotion to the Torah was strong and widespread without being carried to extreme lengths. There is frequent mention of Hasidim in the Psalms (both in the singular and the plural); but the word ' hasid ' meaning ' pious ', ' godly ', was in common use, and does not in any passage in the Old Testament necessarily imply that the person so designated was a member of a particular group. When the writer of 1 Macc. speaks of ' a company of the Hasidim ', he had in mind, of course, a company of persons of the kind indicated by the word hasid; but that there was a regular sect or party known as the Hasidim, in the same definite manner as that in which the later Pharisees or Essenes were a sect or party, is open to question. It is significant that neither ' hasid ' nor ' hasidim ' occurs in the book of Daniel. The name Hasidim seems to denote only those devotees of Torah, amongst the whole number of its adherents, who were most strict in their observance, most uncompromising in their loyalty. That there was any clearly marked line of separation between them and their more moderate co-religionists is a mere matter of speculation. When the Psalmist (Ps. lxxxvi. 2) said: ' Preserve my soul for I am "hasid"', there is nothing to show that he meant to imply that he was a member

[83]

of a special group; he described his own religious attitude by the appropriate adjective. There were doubtless in his time (whenever that was) and in the time immediately before the Revolt (possibly long before) many persons to whom the word 'hasid' was applicable and was applied, as denoting a special type among Jews generally and adherents of Torah in particular. The name was convenient before the time of the Revolt, because then devotion to the Torah, let alone such strict devotion, was not universal. After the defeat of Hellenism, when the Torah had won its complete victory, there was no need of any special name even for its more extreme champions. At a somewhat later date, when the cleavage between different sections of the people in regard to the Torah made itself felt in a changed form, the old name Hasidim was not revived to designate the new party. Instead, they were called Pharisees (see the present writer's *Pharisees*, p. 27 f.); but to all intents and purposes, the Pharisees were the Hasidim over again.

The Hasidim then were the extremists among the defenders of the Torah, and the mass of the people were not hasidim while yet so far 'zealous for the Torah' that they rose in arms at the call of Mattathias. What was the ground of their zeal? What was it that made it an imperious duty to them to imperil their lives for the Torah? It is evident that they felt that their religion was at stake, and no less evident that their religion was something much more than, and very different from, mere performance of prescribed duties at the direction of priests, or even teachers of Torah who no doubt were for the most part priests. If the Judaism of the people in the period from Ezra to the Maccabees had been, as it is usually supposed to have been, a formalism of growing strictness and decreasing spiritual vitality, there would not have been any revolt, for there would have been nothing which anyone would deem worthy of so great a sacrifice as that of life in its defence. It was not the priests as priests, it was Ezra and the Sopherim who taught the people to know and reverence the Torah, as the revelation which God had given to Israel, the Torah as the guide to the doing of his will, the Torah as the enlightener of their minds in all their thought of God. The religion which centred in the Temple and its sacrifices was no doubt venerable, and made a strong appeal to all the conservative instincts in the Jewish nature. But, after all, it could say nothing new, it was but the repetition of ancient ceremonies according to a prescribed ritual, and the passing ages made no change unless to increase the outward splendour of its performance, and perhaps the worldly corruption of those who had the largest share in its maintenance. The religion based on Torah was far different, even though the Torah included in its instructions directions for the proper conduct of the Temple services. Ezra and the Sopherim had made it their object to bring the Torah home to the people as a matter of personal concern to every man, woman, and child. And, though they did not gain the support or even the attention of all the people, yet they certainly did succeed in making a deep impression upon a large number, did awaken and foster in them a strong personal religion, which naturally expressed itself in terms of Torah. And this, though it is seldom recognised in the accounts given by scholars of Judaism in the period between Ezra and the Maccabees, is, if not the most conspicuous, certainly the most important fact in the history of Judaism in that period. How important, and also how little recognised, will be seen more clearly when we come to deal with the Apocryphal literature.

It will be remembered that when Mattathias gave the signal of revolt his words were: ' Whoso is zealous for the Torah, and would maintain the covenant, let him come forth after me ' (1 Macc. ii. 27). Why did he mention the covenant? He had in mind, presumably, the covenant made at Sinai, when the Torah was given to Moses and by him proclaimed to Israel. But that was long ago, and it might be supposed that so ancient a memory could make no fresh appeal, even at so critical a time as that in which Mattathias uttered his challenge. Some light is thrown on the question by a passage in the book of Daniel (ix. 11-13): ' Yea, all Israel have transgressed thy Torah, even turning aside that they should not hear [obey] thy voice. Therefore hath the curse been poured out upon us and the oath that is written in the Torah of Moses the servant of God; for we have sinned against him. And he hath confirmed his words which he spake against us, and against our judges that judged us, by bringing upon us a great evil; for under the whole heaven hath not been done as hath been done upon Jerusalem. As it is written in the Torah of Moses all this evil is come upon

[85]

us'. The book of Daniel, as is generally agreed, belongs to the period of the Maccabean Revolt, and must have been making its message known at the very time when Mattathias started the revolt. If the author of 1 Macc. is right in making Mattathias in his dying words mention Daniel and Hananiah, Azariah and Mishael (1 Macc. ii. 59, 60), it would seem probable that Mattathias had read the book, or at all events that he knew something of its contents. When therefore he called on ' whoso would maintain the covenant ' to follow him, he would have in mind the curse which had been pronounced against all who disobeyed the Torah (Deut. xxx. 1, 19), and of which the reminder had so recently been given. A curse was no light matter in the estimation of the people of those times. And, in this particular instance, the curse pronounced by Moses all those ages ago had, according to the author of the book of Daniel, been the direct cause of all the evil from which the people were suffering at the hands of the persecutors. The Torah had been given on Sinai, and all the people had solemnly promised to obey it: ' All the words which the Lord hath spoken we will do ' (Exod. xxiv. 3). Therefore, anyone who failed to obey the Torah made himself liable to the effects of the curse. And that this was a real ground of apprehension is shown by traces of its influence in the Talmud, belonging to a time much later than the period of the Maccabees. (See Lauterbach, ' Sadducees and Pharisees,' in the *Kohler Festschrift*, p. 187, n. 1.) The appeal of Mattathias had, accordingly, been both to the loyalty and the fears of those who heard him, to their zeal for the Torah on its own account, and to their fear of the consequences if they did not ' maintain the covenant '.

Such then was the nature of the resistance offered to Hellenism by the defenders of the Torah, and it only remains to indicate the character of the victory which they won.

It has been shown above that the watchword of the Revolt was the Torah and its defence; and the final victory was, beyond any doubt, the victory of the Torah over Hellenism. But this was not the only result, as the defence of the Torah was probably not the only motive in the minds of the insurgents. The desire to throw off the foreign yoke and to win the freedom of an independent state must have arisen at a very early stage of the struggle, and have inspired a hope which was by no means identical with the hope of placing the Torah out of danger. It is quite likely that Judas Maccabæus himself, when he stood forth as the first captain of the insurgents in loyal response to the call of Mattathias, saw other possibilities besides that of delivering the Torah from its enemies. It is certain that the struggle, carried on for years with varying fortunes, did not cease until the independence of the Jewish state had been acknowledged by the Syrian court, and Simon, the third of the sons of Mattathias, had been recognised as the head of that state. With the political fortunes of the short-lived rule of the Hasmonean house we are not here concerned; and, for the present purpose, the victory in question is the victory of the Torah over Hellenism.

That victory was complete and final. There was never again any attempt on the part of any ruler to do what Antiochus Epiphanes had tried and failed to do. No doubt Herod the Great would have been very willing to try, and went as far as he dared in that direction; but even he shrank from provoking another Maccabean Revolt, having clearly before his eyes what had come of the first. So far as the Jewish state was concerned, Hellenism was done with; and the Torah was henceforth acknowledged by all as the supreme religious authority, whatever interpretation might be put upon its precepts and its obligations, and whether or not the homage offered to it was sincere. The Torah was, so to speak, the constant factor in the problem of Jewish national life, taken into account by all who in various ways tried to solve that problem. It is important to note this because it often seems to be supposed that the Pharisees, of whom more will be said presently, had, as it were, exclusive rights in the Torah, to such an extent that any book which dealt much with Torah must have been written by a Pharisee. This is an error into which many scholars who have dealt with the Apocrypha and Pseudepigrapha have fallen. A very natural error, but none the less an error. Torah was acknowledged by everyone, by Sadducees no less than by Pharisees, by Zealots no less than by Essenes. It was only when these several parties came to apply their principles to practical objects that their divergent views of what the Torah was became apparent. All the types of Judaism represented

[87]

by the various sects which arose after the Maccabean Revolt took their stand upon the Torah, and from their own point of view were entirely loyal to it.

The victory of Torah was finally won as soon as the early successes of the Revolt made it possible to re-establish the religious observances which had been in abeyance during the persecution and the first fighting. The visible symbol of it was the purification of the Temple and the resumption of its services, which was accomplished just three years after Antiochus had profaned it (1 Macc. iv. 54); and the memory of that re-dedication of the Temple is celebrated even unto this day in the annual festival of Hanuccah. That the Temple was thus made the symbol of victory does not in any way conflict with what was said above (pp. 81, 82) of the relative importance of Temple and Torah. There could be no victory for the Torah which did not make the restoration of the Temple one of its first concerns. After all, the Temple and its services were expressly provided for and enjoined in the Torah, so much so that some have supposed that the whole Torah, as written in the Pentateuch, was, so to speak, focussed in the Temple, and had for its main object to set forth the origin and purpose of the priesthood and the ritual. The Torah, as has been shown, meant a good deal else besides this; but no Jew, whatever he might conceive the Torah to be, would feel other than a deep indignation at the outrage offered to the Temple, and a passionate desire to avenge the insult, wipe out the stain, and restore to its former purity the ancient ritual.

To purify and re-dedicate the Temple was, however, only the symbol of the victory of Torah and the defeat of Hellenism. The actual victory implied much more than could be expressed in the work of restoration of the profaned altar and the cleansing of the desecrated courts. The public life of the nation had to be carried on somehow, and things done which had formerly been done by the officials of the Syrian government or by the Hellenisers among the rulers. All these had now been chased out; and, though complete independence was not achieved until several years had passed since the outbreak of the Revolt, yet the Syrian government never permanently regained the mastery over the Jewish people. There must have been some kind of provisional government, at first very haphazard, and only

[88]

gradually attaining a more regular form. There is mention in the Talmud (b. Sanh. 82a; A. Zar 36b) of a 'Beth Din of the Hasmoneans', but no indication is given of the time at which it functioned. Derenbourg (*Essai*, p. 84) places it under Simon, who ruled from 142 to 135 B.C., and this is quite possible; yet we might expect that the Sanhedrin, established long before the Revolt and presumably in abeyance during the years of strife, would have resumed its meetings in the comparatively peaceful time of Simon.

It is impossible to fix the date of the Beth Din of the Hasmoneans, and it would hardly be worth while to mention it if it were not that the mere existence of a Beth Din implies a judicial reference to the Torah. It shows that there was some official attempt to regulate the administration of justice in accordance with the Torah. And it is natural to suppose that the first attempts on the part of the Hasmonean leaders to govern the Jewish community, even before independence was achieved, would be of such a nature as to conform to the view of the Torah held by those who had begun the revolt in its defence. There is, so far as I know, no positive evidence that this was actually the case; but it is made extremely probable by the fact that John Hyrcanus (135-105 B.C.), the son and successor of Simon, found it necessary or desirable to break with the Pharisees, who in his time represented the view of the Torah which underlay the Revolt, and to join the Sadducees, who by that same time were the party which repudiated the Unwritten Torah and confined their loyalty to the written text. The meaning of the change of attitude on the part of John Hyrcanus would be that he found it increasingly difficult, and at last impossible, to combine Torah with politics on the lines required by the theory of the Unwritten Torah, as expounded by the Pharisees. On the lines of the Sadducees, the Torah was venerated indeed, but its power to interfere in affairs of government was more and more restricted. More will be said of the Pharisees and Sadducees in the next chapter. They are mentioned here only for the purpose of suggesting that in the early years after the Revolt had begun, there was a desire, and to some extent an attempt, to organise the life of the newly formed Jewish state on the lines of what might be called a Torah community, and that to do this was only the logical outcome of the

[89]

' zeal for the Torah ' which had prompted the people to rise in arms to defend it.

In the following chapter we shall study the development of the Rabbinical line of teachers till it comes into the clear light of day in the Mishnah and the Talmud. And only then will it be possible to bring the contents of these several chapters on the Rabbinical line into connexion with the Ethical Teaching for the sake of which alone they have been written.

Chapter V

THE RABBINICAL LINE DOWN TO HILLEL

Within a comparatively short period from the time when Hellenism was defeated and the Torah achieved its victory, we come in sight of the division marked by the famous names Pharisee and Sadducee. It was a division not so much of the people as a whole, as of the leading men; and, although the names were new, the division which they indicated marked the reappearance of two principles which had helped to bring about the Revolt. While the struggle was at its height, the two divergent principles were united in zeal for the common cause; but, when first the religious victory was won and then the political, the representatives of the two principles began to be conscious of their antagonism, and finally came to an open rupture. The two principles were, the exaltation of the Torah as the supreme authority for all purposes, and the desire for the position and functions of an independent state under its own sovereign ruler. The Hasmonean leaders had fought loyally for the Torah, but they were by no means blind to the prospect of their own sovereignty which gradually opened before them as the struggle proceeded. And just in proportion as they inclined towards that dangerous ambition, they awakened the distrust of those who were for the Torah pure and simple.

But the opposition was not on the same lines as before the Revolt. Then, the enemy to be fought had been Hellenism, and against that enemy all friends of the Torah were united, whatever might be their own view of what the Torah was. Now, the opposition was between two parties, both of whom professed, quite sincerely, entire loyalty to the Torah, but who differed in their ideas of how that loyalty should be shown in practice—or, rather, to what extent it should be allowed to influence the conduct of practical affairs. If it be true, as suggested above, that the first attempts at self-government took the form of a desire to set up a sort of ' Torah state ', there was certain to be friction sooner or later. Because such a policy was practically impossible in a state, let alone a kingdom, which

[91]

must necessarily have diplomatic relations with other states. It might have been practicable when Judea was merely a province of the Persian Empire, and had nothing to think of beyond its own internal affairs. Probably that condition of single-minded devotion to the Torah had to a large extent been realised in the Persian days, and remained the ideal, to be striven for against the evil power of Hellenism and to be established again when Hellenism had been overthrown. Those who took this view would naturally look with disfavour upon the policy of national independence, which they must have instinctively felt was incompatible with their ideal, and in regard to which growing experience soon showed them that their instinct was right. If the Hasidim had been in existence in the years that followed the Revolt as in the years that led up to it, they would have taken precisely the line here indicated, for they consistently maintained the position of the Torah, the whole Torah, and nothing but the Torah. Indeed, it is in every way probable that many of the former Hasidim were among those who took the extreme view of the Torah under the early Hasmoneans. The interval of time from the outbreak of the Revolt to the final rupture between Pharisees and Sadducees was at the utmost about sixty years, and there must have been many years during which the divergence was growing which ended in that rupture. Be that as it may, those who took the line of complete all-round supremacy of the Torah were the spiritual descendants of the Hasidim, and they came to be known by the name of Pharisees, a name which probably refers to a minor feature of their practice and does not indicate the real ground of their existence as a separate religious party. (See the present writer's *Pharisees*, pp. 29-36.)

But though the Pharisees took up, or inherited, the position of the old Hasidim in regard to the Torah, they did so with a very important difference. For the theory of the Unwritten Torah was now making its way to acceptance by the teachers (see above, p. 66 f.), and the Pharisees took their stand, as they have maintained it throughout all their history, on the Unwritten Torah. With this powerful instrument in their hands they cherished the ideal of making the Torah applicable to every department of life; and the ideal naturally carried with it the duty of attempting to realise it in practice.

[92]

On the other hand, those whose hopes had been fixed on the thought of political independence, in a kingdom which should hold its own with other kingdoms, were not likely to look with any favour upon a conception of Torah which threatened to swallow up all the minor concerns of life in the one absorbing devotion to religion. The Torah as it had been given to Israel, the written Torah, they loyally accepted. Their fathers had sworn to obey it, and they had no idea of repudiating it. But the Unwritten Torah was quite another thing, an innovation of which no one had ever heard till a few years ago. If the written Torah was becoming more or less out of date and needed to be supplemented by special ordinances, gezeroth, so be it; that had been expressly provided for in the Torah itself (Deut. xvii. 9-11), and had been acted on from time to time. There was no need for anything more. But the Unwritten Torah was an unknown quantity. No one, except those who professed to declare it, could say what it enjoined or forbade, what alterations it would make in the existing practice, what new claims it would make to obedience upon points where the written Torah gave no directions. If it were recognised, life would become impossible except within the narrow range of personal religion. Public affairs, and especially the politics of a self-governing state, could not be carried on if the Torah, in this new and unwarranted extension of its meaning, were owned as the supreme authority. Those who held this view were, naturally, the men who had most to do with public affairs, the members of the great priestly families, the rich and influential whose security was bound up with the fortunes of the state. The party which included all these and took the line in regard to the Torah indicated above, came to be known by the name of Sadducees, a name whose origin is even more uncertain than that of the name Pharisees. But, whatever the two names signified, and however they were acquired, the two parties came into existence in the very early years of the Hasmonean state; and the real ground of the difference between them was and continued to be the validity or otherwise of the Unwritten Torah. Not, of course, as a mere speculative theory, but as involving practical consequences whose range it was impossible to foresee.

The definite rupture between the two parties took place at

some period in the reign of John Hyrcanus (135-105 B.C.), when that prince left the party of the Pharisees and went over to the Sadducees (see *Pharisees*, pp. 36-44). This, of course, shows that the two parties were more or less defined before that time; but naturally the secession of the sovereign from the one party and his adhesion to the other threw them both into more acute opposition. There was never any attempt at reconciliation between them, as indeed the ground of difference was funda-mental; it was in essence that difference, between Judaism as a religion and Judaism as the self-expression of a nation, which has played a part in Jewish history from the time of the Has-moneans down to the present day. Zionism and anti-Zionism are the latest phase of it.

When John Hyrcanus went over to the Sadducees, it is said by Josephus (Antt. xiii. 10, 6) that he annulled all the decrees which the Pharisees had imposed on the people, and punished those who observed them. This exactly bears out what has been said above, that the Torah party, or as we may now say the Pharisees, had striven to impose their own ideas upon the policy of the rulers, by way of setting up a ' Torah state ', and that with this object they had made some use of the Unwritten Torah to extend its range to obligations not defined in the written Torah. The new regulations, whatever they may have been, were, for the time, allowed if not enforced by the govern-ing body; but that they were felt to be irksome and in principle dangerous is shown by the fact that John Hyrcanus annulled them and punished the observers of them as soon as he went over to the Sadducees. He could not have more clearly shown the real reason of his change of policy.

The emergence into definite rivalry of the Pharisees and Sadducees is the most important consequence of the Maccabean Revolt in regard to the religious development of Judaism in the time which followed. We have to follow the line of the Phari-sees, for it was this which connected Ezra and the Sopherim with the Rabbis of the Talmud; and it was only for the purpose of defining the religious attitude of the Pharisees that the above historical sketch has been given.

The Pharisaic line is indicated by a series of names of teachers, twice given in the Mishnah (M. Hagg. ii. 2; Aboth i; and alluded to M. Peah ii. 6). They are grouped in pairs (zugoth),

[94]

and are usually referred to as the Zugoth. There were five of these pairs, each pair following immediately on its predecessor. The names and approximate dates of the successive Zugoth are as follows: I. José b. Joezer of Zeredah and José b. Johanan of Jerusalem, 200-160 B.C.; II. Jehoshua b. Perahjah and Nittai the Arbelite, second half of second century B.C.; III. Jehudah b. Tabbai and Simeon b. Shetah, beginning of first century B.C.; IV. Shemaiah and Abtalion, about the middle of the first century B.C.; V. Hillel and Shammai, end of first century B.C. In the passage M. Aboth i, it is said that each of the Zugoth ' received ' from its predecessor, and what was thus received was Torah. The purpose of that chapter of Aboth was to trace the line of tradition from Moses, to whom the Torah was given on Sinai, through Joshua, the Elders, the Prophets, the Great Synagogue, Simeon the Just, Antigonos of Socho, to José b. Joezer and José b. Johanan, and so on down to Hillel and Shammai. After these, the last of the Zugoth, the line of tradition broadens out by the inclusion of more and more names of teachers, now usually with the title Rabbi, until it becomes the ' multitude which no man can number ' of the Tannaim of the Mishnah, and the Amoraim of the Talmud. This is the line by which the Pharisees justified their claim to be the custodians of the Torah given to Moses; and whereas the earlier stages of the tradition, down to the Prophets, were the common inheritance of all Israel, in the later stages, from the period marked by the name of the Great Synagogue, in other words the period of Ezra and the Sopherim, the tradition becomes Pharisaic. This is true, as shown in the preceding chapters, even though the name of Pharisee only came in during the time of the first or, more probably, the second of the Zugoth.

The two men named in each of the Zugoth are represented as being colleagues in office. One is always called President (nasi) and the other Vice-President (Ab-beth-din). So they are styled (M. Hagg. ii. 2); and it has generally been understood that in the view of the Mishnah the men in question were respectively President and Vice-President of the Sanhedrin. They may have been members of the Sanhedrin in their time, and most of them probably were, but the available evidence goes to show that the High Priest was always the President of the Sanhedrin; and, as the High Priest had a deputy for certain purposes, it is not impossible that this deputy was the Vice-President. Be that as it may, there is nothing to show that the members of the Zugoth held in the Sanhedrin the high offices assigned to them. But that is not to say that the statement of the Mishnah is without foundation. We have seen that away back in the time of the Sopherim there was some sort of a council of the teachers of Torah (see above, p. 44 f.). Its work was interrupted by the period of anarchy caused by the change from Persian to Greek rule, and the consequent influence of Hellenism. When the Sanhedrin was established, in 196 B.C., it necessarily included amongst its members both Hellenisers and defenders of the Torah. Amongst the latter were José b. Joezer and José b. Johanan, the first of the Zugoth. Now it is said (b. Shabb. 14b) that these two made decrees (gāzĕrū) in regard to certain matters, a thing which they certainly could not do on their own authority, and for which the authority of the Sanhedrin is not claimed. Moreover, these decrees were regarded as valid, not merely for the particular adherents of the two Josés, but for the people in general. They were regulations affecting religious practice, which were never afterwards called in question. By what authority were they issued?

Büchler, in his monograph on the Sanhedrin and the Great Beth Din (*Das Synedrion in Jerusalem und das Grosse Beth Din in der Quader-Kammer*, Wien, 1902), has made out a very strong case for the existence, distinct from the Sanhedrin, of a court or council called the Great Beth Din, which had control and supervision over everything connected with the religious life of the people. It regulated the conduct of the services in the Temple, gave authoritative decisions in regard to the Torah and its interpretation, and when necessary made decrees affecting the religious duties of the people. It acted as the supreme court of appeal from the smaller Beth Dins up and down the country. Unless the elaborate arguments of Büchler can be refuted, the existence of the Great Beth Din, at all events in the later years of the Temple, must be accepted as a historical fact. And there is nothing whatever to show that it was of recent formation in those years. On the contrary, such evidence as there is points to a continuous existence even back to the early Hasmonean times, perhaps even to those of the two Josés.

It was regarded as representing the 'Edah' or 'Congregation' (e.g. Num. xv. 24). And it is in every way likely that as a result of the stress laid upon the Torah by Ezra and the Sopherim there should be some attempt to reproduce the Edah as an institution in the form of a council. We have already seen (above, pp. 44-5) that the Sopherim worked as a corporate body, though it is not said that there was a Beth Din in their time. Still, a council of some kind was a practical necessity. The same necessity made itself felt when the Hasmoneans were getting their hard-won kingdom into order. There was, as we have seen (above, p. 89), a Beth Din of the Hasmoneans; and one which made regulations affecting the religious practice of the people (b. Sanh. 82a, A. Zar. 36b). The Hasmonean Beth Din may have been an assembly *ad hoc*, not continuous with the Great Beth Din of later times. But it was evidently of much the same character and competence, and owed its existence not to an arbitrary act of appointment, but to the necessity of the case. Some authority for regulating the religious life of the people was absolutely necessary; and it is one of the main points of Büchler's case that the Sanhedrin never included such regulation amongst its functions. The Great Beth Din served precisely that purpose; and, whether under that name or some other, its existence from at least the days of the Hasmoneans is a practical certainty. Its relation to the Sanhedrin is a question which need not be discussed here. The reader is referred to Büchler's monograph.

Assuming then the existence of the Great Beth Din, in substance and probably in name, from the Hasmonean time down to the destruction of the Temple, A.D. 70, we interpret the statements of the Mishnah concerning the Zugoth to mean that the members of each pair were respectively president and vice-president of the Great Beth Din, and that it was this body which made the regulations associated with their names. If it be objected that this cannot be true of the two Josés, since the first certainly, and the second probably, was dead before the Hasmonean state had been established, then the solution is ready to hand that the Council, whether or not called the Great Beth Din, but having much the same functions, was in existence even before the Maccabean Revolt. There is nothing impossible in this, and something of this kind is needed to

H [97]

explain how the two Josés could be said to have made authoritative regulations affecting the religious life and practice of the people. As president and vice-president of the Great Beth Din, their names would naturally be associated with its official declarations.

Whatever may have been the case before the Maccabean Revolt, it is obvious that, after the overthrow of Hellenism, any council which regulated the religious affairs of the people must have consisted of men who were devoted to the Torah. Presumably the Great Beth Din at the outset after the Revolt was composed mainly of priests, because priests had been from time immemorial the acknowledged guardians and exponents of the Torah, and also because one of the duties of the Great Beth Din was to supervise the conduct of the Temple services. But it nowhere appears that the High Priest took any part in the proceedings of the Great Beth Din, still less that he ever presided over it. By whom it was appointed, and in what way the vacancies in its ranks were filled up from time to time, there is, so far as I am aware, no evidence to show.

It was in the Great Beth Din, so constituted, that the division between Pharisees and Sadducees first made its appearance; and it was there more than anywhere else that the contest between them was carried on during the whole period down to the destruction of the Temple, which put an end to the Sadducees as a party, though individual representatives of their opinions were to be found long afterwards. The reason why the opposition between Pharisees and Sadducees first appeared and continued to prevail in the Great Beth Din was that the primary duty of that assembly was to make the guidance of the Torah effective in the religious life and practice of the people. That this should be so after the triumph of the Torah over Hellenism goes without saying. But the question immediately became urgent—' What really was involved in obedience to the Torah? ' Was it to be restricted to compliance with the precepts of the written text, or was it to include the Unwritten Torah, of which something had already been heard, even before the Revolt, amongst the teachers of Torah, but of which we may suppose that many of the members of the Great Beth Din now learned for the first time? That the Great Beth Din included among its members teachers of Torah following in the succession of the older Sopherim may be safely concluded from the fact that, as shown above, the Revolt was really the work of these same teachers of Torah through their long and systematic instruction of the people, and they could not possibly be left out when the Great Beth Din began to function after the Revolt. It is even probable that in its first years they took the lead, and began to shape its policy in accordance with the Unwritten Torah. For it was obviously decrees based on the Unwritten Torah which John Hyrcanus annulled when he left the Pharisees and went over to the Sadducees. It was only such decrees which he would have any reason to annul. The division between the Pharisees and Sadducees would accordingly show itself at first in an unwillingness and at last in a downright refusal of the Sadducees any longer to follow the lead of the Pharisees; and from this time onwards, i.e. about the end of the second century B.C., the two parties strove for mastery in the Great Beth Din, with various success, from time to time. The succession of the Zugoth, as respectively president and vice-president of the assembly, does not necessarily imply that they held those offices continuously. It is sufficiently in accord with the tradition of the succession to suppose that in the case of a given ' pair ', the two men in question were the leaders, during their period, of the Pharisee party in the Beth Din, and were from time to time, according to the varying fortunes of the two parties, its president and vice-president.

It might seem that the Pharisees would always be in a minority in the Great Beth Din as compared with the Sadducees; for the Pharisees were the innovators with their theory of the Unwritten Torah, while the Sadducees were the upholders of the old theory and, moreover, the defenders of the prescriptive rights and vested interests of the priesthood. The Great Beth Din, however it came into being, must have been mainly composed of priests (see p. 98); and while it is true that not all priests were Sadducees, for José b. Joezer was a priest and certainly not a Sadducee, yet on the whole the priests would naturally be found on the Sadducean side, and would therefore constitute a permanent majority. How then could the Pharisees ever carry out their policy so that decrees could be made by the Beth Din embodying their ideas? That such decrees were made from time to time is shown by the fact that in regard to

[99]

each of the Zugoth it is stated that they ' decreed ' so and so, which means that they procured such decrees to be made by the Beth Din. (See Büchler, *op. cit.*, p. 178 ff.)

It should be remembered that the Pharisees, whatever their number in the Beth Din might be, had an influence with the common people far greater than any which the Sadducees could ever pretend to. The Pharisees, with whom were included all the teachers of Torah, were the successors of Ezra and the Sopherim as the religious leaders and instructors of the people, and the Revolt was very largely the result of that long-continued influence. The Sadducees never did or tried to do anything of the kind. Therefore, when the Beth Din was deliberating on matters of general religious practice concerning the whole people, the Sadducees might differ from the Pharisees upon the particular application of the Torah which they proposed, or the particular regulation which they wished to enact, yet they knew that they were risking a conflict with the people who would certainly support the Pharisees. They would thus allow the Pharisees to carry out their desired reforms, and enact the regulations which they desired. But when matters immediately concerning the Temple and the priesthood were being discussed, the Sadducees were on much stronger ground; and it was only after long struggles, perhaps not until the last few years before the destruction of the Temple, that the Pharisees finally got the upper hand in the Beth Din, and imposed their will upon the Sadducean priests.

The Great Beth Din was the supreme authority for regulating the religious life and practice of the people. But it was not the only institution concerned in promoting that object, and we must now turn our attention to two others, without whose concurrence the Beth Din would have been almost powerless. These other two are the Beth ha-Midrash and the Synagogue.

The Beth ha-Midrash (House of Study) was essentially a place where the teachers of Torah met for the purpose of studying and expounding it. Of course, the ultimate object was to teach it to the people, thus following on the line of Ezra and the Sopherim. But the primary purpose was to determine what should be taught, and if it were a question of religious practice, how the halachah should be defined. The Beth ha-Midrash had no legislative authority like the Great Beth Din, and its decisions, taken by vote, were only binding on its own members so far as they were binding at all. They were, in fact, only resolutions declaring the opinion of the majority upon the question at issue. But evidently the Beth ha-Midrash stood in a close relation to the Great Beth Din, because, when the Pharisees were able to persuade the latter to make a regulation in accordance with their views, that regulation expressed a conclusion arrived at after discussion in the Beth ha-Midrash. That this was so is shown by the fact that there was a Beth ha-Midrash (called the Great B.h.M.) connected with the Great Beth Din, and meeting, like it, in the Temple (T. Sanh. vii. 1). Büchler (*op. cit.*, p. 130) holds that the two were identical, yet it is difficult to see why in that case two names were needed for the one institution. The Beth ha-Midrash had its own place of meeting, because the Beth Din sometimes met there. Moreover, the meetings of the Beth Din where Sadducees were present would not be a suitable place for the discussions in which the Pharisees elaborated their own point of view. Presumably the members of the B. ha-Midrash, being the most learned of the teachers of Torah, would be members of the Beth Din, so that apart from the Sadducees, the two assemblies would consist of much the same persons. But that the B. ha-Midrash was not in theory identical with the Beth Din, whatever it may have been occasionally in practice, seems to the present writer to follow from such evidence as is available.

The B. ha-Midrash, then, was the place of meeting where the experts of the Torah discussed all questions relating to its interpretation, theoretical as well as practical. Probably the B. ha-Midrash in the Temple was the oldest, as it was the highest in rank of all the institutions called by that name. For, just as there were Beth Dins of lower rank and less numerous membership in the various towns and villages, so there was a B. ha-Midrash wherever there was a teacher of Torah and men desiring to study it with him. So, at all events, it was in the Mishnah period; how long before that cannot be determined. The first B. ha-Midrash actually mentioned is that of Shemaiah and Abtalion (b. Joma, 35*b*), which does not seem to have been identical with the Great Beth ha-Midrash. But, after all, it is only natural that men whose whole object in life was to study and teach Torah should gather around them groups of disciples as they might find opportunity. It was only doing what the men of the Great Synagogue had enjoined (Aboth i. 1), and what the whole policy of Ezra and the Sopherim required for its fulfilment. The two famous groups of teachers (and disciples), known as the Beth Hillel and the Beth Shammai, were respectively the Beth ha-Midrash of the two rival leaders. The two groups had their separate organisation; but together they met in the Great Beth ha-Midrash in the Temple, and it was there that they carried on those disputes which are notorious in the Talmud. In the Great Beth Din, where they met the Sadducees, no doubt the followers of Hillel and Shammai presented a united front. In spite of their differences they were all Pharisees.

We turn now to the Synagogue*, the third of the institutions mentioned above which were concerned with the teaching of Torah. Something has already been said (above, pp. 58, 81 n.) of the way in which the Synagogue probably came into existence, viz. as a development of the meetings for the public reading and exposition of the Torah. And the question might naturally be asked what was the need of the Synagogue when the Beth ha-Midrash provided for the study of Torah? Especially seeing that the common people could, and often did, attend to hear the exposition of the Torah given by the teachers in the Beth ha-Midrash. To say that the Synagogue provided for public worship as well as for instruction in Torah, and that the Beth ha-Midrash did not, is true, but to a Jewish mind would not be the full or exact truth. Wherever Torah was, there was religion, as much in the Beth ha-Midrash as in the Synagogue. And, if the Synagogue began by being a place for the public reading and teaching of Torah, the Torah which was read and taught was the revelation which God had made to Israel, and its first implication was that God should be worshipped. Therefore prayer became, or perhaps already was from the very beginning, an integral part of the proceedings in the weekly meetings for the reading of Torah; it most certainly was so in the synagogues and has continued to be so down to the present day. And the non-Jewish reader would make a mistake if he supposed that there was a sort of opposition or even

* For an exhaustive account of everything connected with the Synagogue, see S. Krauss, *Synagogale Alterthümer*, 1922; and, especially for the history and form of the liturgy, L. Elbogen, *Der jüdische Gottesdienst*, 1924.

division between the devotional and the intellectual portions, between the prayers and the teaching of Torah. In form, no doubt, there was, but in substance there was not. The whole mind of the worshipper was directed to the God who had given the Torah; and if the Torah was taught, it was that the worshipper might know more of God and of his will and so might the better serve him. Ezra and the Sopherim did not set out to teach the people a code of laws, but to make them religious, to make them realise who God was, in what relation they stood to him, what they should do, and what they should be as a faithful people. It was as the result of such teaching carried on through centuries, by the Sopherim, the Hasidim, and last, but by no means least, the Pharisees, that the worshippers in the Synagogue came to think of God and to address him as ' Our Father which art in heaven '.

The first beginnings of a liturgy, of some orderly arrangement of prayers, are traceable, or are attributed, to the Sopherim; and though perhaps nothing in the existing liturgy is in its present form of so great an age, it is not at all improbable that the Sopherim may have taken the first steps in that direction. But however that may be, we are on safe ground in assuming that the Pharisees when they appeared developed the Synagogue into the form in which it appears in history. How far it had already developed from its earliest beginnings by the time that the Pharisees became a definite religious party there is no evidence to show. But they found in it an institution exactly after their own hearts; and whether or not they needed to modify what they found already in existence, they certainly made it their own from that time onwards. They were the successors of the Sopherim, and cherished the same ideals. The Synagogue in their hands was the instrument by which they could work for those ideals more effectively than in any other way. Apparently they had the field entirely to themselves. The Sadducees never had anything to do with the Synagogues. They worked through the Temple, and such influence as they had upon the people at large was only exercised through the Temple services. Even these, at all events in the last years before the destruction of the Temple, had to be performed in accordance with the views of the Pharisees, for fear of the people who always supported them. No other religious party concerned itself with the religious teaching of the people. And, as synagogues increased in numbers under the fostering care of the Pharisees, these became more and more effectually the trusted and beloved leaders of the people, and their influence more and more powerful. The Pharisees and the Synagogue went hand in hand and were for ever inseparable.

It cannot be too often repeated that the Synagogue was a laymen's church, a congregation meeting for worship and instruction and not depending in the slightest degree upon the ministration of priests or the performance of any ritual. The Synagogue had no sacraments nor any consecrated persons to administer them. The priest had no function except in connexion with the Temple and its services, and no privileges except such as were derived from his office as a servant of the Temple, or the descendant of such in later times. The Judaism which has come down through the centuries, the Judaism of which the Synagogue is the chief and most characteristic embodiment, is not and never has been a priestly religion. To say that it is, as some still continue to say, is, in the words of Martineau (in another connexion) 'to give expression to the largest falsehood that can be framed'.

It was through the Synagogue that the Pharisees were able to minister to the religious needs of the people as a whole. For synagogues could be established wherever there were Jews, and gradually made their appearance in every town and village in the land, besides spreading into the Diaspora whereever Jews had migrated or had been carried by force. The presence of one or more synagogues in every centre of population where there were Jews could not fail to exert a powerful influence upon the members of each Jewish community, even though, as is only likely, not every Jew went to synagogue. There might be one synagogue or several in one town, but there was no other place of worship for Jews to go to. There was not, as in a modern Christian city, a large variety of places of worship amongst which the worshipper can choose the one he will attend, or stay away from. It is true that in a great city like Rome different groups of Jews had their own synagogue; but in regard to what was done in them, one synagogue was much like another. The order of prayers, Scripture reading, and discourse did not greatly differ—at all events in the centuries with which we are concerned. The meaning of which is that the development of the Synagogue was not left to chance or the caprice of each separate congregation, but was controlled by a central authority. It is true that the members of any one synagogue managed their own affairs for themselves, and in the service of worship depended on no one outside their own ranks. But the whole theory of the Synagogue, then as now, was that those who met within its walls for worship did so not as a fortuitous company of individuals, but as belonging to the community of Israel. In the countless assemblies every Sabbath all Israel was worshipping at the same time, in theory if not in practice. The order of the service as it came to be embodied in the liturgy was therefore, in its main lines and apart from local differences, the same for all; and for the same reason the prayers are now read only in the Hebrew language and not in the vernacular of each particular country. But this takes us to a later date than that of the period with which we are concerned.

It may have been thought that it was not necessary to spend time, as has been done above, in explaining the function of the Great Beth Din and the Beth ha-Midrash; but after this account of the Synagogue it now becomes possible to explain the relation of these three institutions to each other, and to show how each of them had its part in the work of making the Torah effective in the life of the Jewish people. The relation was briefly this: In the Synagogue the people were taught; in the Beth ha-Midrash the teachers of Torah determined what the Torah really meant and what, therefore, must be taught; the Great Beth Din gave directions that it should be taught. This compressed statement needs some expansion in order to make it true to the facts. The most important of the three institutions was the Synagogue, because it was there that the work of the other two found its practical application. The purpose of the whole organisation was the religious instruction of the people by means of the Torah, the purpose which had been in the mind of Ezra and had been consistently and continuously carried out ever since his time, first by the Sopherim and later by the Pharisees. In the Synagogue service the Torah was made effective in two ways, first as providing the incentive to worship, and second as being the subject of exposition. To learn Torah without being moved to pray to the God who had given the

Torah was, in the Synagogue, an impossibility. To worship him without also seeking to learn even more of him and his ways and will, was also an impossibility. The Synagogue existed and has always existed to meet this twofold need. It gathered Israel to pray, and it taught him concerning God to whom he prayed.

In regard to the prayers in the Synagogue, the general order followed was the same in all, at all events in the period with which we are concerned. The theory was, as stated above, that the whole community of Israel gathered in the Synagogue at the appointed times, and all prayed together, if not in precisely the same words, yet on the same general lines. It was clearly the function of the Great Beth Din to fix those general lines, so that there might be a uniform order in all synagogues. Small local variations there might be, and were; but in all the references in the Talmud to the prayers in the Synagogue, the theory of one uniform order is assumed throughout. Particular prayers are referred to, and such reference would have no meaning unless those prayers were known to all Israel as being included in the service of every synagogue. It is said (b. Ber. 33a) that some of the prayers were instituted by the men of the Great Synagogue, i.e. the Sopherim, and, whether that statement is historically true or not, it points clearly to a central authority and not to a separate congregation, in the ordering of the prayers. For many centuries there has not been a central authority in Jewry; but so long as there was such an authority, either the Great Beth Din in Jerusalem or its lineal descendants in Jabneh, Usha, and Tiberias, it was that body and no other which ensured the uniformity of the synagogues in the order of the services. Of course, the Great Beth Din had many other functions besides that of supervising the synagogues and ordering the service in them; but the point at present is that such particular function belonged to it and to no other body.

The Great Beth ha-Midrash acted as a sort of advisory board to the Great Beth Din, preparing the way by thorough discussion for the subsequent decisions of the legislative body. The primary purpose of the Great Beth ha-Midrash was to study the Torah, in the minutest detail and from every point of view, by the help of the most learned and experienced teachers. It was they who defined the halachah, and it was they who gave the closest attention to the gradual formation of the liturgy. The minute regulation of the prayers, which non-Jewish critics often regard as a hindrance to devotion and one more proof of the mechanical formalism of the later Judaism, was only due to the care most properly taken by the religious leaders to ensure that the liturgy which they were preparing for the use of all Israel should be suited to the wants of all Israel. Unless all liturgical worship is to be condemned as a hindrance to devotion, the preparation of a liturgy, whether Roman, Anglican, or any other, must call for very careful deliberation; and those who in each case were responsible for the form of such liturgy would be failing in their duty if they did not discuss, in very minute detail, what was to be included and what was to be left out, who was to say this, and who was to say that, and what should be said by one or by the other.

The Great Beth Din and the Great Beth ha-Midrash were, as their names indicate, the highest in rank of all the bodies so called. There was a smaller Beth Din in every town, and a smaller Beth ha-Midrash wherever a teacher and a group of students could get together, usually in connexion with a synagogue. Questions of interpretation of Torah, problems of halachah, anything affecting the religious life and practice of the people in this or that locality, were brought in the first instance before the local Beth Din or the local Beth ha-Midrash, and only in cases where the answer received did not satisfy were carried on appeal to one or other of the two High Courts in Jerusalem. Decision there was final, and such decision was presumably made known in the several localities (if it was of general and not merely individual concern) through the local Beth Din or Beth ha-Midrash, or possibly announced in the synagogue. In this way, the system by which the Torah was made effective and brought to bear upon the people as a whole was thoroughly organised. The Pharisees and the teachers of Torah had the control of the system, as they were the men who most deeply felt the sacredness of the work in which they were engaged. It was the intensive culture of religion, by men of clear purpose, strong will, and resolute devotion to the service of God as they understood it. And while it is true that they could only lead those who chose to follow them, and that not the whole community did so, it is not wonderful that they exercised a very powerful indirect influence over the great majority of the people. The Hasmonean Revolt was not an isolated display of enthusiasm, it was the result of all that had been done since Ezra and by the Sopherim for the religious training of the people. And that the same work was carried on afterwards by the Pharisees and the Rabbis, with no less zeal and thoroughness, is the explanation of the fact that the Judaism which survived the catastrophes of the fall of Jerusalem and the revolt of Bar Cocheba, and that has come down through the centuries, was that type of Judaism which worshipped in the Synagogue, sought truth in the Beth ha-Midrash and justice in the Beth Din, and all three in the name of the Torah and in the service of God.

Chapter VI

THE ETHICAL TEACHING ON THE RABBINICAL LINE

(A) THE HALACHAH

WE have now surveyed the gradual development of the principle laid down by Ezra in regard to the application of the Torah to the life of the people, and have seen how, in the hands of the Sopherim and their successors, the Pharisaic teachers, it was organised into an elaborate system. Torah was brought immediately home to the people in the synagogues; the meaning of the Torah, the precise sense in which it was to be understood and applied, was worked out in the Beth ha-Midrash; the authority which gave binding force to the conclusions so arrived at was that of the Great Beth Din. It must, of course, be remembered that no one was obliged to submit to that authority. No one need become a Pharisee, and no one need put himself under the discipline of the system if he did not wish to do so. No one could be, or ever was, compelled to attend the synagogue, still less to listen to the discussions in the Beth ha-Midrash; and a man who so absented himself would not directly come under the influence of the system at all. But if a man did choose to put himself under the discipline of the organised teaching of Torah, then for him the Torah was what the accredited teachers explained it to be, its requirements and its prohibitions were such as they set forth, and they were binding on him because the Great Beth Din endorsed them with its authority. Such binding force, however, even in the restricted sense here indicated, only concerned the halachah; the haggadah was never subject to control, and the teacher of haggadah was free to declare whatever he found in the Torah, while the hearer was free to receive it or not, as he thought fit; of course within the limits of the fundamental beliefs of Judaism. Those who listened to Jesus in the synagogue at Nazareth (Luke iv. 16-30) disapproved of what he said; but he was not stopped on that or any other occasion, even in the very last days of his life when he taught in the Temple.

We are now, after the survey contained in the preceding chapters, in a position to deal with the question: What was the nature of the ethical teaching given by those whose method and organisation have been described? More particularly, What precisely did they teach? The whole object of this book is to compare the ethical teaching to be found in the Rabbinical and the non-Rabbinical literatures respectively, and the natural way in which to do this would seem to be to show that the Rabbis taught so-and-so, and the various non-Rabbinical writers taught so-and-so upon any given subject. For this purpose the haggadah is, on the face of it, more adapted than the halachah; because the haggadah is exposition of Torah on the non-preceptive side, the result of the free play of devout meditation upon sacred themes, including the whole field of ethics along with much else. And the difficulty, always urged by the non-Jewish scholar, is that the haggadah as we now have it is contained in compilations which were not written down till long after the period with which we are concerned; and, further, that though some of the teaching therein contained is much older than the date of its compilation, little, if any, of it is older than the time of Hillel. For the earlier period from Ezra to Hillel there is no authentic haggadah, none even that could be claimed as belonging to that period. What, then, is there which can be set up for comparison with the ethical teaching of the Apocryphal literature which belongs to the centuries during which the Rabbinical literature is, in this respect, a blank? This is a question which must be fairly faced, being a very proper and natural question, and one, moreover, of which the evasion would invalidate the whole argument of this book.

The answer, in brief, is this: First, that although there is no haggadah directly available for the period Ezra to Hillel, the study of the halachah throws a great deal of light upon the ethical teaching given in that period, so that that period is by no means a blank on the Rabbinical side; and second, that it is possible to infer from the ethical teaching given respectively before and after that period, what it probably was during the period. It will be convenient to devote a separate chapter to each of these two arguments, the more so because the ethical aspect and value of the halachah are hardly known except to

Jewish scholars. In this present chapter, accordingly, we shall study the halachah for the light it can throw on the ethical teaching of the period with which we are concerned, and reserve for the following chapter the discussion of the ethical teaching in the haggadah.

It has been explained above (p. 53) that the halachah was the definition of the precise way in which a commandment of the Torah was to be performed, a definition given on the authority of the accredited teachers, and to be accepted by all who submitted to the discipline of the system described in the preceding chapter. So long as a halachah remained in force, it was a definite and precise law; and non-Jewish critics of Judaism have usually supposed that the whole body of halachahs, increasing from age to age, formed a rigid system the pressure of which constituted the ' burden of the Law ', as they have learned from Paul to describe it. As a matter of fact, however, the halachah was not unalterable, and was actually altered in many cases, as will be shown presently. On the face of it, one would suppose that in regard to many of the commandments of the Torah obedience would be a simple matter requiring no definition of halachah. There was the commandment, in so many words, as, for instance, in regard to the Sabbath, ' in it thou shalt do no manner of work ' (Exod. xx. 10), actually in the Decalogue. What could be more obvious than that the proper way to fulfil this commandment was literally to do no work of any kind whatsoever? Yet a halachah was felt to be necessary even on so plain and explicit a commandment, and not one halachah only but, in course of time, a huge mass of halachahs all directed to the object of defining the right way of keeping the Sabbath in accordance with its true purpose. One whole treatise of the Talmud, and that by no means the shortest, is taken up with the discussion of the halachahs relating to the Sabbath. The same is to be found in regard to very many other commandments in the Torah. In all these cases the halachah, by giving a definition of what had not been defined, by making exceptions in what had been stated generally, by including what had not been mentioned, and the like, did modify the commandment as set forth in the written text, and was expressly intended to do so. An exact literal compliance with the written word of the Torah tended to become more and more impossible as time went on, and the Torah was in danger, as already remarked, of becoming an archaic relic, which all might venerate but which no one could obey. The Sadducees were quite willing that it should be so, and held that what was necessary for the guidance of those who lived under the Torah should be provided by ordinances made by the priests on their own authority. (See above, p. 69.) The Pharisees met the difficulty by developing the theory of the Unwritten Torah (see above, Bk. II, Ch. III, under that title), and all the elaboration of the halachah, after its first simple beginning, was the result of applying the theory of the Unwritten Torah.

The foundation of that theory was the belief that the Torah, as the divine revelation, was contained not in the written text alone, but in the text and the Oral Tradition together. From which this conclusion followed, that the written word by itself was not in every case decisive; it might be modified, or even set aside, in order that the real intention of the Torah, the full divine revelation, might be accomplished. This conclusion, that the written word of the Torah might be modified or even set aside, or even annulled (as was sometimes done), was deliberately drawn and consistently acted upon by the teachers who developed the halachah; and that they should do so will only seem strange to those who believe that Judaism in its practice is or even was tied down to the bare letter of the Torah. The leading teachers of the halachah knew as well as Paul did, and long before him, that ' the letter killeth but the spirit giveth life ' (2 Cor. iii. 6). The precise purpose with which they formulated the halachah was to prevent the letter from killing, and to open the way for the spirit to give life. And this is what actually followed from their labours on the halachah, though certainly not according to Paul's ideas.

The gradual adoption of the theory of the Unwritten Torah made possible the development of the halachah, so as to make the real intention of the Torah applicable not only to the changing conditions of life but also to the changing ethical conceptions arrived at, as the moral standard was raised or its requirements more clearly discerned. The development of the halachah was towards a higher ethics, and not at all towards a mere multiplication of ceremonies. If the ethical purpose was not the only one, it was by far the most important, and never for long lost sight of. And by the 'ethical purpose' is meant the intention to make the Torah in its highest discernible meaning effective for the guidance and enlightenment of all who lived under it. The written Torah was good for the age in which it was given, or in which it was first read; but the written Torah alone could not suffice for later ages. The development of the halachah virtually amounted to the declaration (in any given age): 'This is what the Torah means *now*. This is what it says to us who are living at this present time. This is what we must do if we would do the will of God as he has revealed it to us'. Every Jew, according to a well-known Rabbinical dictum* should regard himself as having been actually present at Sinai when the Torah was given. The Torah was given to him, not only to his far-off ancestors. God's command is to him personally, and the halachah only serves to make clear to him what the divine will is and how he ought to obey it.

The teachers who introduced the conception of the Unwritten Torah, and thereby broke the connexion between the halachah and the written text, were quite aware of the extreme gravity of the step they were taking. They intended to modify the written commandment in various ways, and in course of time actually did so in numberless cases. Yet they had before them the plain injunction (Deut. iv. 2): 'Ye shall not add to the word which I command you, neither shall ye diminish from it; that ye may keep the commandments of the Lord your God which I command you'. Of course, a theory which justified a departure from the written word would justify a disregard of this particular written word; but the real justification of the procedure was 'that ye may keep the commandments of the Lord your God'. If the commandment could not be kept according to the strict letter, the true intention of the commandment could be fulfilled by departure from the letter. And, whatever was done by means of the Unwritten Torah to modify, or even abolish, the written word of a commandment, it was always done for the purpose of fulfilling the real intention of the commandment, to make the Torah effective instead of

---

* It is stated in the Mishnah, Pes. x. 5: 'Every man is bound to look on himself as if he had gone forth out of Egypt'. His presence at Sinai would follow as a matter of course.

letting it become obsolete because impracticable. Weiss* (*Dor, dor*, ii, p. 53) says very truly that 'it was easy for the teachers to treat the injunction " Ye shall not add ", etc., as clay in the hands of the potter '; but in doing so they certainly did not feel that they were disloyal or anything but intensely loyal to the real Torah as they understood it.

The authority to suspend or annul or modify the written word of the Torah was claimed for the Great Beth Din alone, and was never allowed to any minor Beth Din, still less to any individual teacher. But for the Great Beth Din it was claimed, and the claim was maintained so long as there was any court which could be so called. The claim was based on the text (Deut. xviii. 15): ' The Lord thy God shall raise up a prophet like unto me from the midst of thy brethren. To him shall ye hearken '. This is explained in Siphré (ii, § 175, p. 107*b*, ed. Friedmann) to mean ' Even if he tell thee to transgress any one of the commandments which are given in the Torah, like Elijah on Mount Carmel, according to the need of the hour, hearken to him' (cp. also b. Jebam, 90*b*). The Great Beth Din was not a prophet, but we have already seen (above, p. 72 f.) that 'Prophecy was taken from the Prophets and given to the Wise, and it has not been taken away from these ' (b. B. Bath. 12*a*). ' The Wise ' are the teachers of Torah, as may be seen on every page of the Mishnah. The argument accordingly is that in virtue of what was taken from the Prophets and given to the Wise, the Beth Din, representing the Wise, became entitled to the implicit obedience enjoined in Deut. xviii. 15, even to the extent of ordering the transgression of any one of the commandments contained in the Torah. And the argument was further strengthened by the injunction (Deut. xvii. 9-11): 'And thou shalt come unto the priests, the

* On the whole subject of the modification of the written Torah, the reader (if he can read modern Hebrew) should study the invaluable chapter in Weiss, *Dor, dor ve-doreshav*, vol. ii, pp. 53-71, in which he discusses the question in all its bearings, with ample illustration. I do not know of any such comprehensive treatment of the subject elsewhere. For much of what is contained in the present chapter I have gladly followed the guidance of Weiss. Reference may also be made to Lauterbach's essay on *The Ethics of the Halakah*, 1913, which, however, does not cover the whole field; and to M. Bloch, *Die Ethik in der Halachah*, Wien, 1906, which does indeed cover the whole field, but is hardly more than a bare outline.

Levites, and unto the judge which shall be in those days, and thou shalt inquire, and they shall show thee the sentence of judgment; and thou shalt do according to the tenor of the sentence which they shall show thee from that place which the Lord shall choose; and thou shalt observe to do according to all that they shall teach thee,' etc. It will be remembered that this text was used by the Sadducees to justify the making of ordinances by the priests in cases where the written Torah was not explicit or practicable. The difference between the Sadducees and the Pharisees in this respect was that the former did not pretend that the ordinances of the priests were Torah, while the Pharisees insisted that unless the ordinances were Torah they were not binding (see above, p. 66 f.). They therefore had no difficulty in identifying ' the judge which shall be in those days ' with the Great Beth Din, so as to transfer to the latter the implicit obedience required in the Torah to be accorded to the former.

The above arguments were used to justify a claim already made and put into practice. It does not seem likely that any interpreters of the Torah would have arrived at such a conclusion by a mere study of the texts. The practical necessity of finding some way of bringing the Torah into effective use must have been felt before the arguments were devised by which the means adopted could be justified. Be this as it may, it is certain that the practice of modifying the written word of the Torah, by suspending or even abolishing it in this or that case, can be traced far back in the period which ends with Hillel. A striking instance of such practice is provided by the case of the Sabbath law. The written word is quite explicit: ' In it [the Sabbath] thou shalt not do any manner of work ' (Exod. xx. 10). The teachers of Torah formulated in reference to that prohibition the rule that for the purpose of saving life every law pertaining to the Sabbath may be, indeed must be, disobeyed (*pikkuaḥ nephesh doheh eth ha-Shabbath*). It was not merely excusable to break the Sabbath in order to save life, it was an imperative duty to do so; and the duty must be fulfilled at once without waiting for permission from any authority (b. Joma, 84*b*). There are various discussions in the Talmud as to the Scripture basis for this regulation, being as it was obviously necessary on grounds of humanity and no less obviously a flat contradiction of the word of the Torah. The discussions were not for the purpose of justifying a new departure, but for the purpose, hardly more than speculative, of finding some support in Scripture for a principle and a practice which had long been accepted and acted on. The first mention of a case in which the Sabbath was deliberately broken for the sake of saving life is in the well-known story of Hillel being found in the snow (b. Joma, 35*b*), and there it is taken for granted that of course the Sabbath must be broken to save a human life. There is no hint that Shemaiah and Abtalion, in breaking the Sabbath on Hillel's account, were introducing a new practice. It evidently seemed to them the obvious thing to do; and no one at the time or afterwards challenged their action as a violation of the Sabbath. The principle on which they acted must have been recognised at least so long before their time that any question of its validity had been forgotten, but there must have been a time when it was first formulated. For, if it had been a recognised principle at the outbreak of the Maccabean Revolt there would have been no reason why the band of insurgents should have died because they would not fight on the Sabbath (1 Macc. ii. 34-38). If the Sabbath was to give way to the saving of life, it obviously covered the case of fighting in self-defence on the Sabbath. Mattathias and his friends drew the conclusion that for the sake of all that was imperilled fighting on the Sabbath must be allowed, and proceeded to act on that conclusion. It seems natural to suppose, although there is no direct evidence on the point, that the principle, ' the Sabbath must give way to the saving of life,' was formulated as a generalisation from what had happened during the Revolt; and it is tempting to suggest that the ' Beth Din of the Hasmoneans ' (see above, pp. 89, 97) was the authority who enacted it.

Here we have a clear case in which an explicit commandment of the Torah was set on one side—or, rather, annulled altogether; for the principle introduced was intended to be permanent, and there has never been any attempt to go back on it. The reason why it was annulled was this: That the teachers of Torah were raising the ethical standard and recognising a higher value and a greater sacredness in human life. The Sabbath was indeed a divinely given institution, to be reverenced accordingly; but human life was more than an institution, as every human being was made 'in the image of God'. The Sabbath was given to man for his good; man himself was higher than the Sabbath, and in the last resort the Sabbath must give way. The declaration: 'The Sabbath was given to you, ye were not given to the Sabbath,' is found (Mech. Ki Tissa, 103*b*) and repeated (b. Joma, 85*b*) in almost exactly the same words as in the Gospel (Mark ii. 27). The similarity between sayings of the Rabbis and sayings of Jesus will be discussed in a later chapter.

This instance of the abrogation of the Sabbath law in the interest of humanity has been dwelt on at some length, both as an illustration of the power claimed and exercised by the teachers of Torah, acting through the Beth Din, to modify and even annul the written word of the Torah, and also as showing that this was done on ethical grounds. It will be possible to deal more briefly with some other cases in which the written word of the Torah was set aside. In the chapter above referred to (*Dor, dor, etc.*, ii. 53-71) Weiss gives a list of ten principles according to which the departure from the written text or its actual abrogation was carried out in practice. Of these, the first five are concerned with the reasons why such departure was allowable; the second five are concerned with the method of application, and need not be discussed here. The first five principles are as follows (the letter of a commandment of Torah may be departed from or annulled):

(*a*) Because of the needs of the time.

(*b*) For the adjustment of human relations.

(*c*) For the raising of the standard of religious and moral life.

(*d*) Because of human weakness.

(*e*) When the reason for a law no longer operates.

We will take these five reasons in order.

(*a*) The needs of the time (*ha-sha'ah tzerichah lecach*). On this ground various actions recorded in Scripture are justified, e.g. that of Abraham offering Isaac on Mount Moriah, and Elijah on Mount Carmel in building an altar, etc., cases which in a sense were of only theoretical interest. Much more to the point was the case of Ezra, who ordered by a proclamation that ' whosoever came not within three days, according to the counsel of the princes and the elders, all his substance should be forfeited and he himself separated from the congregation of the captivity' (Ezra x. 8).

There was certainly no warrant in the written Torah for so high-handed a proceeding, for the Torah regards the taking away of a man's wealth, otherwise than by process of law, as plain robbery. Nevertheless, it was held, Ezra acted rightly because he was faced with an emergency, and what he did then was not taken as a precedent. All that the Torah said on the subject of rights of property held good, and was not affected by what Ezra had done. Cases of this kind are hardly more than instances of special pleading, and amount only to saying that in such and such an event there was no help for it but to do what was done, Torah or no Torah. The plea may be admitted without troubling to find a Scripture proof.

(b) The adjustment of human relations (*tikkun 'olam*). This was one of the main purposes for which the halachah was developed, and although a departure from the written word of the Torah was not always required, such departure was freely resorted to if the end could not be attained without it. Under the head of *tikkun 'olam* are included all warnings intended to keep a man from transgressing before he actually comes to the danger. These are what are meant by ' the fence for the Torah ', which the men of the Great Synagogue ordered to be set up (M. Aboth, i. 1), and a popular proverb is often quoted by way of illustration: ' Go away, Nazirite, round the vineyard, do not approach it ' (b. Shabb. 13a and often). So also things were forbidden not because in themselves they needed to be forbidden, but because they might be mistaken for such; and here again a popular proverb expressed the principle: ' keep far from what is ugly [repulsive] and from what looks ugly ' (b. Hull, 44b).

In regard to social relations, the principle of *tikkun 'olam* was applied in mitigating the severity which would be caused by the literal adherence to the written word of the Torah. Wherever a loss would be involved, either of money or other value, the amount of the loss was made as small as possible— at all events, smaller than the strict letter would require. Such regulations cannot be shown to have been made exclusively in the pre-Hillel period, and it is not here contended that all of them were. But certainly some of them were. The most famous case is that of the *lex talionis* (Exod. xxi. 24): ' An eye for an eye,' etc. The literal carrying out of this law would, of course, imply the actual loss of eye, hand, or foot by the offender in return for

what he had done to his victim. Instead of this savage retalia-
tion a money fine was imposed, and there is nothing to show
that the literal penalty was ever inflicted. The Mishnah
(B. Kamma, viii. 1) says that if a man strikes out the eye, or cuts
off the hand or the foot of another man, he is liable for damages
to the amount of the loss. It is as if the injured man were a slave
for sale in the market, and his value after the injury is compared
with his value before the injury. The difference is the amount of
damages to be paid. The discussion of this in the Talmud makes
no allusion to any enactment by which the money payment was
substituted for the infliction of actual bodily injury. Instead, it
remarks on the cruelty and also the futility of literal fulfilment
of the law, and seems to suppose that no one could ever have
dreamed of such barbarity. There are several instances in which
modifications of the written word of Torah are ascribed to one
or other of the Zugoth (see above, p. 96), and if there had been
the memory of such a change in regard to the present case, it was
sufficiently important to call for special mention. No decisive
answer can be given to the question When was the change
made? But, until clear proof can be given to the contrary, it
seems most probable that the date should be placed in the far
past of the Ezra-Hillel period, certainly not in its latest years.
Whenever the change was made it was clearly due to the
motive of humanity, partly because the penalty in its literal
form was cruel to the offender, and partly because the infliction
of it tended to brutalise the person who carried it out and the
society which sanctioned it. Thus, the clear and emphatic
injunction contained in the written word of the Torah was
deliberately annulled on grounds of humanity.

   Of a somewhat different kind, but the most often cited
instance of the abrogation of the written word of the Torah,
was the institution known as Prosbol, the author of which was
Hillel. This was a kind of legal fiction whereby the cancelling
of debts in the seventh year (Deut. xv. 1-3) was avoided. If
debts were to be cancelled, as the written Torah required that
they should be, the natural result was that when the end of the
sixth year was approaching a man would not lend to his neighbour, and thus the neighbour would be deprived of the help
which a loan would have been to him. To lend to the needy
was itself enjoined in the Torah, and commended in Scripture

generally. In Hillel's view it was more important to keep open the door for practical benevolence than to insist on a literal adherence to the letter of the Torah, which would effectually close it. This was strictly in accordance with the principle of *tikkun 'olam.*

So also were regulations made in the interests of peace and goodwill, *darkē shalom,* in social and domestic relations, and between Jews and their non-Jewish neighbours. These were not necessarily abrogations of the Torah, but they were certainly amplifications in the direction of goodwill and brotherly love; and whether or not they, or any of them, were made in the Ezra-Hillel period, they illustrate the tendency to interpret the Torah in the ethical direction which has already been traced in that period.

(*c*) Modification of the written Torah for the sake of raising the religious or moral standard. Under this head Weiss (*op. cit.,* p. 58) remarks that ' it was fitting that those who made decrees and ordinances should consider the religious and moral condition of the people, and should weigh in the balance of their wisdom the regulations which they approved. For there are some things which are (theoretically) compulsory but are not possible, and there are others which are possible but not compulsory. For this reason they sometimes refrained from making a decree or an ordinance because the result would be loss which could not be borne, or great injury in which case it would be impossible. . . . At all times they hesitated to make an ordinance upon anything which would be more than the people could bear. And they made a general rule that " no ordinance is to be laid on the people unless the majority of the people are able to bear it "' (b. B. Bath. 60*b* and often). Various deductions are made from this principle into which it is not needful to enter. But those who are accustomed to hear and speak about 'the burden of the Law' might usefully consider this principle.

(*d*) Concession to human weakness. This means the relaxing of a prohibition, on the ground that if it were insisted on, men would, by the weakness of their nature, very often transgress the prohibition. It was better, said the wise (surely with wisdom) that Israel should sin in error, if they must sin, rather than deliberately as they would do if the prohibition were rigidly insisted on (b. Betz. 30*a*). On this principle various concessions were allowed which made for good relations with fellow men, particularly by way of not giving offence.

(*e*) When the reason for a law had ceased to operate. This is obvious, but it is also important as showing how the teachers who developed the halachah were careful to keep it adjusted to the changing conditions of the time and the changing religious and moral conceptions in the minds of themselves and of the people whom they taught.

It is obviously impossible to survey the whole body of halachah in order to show in every case its ethical bearing. The main point is that it always had an ethical bearing. Indeed, that is the main reason why there ever was a halachah at all. If it had been possible to obey the written word of the Torah literally, there would have been no need of a halachah to say how it should be done. But, partly because the written word could not be literally obeyed and partly because it ought not to be obeyed, and partly because its directions were often far from clear, it was necessary to state its intention in a form that could be obeyed and that was in accordance with the ethical conceptions of the teachers of Torah. The whole mass of halachah is the result of treating the Torah from that point of view; and the ground purpose of it all was to make possible the fulfilment of the Torah in its real intention, as completely as possible and by as many as possible of those who recognised its authority.

If this is borne in mind, certain misunderstandings will be avoided by which non-Jewish critics of the halachah have sometimes been led to wrong conclusions. They point to what they call evasions of the law—such, for instance, as the *erub*, by which several houses in a court can by a symbolic act be treated as one house, for the purpose of Sabbath observance, or the several courts in a street as one court, for the same purpose, or the 2,000 cubits of a Sabbath day's journey be extended to 4,000 cubits, again by a symbolic act. But these are not evasions of the law, they are the substitution, conscious and deliberate, of action which will realise the true intention of the Torah for action according to the mere written word which will not, even if it were possible, realise that true intention. If the teachers of Torah had ever admitted that they were bound by the strict letter of the Torah, then the *erub* would have been an evasion, and so more or less would every halachah in the Talmud. It was precisely because they felt themselves to be not tied down to the written word of the Torah that they were free to develop the halachah, and to make of it an interpretation of the real intention of the Torah as nearly as they could in accordance with their own ethical conceptions.

Another misunderstanding to be carefully avoided is this, that the teachers of Torah, according to their own principle, were free to teach anything they pleased, and could have repealed every commandment in the Torah if they had been so minded. Thus, for instance, it is well known that the teachers of Torah did a great deal to make divorce difficult, to protect the wife against the caprice of the husband, to mitigate the hardship of her position, and they expressed their strong regret that divorce should ever take place. Why then did they not abolish divorce, seeing that they were not bound by the written word of Torah, and could apparently make it say whatever they wished it to say? The answer is that they were the guides of the people, making laws (in the form of halachah) which would be binding on the people; they had the duty of teaching Torah, not of teaching something of their own invention. The Torah was divinely given, and the Torah recognised divorce and even enjoined it. If the teachers had been drawing up an entirely new code of laws for a new human society, they would have been free to leave out divorce and make no provision for it. But whatever they might have done in that case, they were as teachers confronted with the Torah as an actual fact, and the permission of divorce as an undeniable part of its contents. All that they could do was to make the actual procedure of divorce conform as closely as possible to the requirements of justice to the weaker party and sympathy with the sufferer, and to ensure that it should not be carried out 'unadvisedly or lightly'.

It is recorded that the Beth Shammai held that divorce was permissible only on the ground of unfaithfulness, while the Beth Hillel held that a man might divorce his wife even for a trivial cause, simply because he wanted to. Hard things have accordingly been said of the low morality indicated in the latter opinion. But those who held that opinion, including presumably Hillel himself, were stating their view of what the law was, the law, moreover, according to the written text of

[122]

the Torah, they were not stating what they would like it to be; and all the halachahs which they and their predecessors and followers devised on the subject were intended to bring the unavoidable fact of divorce within the range and under the influence of ethical and not merely legal principles. In other words, they were trying to realise and make effective in the social life of the community what they deemed to be the real intention in this particular matter of the Torah as God had given it.

After what has been said in this chapter already, it will not be needful to enlarge further on the ethical value of the halachah. Whatever may have been the effect upon those who recognised the system and lived under it, a question which will be considered later (see below, p. 138 f.), it is clear that the whole intention of the halachah in all its vast development was ethical. In the case of some halachah affecting some small detail of practice the ethical intention may not be obvious; but if such a halachah is considered in its relation to the whole of the halachahs on the subject with which it deals, then the ethical purpose becomes apparent. If this were realised, a good deal of the amusement found by some in the fact of serious discussion about, for instance, an egg laid on the Sabbath day, would be seen to be rather pointless.

But the question may naturally be asked, and it is well worth considering, What really led to the halachah, and why was it always developed in the ethical direction and not as a mere elaboration of ritual acts?

The written Torah was made by Ezra the supreme authority for the religious life and practice of the Jewish community, and it was studied and applied with this end in view by the Sopherim and the later teachers, as has already been shown at length in the preceding chapters. Now during all the period from Ezra to Hillel the Canon of Scripture was being gradually brought to completion (see above, Bk. I, Ch. II, p. 7), and more particularly the prophetical books had assumed their present form, probably about 250 B.C. This implies that the contents of these books were more available for study; and no doubt the main reason why they were collected and edited was that they might be studied. It is quite certain that none were more intent on the study of the prophetical books than the teachers of Torah,

[123]

because, although prophecy was not technically Torah, yet prophecy and Torah both came from the same God and were, each in its own degree, his revelation to Israel. The prophets were teachers of righteousness, whatever else they were, and they gave their teaching in the form of direct appeal to the moral and spiritual nature of those to whom they spoke. They exalted goodness and denounced sin, in the name of the One Holy God, and called on those who would serve him aright to walk worthily of their high calling, ' to do justly and to love mercy and to walk humbly with their God' (Micah vi. 8). No one has ever questioned that the prophetical books are full of noble and lofty ethical teaching, and there is no need to labour the point. All that teaching was present to the minds of the teachers of Torah, and by them diligently studied and taken to heart. The effect upon them, as it is the effect upon all who learn from the prophets, was to raise their moral standard and make clearer their discernment of what it implied. The very last thing in their minds was to disparage or disregard the teaching of the prophets, as if it were something alien from their own principles or from the Torah, which for them was supreme. On the contrary, they brought to the study of the Torah the inward light which had come to them through the prophets and which enabled them to see more deeply and more clearly what the Torah really meant.

Now the whole object of the halachah was to train the people to do the will of God in exactly the right way. We have seen (above, p. 52 f.) that in the type of Judaism which we are considering, the greatest stress was laid upon *doing*. To do the will of God was the one essential, whatever else there might be in religion. It was not enough to learn what the will of God was, or to believe this or that about him, no matter how sublime that might be. God was not served unless man gave himself to that service in the most complete and effective way possible, and that was by the conscious deliberate act of doing his will. If the teaching of the prophets had been taken to heart and put in practice by those to whom it had been addressed, God would have been truly served. But the words of the prophets had fallen upon deaf ears; and as the result of the disregard shown to the warnings, pleadings, and threats of the prophets, the calamity of the Exile had come upon Israel. Had the prophets then

[124]

spoken in vain? So far as regarded the people of their own generation, they certainly had. But they spoke the word of the
Lord. Had *He* spoken in vain when he sent them on his errand?
Was it not said by one of them, speaking in his name (Isa. lv. 11):
' So shall it be with my word that goeth forth out of my mouth;
it shall not return unto me void, but do that which I please
and prosper in the thing whereto I sent it '. As the teachers of
Torah read the lesson of the past, it was clearly for them as the
successors of the prophets to give effect to this declaration by
making the prophetic teaching effective as it had never been.
They did this in the only way which was open to them, viz.
by applying to the Torah the prophetic ideas, and interpreting
it accordingly. The halachah was the first result, and the ethical
direction of the halachah was the second result. That there
should be halachah at all was in itself a sign that the written
Torah was felt to be insufficient for its purpose of guiding and
uplifting the religious life of the people. And that the halachah
should be developed always on ethical lines is the clear evidence
that the teachers were reading the Torah in the sense of the
prophets. It is idle to complain that the teachers of Torah did
not follow the prophets in their freedom of utterance, but cast
their teaching into the form of halachah. To follow the prophets
in merely proclaiming the word of the Lord would be to fail
as the prophets had failed, and to do so even with that prophetic failure before their eyes. What was wanted now was to
get the thing done, to get the will of God obeyed, to train men
actually to do what was enjoined, and not to think that they
could get off by merely hearing about it. So far as the Torah was
the revelation of the divine will, it was there to be obeyed, and
the halachah was the manifold direction how to obey it. And,
because the halachah was developed always in the ethical
direction, it represented the union of Torah with prophecy,
Torah on its preceptive side interpreted in the light of prophetic illumination. The whole system of which halachah is the
essential feature was, and was intended to be, a discipline,
a practical training in the doing of right acts and refraining
from wrong ones; and its purpose would not have been accomplished by the mere utterance of lofty teaching, even as lofty
as that of the prophets. The teachers of Torah on the lines of
halachah knew very well what they were about; what they did

and what they avoided doing was their deliberate choice, and they carried out their ideas without wavering, no matter what those who would not accept their system might say of them.

It was not for nothing that ' Prophecy was taken from the prophets and given to the Wise and not taken away from these '. Halachah is truly the application of prophetic ideas to the interpretation of Torah, and that is its chief meaning. But it should be added that as the Canon of Scripture was gradually formed, all the ethical influence of the other books, notably the Psalms and the Wisdom literature, was added to that of the prophets, and had a share in the ethical development of the halachah. Which only means that gradually the whole of Scripture was available and became effective in deepening and widening the ethical discernment of the teachers of Torah, and gave them the lead which they followed in working out the halachah.

It is of the greatest importance to realise and keep in mind the ethical meaning of the halachah, and to understand that it never was a mere code of rules to be blindly accepted and mechanically carried out. It was all part of a great scheme whose purpose was the complete and faithful service of God by doing his will in every relation and every act of life. And because this aspect of the halachah is seldom if ever known to non-Jewish scholars, and still more seldom understood, it has been made clear, it is hoped beyond the possibility of misunderstanding, in the present chapter.

CHAPTER VII

THE ETHICAL TEACHING ON THE RABBINICAL LINE

(B) THE HAGGADAH

THE ethical teaching on the Rabbinical line is presented more clearly in the haggadah than in the halachah, chiefly because halachah is not primarily instruction, but direction, while haggadah is instruction and nothing else. The halachah assumes the duty of doing the will of God, and indicates the right way of doing it. The haggadah meditates on the Torah, and draws forth the truths and ethical lessons which it contains. The halachah, as we have seen in the preceding chapter, was developed on ethical lines from first to last, but the ethical ideas were applied to the halachah, without being definitely stated. In the haggadah they form a large part of the subject-matter, though even there they are not formulated into a system. There is no system of any kind in the haggadah, while yet certain main lines and leading thoughts can be traced throughout its whole extent. These will serve better than anything else to indicate what the ethical teaching in the Rabbinical literature really was. So far as that can be ascertained, it will provide the means of answering the question raised above (p. 110) as to the teaching given during the Ezra-Hillel period for which no authentic haggadah is extant. It will be the purpose of the present chapter to set forth the Rabbinical Ethics so far as they have not been dealt with in the preceding chapter.

It goes without saying that the basis of all the Rabbinical Ethics is the Old Testament; and the chief difference between the earlier and the later body of teaching is in the working out of ethical ideas, not in the ideas themselves. As has been well said: 'To the eternal glory of the Old Testament, the great texts, " love thy neighbour as thyself," " hate not thy brother in thy heart," " avenge not," " bear no grudge," " love the stranger," are part of the Hebrew law of holiness. There was little left for religion in subsequent ages except to draw out the

[127]

full consequences of these and similar injunctions. Nothing that has been added can compare in sheer originality and power to the first formulation of these great principles' (Abrahams, *Studies in Pharisaism, etc.* i, pp. 150-1). These words were written with special reference to the subject of forgiveness, but they apply equally to the whole field of Rabbinical Ethics. What was new in the later teaching would not have been there at all if it had not been suggested by, or implied in, something already contained in the earlier teaching. But what was new in the later teaching was there because the teachers devised it as a more effective way of bringing home to those whom they taught the meaning of what was old. The haggadah was one part of the whole system, of which halachah was the other part, whose object was to train men in doing and being what God would have them do and be. The teachers of Torah, whose function it was to administer this system, were above all things practical teachers whose aim was to make good men and women; they were not speculative philosophers, or even theoretical moralists. They gave their teaching to the people assembled in the Synagogue, and worked it out in the Beth ha-Midrash; and neither the one institution nor the other was a school of philosophy. Behind the learning and teaching was always the doing.

The Rabbinical teachers used no terms corresponding to those usually found in ethical treatises. They never spoke of the Ethical Ideal, nor the Moral Law, nor the Summum Bonum, nor yet of conscience, nor even of religion as a general term. But they were well aware of what is implied in those words, and their hearers also were aware. Which means that what they enjoined was not blind subservience to an external law, but the willing obedience of free moral agents, knowing whom they served, and why they served him.

The object towards which all the labours of the teachers was directed, the ideal towards which they pressed forward without ever fully attaining it, was that those to whom the Torah was given should make a complete response to it, so that as a divine revelation everything revealed should fulfil its purpose. If anyone came short of reaching this ideal, as indeed no one fully succeeded, then in his case the intention with which the Torah had been given was not completely realised, there was still something to be learned, something to be done. And this is what is meant by the innumerable allusions to *Talmud Torah* as the highest exercise of the human spirit. To render that phrase by 'study of the Law' is to miss nearly the whole of its meaning. Superficially, even, the rendering is not correct, because 'Law' gives a wrong direction to the thought. *Talmud Torah* is far deeper and wider. If a Jew were to imagine what life would be without Torah, and were then to realise what the difference was when the light of the divine revelation irradiated every remotest corner and every smallest detail of life, then his contemplation of that difference, his growing comprehension of it, and his conscious reaction to it, would be his *Talmud Torah*. Something like what is here suggested hovered before the minds of all those who held the Rabbinical conception of religion in terms of Torah, all who held that conception for themselves and who strove to impart it to others. Something like this is the ultimate clue to the meaning of the whole of the Rabbinical literature. After what has been said in the preceding chapters it will be clear that the idea here expressed is the direct outcome of the work of Ezra, its development at the hands of the Sopherim and their successors, who gradually perceived and unfolded the inexhaustible contents of the original concept of the Torah.

Our present concern is with the contents of the Torah as ethical teaching—that is, its application to life as the service of God. That teaching was given partly by illustration of specific virtues and their opposite vices, of which more will be said presently, and partly by laying stress on certain leading ideas and principles which serve to give definite direction to the teaching. These leading ideas will be formulated and explained before going on to the teaching in regard to the specific virtues.

The principle of widest scope may be expressed in the form that the true life of man is to be like God. 'Imitatio Dei' is a phrase often used by modern Jewish writers, and obviously suggested by 'Imitatio Christi'; but the idea of imitation of God by man is far older, though the abstract term does not occur in the Rabbinic sources. The nearest approach to the thought underlying it is in the two words *Kedushah* and *Hasiduth*, Holiness and Saintliness, words which are closely associated and often thought of together*. And the reason why these are taken to be the equivalent of the idea of Imitation of God is given by the text (Lev. xix. 2), ' Ye shall be holy, for I the Lord your God am holy'. Whatever may have been the original meaning of ' holy ' in this passage and elsewhere, it was understood by the Rabbis to denote the moral perfection of God, that in his nature to which the nature of man in some degree corresponded, so that there could be some likeness between them, however faint. Man was created in the image of God (Gen. i. 27), and therefore the possibility of becoming in some respect like him was present from the beginning. To attain to such likeness, as far as possible, was the true end and aim of life; and the range within which it was possible was indicated by the terms *Kedushah* and *Hasiduth*.

These terms denote much more than qualities of character, they imply actions which manifest that character. Therefore, to imitate the holiness of God is to do such things as he does, it is not to aspire to a static perfection. The end in view is not mystic contemplation, but consecrated action. Thus it is said (Mech. 37*a*), in commenting on ' I will praise him ' (Exod. xv. 2), 'Abba Shaul said†: "I will be like him ". As he is merciful and gracious so be thou merciful and gracious'. Again it is said (Siphré ii. 85*a*): ' " To walk in all his ways." These are the ways of the Holy One, blessed be He, as it is said (Exod. xxxiv. 6, 7): " The Lord, the Lord, a God full of compassion and gracious, slow to anger and plenteous in mercy and truth, keeping mercy for thousands, forgiving iniquity and transgression and sin, and clearing, etc."; and it says (Joel iii. 5; ii. 32 A.V.): "Every one that calls on‡ the name of the Lord shall be delivered ". But how is it possible for a man to be called by the name of the Lord? But as the All-present is called merciful and gracious, so be thou

---

* On *Kedushah* and *Hasiduth*, see Schechter, *Some Aspects of Rabbinic Theology*, ch. xiii, p. 199 f. I am much indebted to Schechter's guidance in what I have said under this head.

† Abba Shaul interpreted the word *anvehu*, ' I will praise him,' as if it were to be read *Ani ve hu*, 'I and He'. Abba Shaul knew perfectly well that this was not grammatically possible; he read it so in order to bring out his point. Haggadic exegesis very often deals with a text in this manner and for this purpose.

‡ Schechter points out that the Rabbis must have read in the text of Joel *jikkārē* where the Mass. text has *jikrā*.

merciful and gracious, giving freely to all; and as the Holy One blessed be He is called righteous, as it is said (Ps. cxlv. 17): " The Lord is righteous in all his ways and gracious in all his works," so be thou righteous. As the Holy One, blessed be He, is gracious in all his works (*ibid.*) so be thou gracious. Therefore it is said (Joel, *ib.*): " Every one that is called by the name of the Lord shall be delivered "; and it says (Isa. xliii. 7): " Every one that is called by my name I have created him for my glory, I have formed him, yea I have made him". And it says (Prov. xvi. 4): " The Lord hath made everything for his own sake ".' It is pointed out by Schechter, in the chapter referred to above (*Aspects*, p. 204), that the ' Imitatio Dei ' does not extend to all the divine attributes, and he mentions a passage (*Midrash ha Gadol*, p. 549) which runs as follows: ' This is what Scripture says (Ps. lxvi. 5): " Come and see the works of God, he is terrible in his doing to the children of men". This verse was said in reference to the devious ways by which the Holy One, blessed be He, manages his world, and it is one of four attributes which it is not well for flesh and blood to make use of but the Holy One b. H. alone. And these are they: Jealousy, vengeance, exaltation, and a devious way'. This passage is very late in date, but at least it clearly states, what is true of the older teaching with which we are concerned, that the imitation of God which is enjoined is restricted to the attributes of mercy, etc., as enumerated above.

All the passages quoted above in reference to *Kedushah* show how fundamental in Jewish thought was the principle, ' Ye shall be holy for I am holy'. Its most characteristic development remains yet to be noted, viz. the advance from ' being holy ' to 'making holy'. The effect of this advance is to lay stress on the need of action in order to fulfil the requirement of holiness. The point is well brought out in a passage (Siphra, 86c) which runs as follows: '"And the Lord spake unto Moses, saying Speak unto the children of Israel and say unto them Ye shall be holy " (Lev. xix. 2). Teaching that this portion [*parashah*] was spoken in the congregation. And why was it spoken in the congregation? Because most of the main principles [*gūfē*] of the Torah are implied in it. " Ye shall be holy." Be separate. " Ye shall be holy for I the Lord your God am holy." Meaning, " If ye make yourselves holy I will account it as if ye made me holy.

And if ye do not make yourselves holy, I will account it as if ye did not make me holy ". Or does it mean only " If ye make me holy then I am holy, and if ye do not make me holy then I am not holy "? We learn to say " I exist in my holiness whether ye make me holy or do not make me holy ".' To make holy is to do such things as bear witness to the holiness of God, and obviously these can only be done by those who strive to be holy as he is holy. But these actions are not confined to works of mercy and the like. They include all acts by which a man affirms his loyalty to God, declares himself on God's side, and they are all summed up in the famous phrase, *Kiddūsh ha-Shem*, ' hallowing the Name,' or, more correctly, though not verbally exact, ' hallowing God,' making him holy in the sense of the passage from Siphra just quoted. The ideas contained in *Kiddush ha-Shem* and its opposite *Ḥillūl ha-Shem*, ' profaning the Name,' have been of immense importance, not merely in Jewish ethical teaching, but in the practical living of Jewish lives all down the centuries to the present day. The idea underlying *Kiddush ha-Shem* is that man hallows God by a virtuous life, so that every single virtuous act is in itself a *Kiddush ha-Shem**; because by such actions man honours God, and so to speak proclaims him before men. Man does not make God holy in the sense that otherwise he would not be holy; God remains ever in his holiness whatever men may do or not do. But those who formulated the term *Kiddush ha-Shem* ' clearly recognised that the moral principle inherent in God became for every individual, not indeed objectively but subjectively, a reality only in so far as it was an active power in his life, when it made him a moral man, and thereby awakened a moral life in others. This alone is the meaning of the concept *Kiddush ha-Shem* and the opposite that of the correlated *Hillul ha-Shem*, terms which down to the present day are taken very seriously in Judaism. Every honourable act is a victory of the God-idea, and at the same time a " hallowing of God before all men; while every base act is a defeat of the God-idea, a desecration " of God before all men' (Perles, *op. cit.*, pp. 69-70). This well brings out the deepest meaning of *Kiddush (Hillul) ha-Shem*, as

* For an admirable explanation of *Kiddush (Hillul) ha-Shem* see Perles, in his critique of Bousset's *Religion des Judentums* (pp. 68-71), and the references there given.

it was present in all ages of Jewish thought; but the earlier applications of the term, especially *Kiddush ha-Shem*, were in connexion with martyrdom, the voluntary sacrifice of life for the sake of God, and in order to be faithful to him. The source of the two terms is (Lev. xxii. 32): ' Ye shall not profane my holy name, and I will be hallowed in the midst of the children of Israel; I am the Lord which hallow you, which brought you forth out of the land of Egypt to be unto you for a God. I am the Lord '. But perhaps an older source is (Isa. v. 16): ' The holy God is hallowed by righteousness '. This at all events gives the connexion between the holiness of God and the active, not merely passive, hallowing of him by the life of man. The application of *Kiddush ha-Shem* to surrender of life rather than be unfaithful to God is found in Siphra, *Emor.*, p. 99*d*, ed. Weiss, and is illustrated there by an incident of the persecution under Trajan (Pappus and Lulianus). But it is clearly foreshadowed in the Old Testament. The passage in Siphra expressly mentions the example of Hananiah, Mishael, and Azariah (Dan. iii) as a case in point; and when a psalmist says (Ps. lxxix. 2): ' *For thy sake we are killed all the day long* ', he had the thought though not the words. From these roots in the Old Testament there grew up the idea of *Kiddush ha-Shem*, and of its opposite *Hillul ha-Shem*, first in the special case of martyrdom, and then in the more general sense explained above, but it is not possible, I believe, to mark the date when they first emerged in Jewish usage. The words of Abtalion (Aboth i. 10) seem to show that in his time, the end of the last century B.C., the term *Hillul ha-Shem* was already current, and presumably also *Kiddush ha-Shem*. However that may be, these two great conceptions, together with that of *Kedushah*, from which they are derived, stand as the eternal pillars of the Ethics of Judaism, at all events of that type of Judaism with which we are at present alone concerned. And they do so because they express the thought of life as the service of God, the life that he gave consecrated to him in every act, word, and thought by man who was made in his image, and whose ideal was to be like his maker.

From this view of the foundation of Jewish Ethics it is easy to derive the motive with which right actions should be done, and here again we find a general principle expressed in what became a technical term. This is *lishmah*, which means that a

right action is to be done ' for its own sake '*, and not for any
lower motive. A variant on this is *le shem Shammaim*, ' for the
sake of heaven (God) '. The two together express the thought of
conscious devotion to the service of God, obedience to his will,
etc., with single-minded sincerity and with no ulterior motive.
Whatever a man ought to do was a commandment (*mitzvah*),
whether precisely defined or not. It was a mitzvah to keep the
Sabbath, it was also a mitzvah to do good deeds and show
kindness. God had the right to command, and what he commanded was there to be done—or not done, as the case might
be. What was to be man's attitude towards the mitzvah, the
spirit in which he was to do it? It was possible to feel it as an
irksome task, which he would not perform except for fear of
consequences, or in the hope of gaining some reward for doing
it. The Rabbinical Ethics rules this out, quite definitely, and
teaches that a man ought to perform a mitzvah simply because
he loves God and there is no better way of showing his love
than by doing what God enjoins. The same thought is expressed, in a very different connexion, in the saying: ' If ye
love me, ye will keep my commandments' (John xiv. 15). In
Judaism this attitude of mind was expressed in the term ' the
joy of the commandment' (*simhah shel mitzvah*), which implied
joy that the commandment had been given, and joy in fulfilling
it. Whatever the mitzvah might be, however hard, or dangerous, involving the sacrifice even of life itself, it was an opportunity sent by God of showing love to him, not by grudging
obedience nor by hope of reward, but by the eager acceptance
of the opportunity with grateful adoration of him who had
sent it. When R. Akiba was being tortured to death, he recited
the Shema. The executioner was astonished to see him laugh
in the midst of his agony. On being asked the reason why he
did so, 'he replied: "All my life have I tried to fulfil the commandment Thou shalt love the Lord thy God with all thy heart
and with all thy soul and with all thy might. I have loved him
with all my heart and with all my wealth. But to love him with
all my soul I found not. And when I come to ' with all thy soul '
and the hour of reciting the Shema is at hand, and I can say it

* *Lishmah* properly means ' for her sake', the feminine suffix referring to
mitzvah, which is feminine. *Mitzvah*, in the wider sense, included everything
that a man ought to do.

with undivided mind, therefore I recite it and laugh ". He had not finished before his soul departed' (j. Ber. 14*b*). That is the classical example of *simhah shel mitzvah* at its highest, but it was not reserved for the martyrs. It was there for everyone who fulfilled a mitzvah from love to God and from no lower motive. To serve him from love was the highest motive of all. Abraham served him from love; Job only served him from fear (j. Ber. *ibid.*).

It is so often asserted that in Jewish Ethics the motive for service of God was hope of reward or fear of punishment that it will be well to deal expressly with the point. Certainly much is said by the Rabbis about reward, and merit; but no less certainly they refused to allow these to constitute the motive for right action. The famous saying of Antigonos of Socho (Aboth i. 3): ' Be not as servants who serve their master on condition of receiving a gift, but be as servants who serve their master not on condition of receiving a gift', stands at the very beginning of the specifically Pharisaic ethical tradition, and the thought expressed in it is found all along the line of that tradition. ' Say not I will study Torah that I may be called wise, that I may sit in the lecture-room [*yĕshībāh*], that I may live long in the world to come, . . . learn nevertheless, and the honour will come in the end ' (Siphré, ii. 84*b*). In other words, learn for its own sake. The reward is doubtless a reality, but it is not to be a motive. R. Eliezer b. Horkenos explains the words ' that delighteth greatly in his commandments ' (Ps. cxii. 1) to mean ' delighteth in the commandments, but not in the reward of the commandments ' (b. A. Zar. 19*a*); upon which follows immediately a reference to the saying of Antigonos cited above, not as an individual saying, but as a quotation from the Mishnah. It was never the case that the expectation of reward for performing a commandment was allowed to be a motive for doing it, though, among the many hundred teachers whose words are recorded in the Talmud and Midrash, someone may have said something to that effect.

Then what was the relation of ' reward ' to commandment?* The reward was simply the better condition which a man who performed a commandment was in as compared with what he

*For a full discussion of the meaning of reward and merit in the Rabbinical ethics, see my *Pharisees* (pp. 128-135).

[135]

would have been in if he had not performed it. This was a development of the ancient words: 'That it may be well with thee' (Deut. v. 33). In what precise way it was 'to be well with thee' was variously interpreted from age to age; beginning with the material prosperity of the older Scriptures and becoming more and more spiritualised in the Talmud and Midrash. The point lies, however, in the fact, not in the manner, of its 'being well with thee'. The fact had its source in the justice of God, to whom it could not be indifferent whether a man did his will or neglected or refused to do it. The man himself stood in a different position in regard to God as the result of his acting in one way or the other. Now the essence of the act consisted in its being done solely from love to God, as we have seen. The mere performance of what was commanded, as an *opus operatum*, without the single-minded intention of serving God thereby, was ethically worthless, if indeed it was not an actual sin. Obviously, therefore, an act done for the sake of reward would defeat its own end, because the first essential would be wanting, and would rightly do so because there ought not to have been an 'end'. And this is what is really meant in the saying quoted above (p. 135): 'Learn, for its own sake, and the honour will come'. Learn Torah for its own sake, perform the mitzvah for its own sake, simply because so and only so is God perfectly served, and then 'it shall be well with thee', as he shall see fit.

Such was the ideal of true motive which was always maintained in the Rabbinical Ethics; and that severe demand was the result of trying to realise in act the meaning of 'Thou shalt love the Lord thy God with all thy heart and with all thy soul and with all thy might'.

It has been said above (p. 128) that the 'whole duty of man' on the lines of the Rabbinical conception of religion was to make a complete response to the Torah, learning what it taught and doing what it enjoined. Nothing which it contained was to be neglected as if it did not matter. God had given it all. But, while all was thus of equal obligation, so far as it was a command to do or refrain from doing, yet there was a clear difference in the character of the things commanded. Some commandments related to the ritual, of sacrifices, purifications, offerings, and the like; some were laws for the regulation of the life of the community, such as laws relating to property, inheritance, marriage, contracts, civil wrongs and criminal offences, and many others; and some were commandments relating to the conduct of man towards his fellow man; such as ' thou shall not hate thy brother in thy heart '. All these were commandments, mitzvoth; and whatever was a mitzvah was a thing to be done, for the motive and on the general principle already explained in this chapter. It was the object of the teachers of Torah to make clear how these several mitzvoth were to be performed, and here we come across another general principle which they applied to the interpretation of Torah.

It was obvious that some mitzvoth, especially the negative ones—' Thou shalt not '—could be defined in such a way that the exactly right action could be distinguished from others that were not exactly right. But others were so general and inclusive that they could not be defined. It was possible to define how the Sabbath ought to be kept, although an immense number of halachahs were needed for the purpose. But it was not possible to define how the mitzvah ' thou shalt love thy neighbour as thyself ' was to be fulfilled, or ' honour thy father and thy mother ', or the general requirement to do good deeds, to show kindness, or the supreme mitzvah of all—' Thou shalt love the Lord thy God '. The general principle which was applied to this distinction between mitzvoth was this, that so far as it could be defined it must be defined, but so far as it could not be defined it must be left to the conscience of the individual. A mitzvah thus left undefined was called ' a thing committed to the heart ' (*dabar masur laleb*)*. The phrase is found in Siphra (p. 88*d*, end) and often in the Talmud (b. B. Mez. 58*b*, and parallels). In the passage in Siphra (*loc. cit.*) it is connected with ' Thou shalt fear the Lord thy God ' (Lev. xix. 14, and elsewhere), added after the commandment. Rashi (on b. Mez. 58*b*) explains it to mean that the mitzvah is ' committed to the heart ', because only God can read the heart and can know if the action is really good. This is true, but it does not apply to other cases when ' thou shalt fear the Lord thy God ' follows on a mitzvah. (See Lazarus, *Ethik d.*

* On this phrase see Perles, *Critique of Bousset*, p. 65, for a very clear explanation.

Judentums, i, p. 400.) The real point of the phrase 'committed to the heart' is that the mitzvah so described cannot be exactly defined. For the mitzvoth so described are not always accompanied by the words 'Thou shalt fear the Lord thy God'. What it really amounts to is this: So far as a mitzvah could be defined the halachah was the definition of it; but the whole duty of man was not and could not be summed up in so many and such and such halachahs, and only the conscience and moral discernment of the person concerned could show him what he ought to do. A man was not at liberty to say 'I am only bound to do this and that which is defined in a halachah, or to refrain from such acts as are definitely forbidden', as if all the rest of his possible actions were morally indifferent. He was at no point outside the range of ethical principles. If there were no defined halachah at all, he would still be within the range of the supreme and inclusive mitzvah, 'Thou shalt love the Lord thy God'; and the effect of defining halachah upon this or that point was not to weaken or cancel that supreme obligation, but only to make clear that in regard to this or that particular action it meant so and so, the obligation ought to be met in this or that particular way. Where no such definition was given, the original obligation remained in full force, and the right way of meeting it was left to the conscience which owned the obligation and the devotion to the will of God which made his service a joy. Thus the 'things committed to the heart' cover the whole field of ethics where the mitzvoth are not defined in a halachah, and by the nature of the case no exact list of such actions could be drawn up or was ever thought of. But prominent among such actions are the doing of kindnesses (*gemiluth hasadim*) and good deeds generally, the honouring of father and mother, love to one's neighbour, and, of course, love to God, so far as it was not defined by halachah.

In the view of the teachers of Torah the ethical life of man was not merely the adding together of so many detached and prescribed actions; it was a continuous process consciously directed to the service of God by doing his will, and only at certain points and in certain acts was that service defined in a particular way. The defining of actions by halachah was intended to be a direction to a man for the right doing, in a given instance, of that which he always desired to do, viz. the

[138]

will of God. It was not a compulsion laid on him from without, unless the initial obligation to serve God at all was a compulsion laid on him from without, instead of being the instinctive response of his soul to the love of God. The halachah was guidance given him; a discipline certainly, but a discipline which he gratefully accepted because he trusted in the wisdom of the teachers who had given it for his guidance. The discipline would only become irksome and the 'Law' a 'burden' if he distrusted that wisdom and doubted the validity of the whole system. Which is exactly what Paul did; and those who have learned from him to speak of 'the burden of the Law' are only bearing witness to their ignorance of what the religion of Torah really meant to those who lived by it.

From this point onwards the field of ethics is divided between mitzvoth, the fulfilment of which is defined in a halachah (or several halachahs) and mitzvoth, the fulfilment of which is not defined but 'committed to the heart'. The ethical bearing of the halachah has already been explained in the preceding chapter, and need not be further dwelt on. But before going on to treat of the other branch of ethics, the non-halachic, one more general principle should be noticed, which serves to connect them together. It has been pointed out above (p. 136 f.) that some of the mitzvoth were intended to regulate the life of the community in such matters as contracts, property, inheritance, criminal offences, and the like. When these were defined in one or more halachahs, the halachah was in the strictest sense of the word Law, with definite penalty for its violation. The sanction of the law was the authority of the Great Beth Din, which declared that in such and such a case the Torah commanded so and so. In a community whose life was regulated by civil and criminal law so formulated, the rights and duties of each member of the community were precisely defined, and it was the duty of every judge who administered the law to give his decision between the contending parties before him without fear or favour, declaring simply what the law required him to say. He must not be influenced by any other considerations, such as sympathy with the oppressed or his own opinion that the law was a hard one. All this, of course, is of the essence of upright administration of the law, in any law-respecting country.

Now if a man brings an action against another man, he asks the court to say that he is rightfully entitled to so and so, compensation, damages, or what not, and the judgment awards him what according to the law he is entitled to have, or allows him to do what he seeks to do; in any case the law defines his right and authorises him to act accordingly. Obviously he does no wrong if he acts in accordance with the judgment given in his favour. But Rabbinical ethics was not satisfied with this, and looked with approval on a man who did not insist on his strict legal rights. Such a man was said to act ' within the limit of the judgment' (*liphnim misshurath ha-din*). And the reason why his action in so doing was approved was that in this way brotherly love was promoted between those who were at variance with each other. The phrase 'liphnim misshurath ha-din' is found (Mech. 59*b*) in an exposition of Exod. xviii. 20; but it is there used as an already familiar term, and its connexion with the text is merely arbitrary haggadah. Several examples of it are found in the Talmud (b. B. Mez. 99*b* end, and often). The sense is always that of refraining from insisting on one's legal rights. A not unlikely source of it, in thought though not in word, is: ' And thou shalt do that which is right and good in the sight of the Lord, that it may be well with thee ', etc. (Deut. vi. 18). Rashi, *ad loc.*, says that this means ' agreement, and "liphnim misshurath ha-din" '. Agreement is reached when two parties who are at law with each other make up their difference and become friends. The judgment of the court would have been for the one and against the other; that would be strict law. By agreement (*pesharah*) they refrain from insisting on strict law, and friendship is re-established. The text (Deut. vi. 18) is used to support a distinction between law and equity in the Rabbinical jurisprudence, by laying stress on the two words ' right ' and ' good ' and the difference between them*.

The general principles which have been reviewed in the foregoing pages give a clear indication of the character of the Rabbinical ethics as a whole, of the manner in which it was developed on the basis of the Torah, and of the main direction

* See an essay by M. Eschelbacher on 'Recht und Billigkeit im Jurisprudenz des Talmud' in the Hermann Cohen *Festschrift*, 1912, pp. 501-514, especially p. 503.

of that development. We shall now go on to consider the ethical teaching in relation to several specific virtues, and more particularly those which are not defined in halachah but are 'committed to the heart'. The following are not arranged in any logical order, but they include some of the most important subjects of Rabbinical ethics: (1) Good deeds, and the doing of kindness. (2) Love to one's neighbour. (3) Truthfulness and sincerity. (4) Honesty. (5) Forgiveness. (6) Honour to father and mother. (7) Chastity.

(1) GOOD DEEDS, and the doing of kindness (*maasīm tobīm* and *gemilūth hăsādīm*). Rabbinical ethics always laid great stress on good deeds, and the term may be said to have almost become a technical one, though hardly perhaps to be described as a specific virtue. Its use is seen in such phrases as 'Repentance and good deeds are as a shield in face of punishment' (Aboth iv. 13); '. . . even though he possess Torah and good deeds, he has no portion in the world to come' (*ib.* iii. 15). The combination 'good deeds' does not occur in the Old Testament, but, of course, the thought implied in the words is found everywhere in Scripture. Possibly the source of it is: 'Turn from evil and do good' (Ps. xxxiv. 15), which closely corresponds to the first quotation from Aboth, just given. The words in the Psalm are quite general, and apply to any and every action which can be called good. But the connotation of 'good deeds' in the Rabbinical ethics is no less wide. True, the Rabbis understood by a 'good deed' an action performed in fulfilling a mitzvah, so that it might seem as if 'good deed' were in some way restricted and specialised by being brought into relation with Torah. But there is no such restriction of meaning. As we have seen, a mitzvah is any act enjoined in the Torah; and, while many mitzvoth are defined by a halachah, the others are 'committed to the heart'. The general mitzvah, 'to do good,' loses none of its validity because at certain points it is defined by a halachah.

It is easy to understand why such great importance was attached to 'good deeds' in the Rabbinical ethics. Indeed, that it should be so follows naturally from the principle, explained above (p. 51 f.) and often referred to, that the first essential is to *do* the will of God. Nothing whatever must take precedence of that; for even the study of Torah, which Akiba held to be a higher duty than action, was only to be so regarded because it led to action, to the doing of good deeds (b. Kidd. 40*b*. See parallels in Bacher, *A. d. T.* i, 303, n.3). An act (*maaseh*) is a man's expression of himself, the exercise of his will, his mark made upon the sum total of things about him; and an act whereby he fulfils the will of God as revealed in the Torah is his own conscious and intentional service of God. Such an act is necessarily a ' good deed', and this is what is meant by 'good deeds' in the Rabbinical ethics. The more of such ' good deeds' a man has performed, the more complete has been his service of God; and when it is said that God weighs and counts the good and the bad deeds of a man, and even writes them in a book (so in some late midrashim cited by Weber, *System, etc.*, p. 271), that only means that, being just, God takes account of how a man has or has not served him. The figure of speech used to enforce the thought is one thing, the thought is quite another, and the failure to distinguish between them leads to a complete misunderstanding of what the Rabbis really taught on the matter*. There was never any idea of a bargain between God and man, and in the last resort ' salvation ', or, as the Rabbis would say, ' a portion in the world to come,' depended on the free grace of God. It was not the payment of a credit balance of good deeds. Doubtless the ' good deeds ' were not without significance in the sight of God, and doubtless there was a ' reward ' for them; but there was not, in respect to either, the ' degraded and mechanical conception ' which non-Jewish critics have usually supposed.

Closely allied to ' good deeds ', forming indeed a special branch of them, is ' the doing of kindnesses ' (*gemiluth hasadim*). As in the case of ' good deeds ', so also here the exact form of the term is not found in the Old Testament, while the thought is of constant occurrence. But the term itself is found as early as the third century B.C., in the maxim of Simeon the Just (see above, pp. 60-1): ' Upon three things the world standeth: upon Torah, upon Service, and upon the doing of Kindnesses ', ' gemiluth

---

* Dr. Maldwyn Hughes, in his *Ethics of the Apocryphal Literature*, p. 76, writes: ' We have not here the degraded and mechanical conception of the Talmud, according to which salvation depended on there being a balance of good deeds to a man's credit, when his righteous and unrighteous acts had been set over against each other as in a ledger account '.

hasadim ' (Aboth i. 2). Simeon the Just was one of the last of the Sopherim, so that his use of the term is evidence of its age. It does not seem to have been formed on the model of any Old Testament phrase. In a statement (b. Jeb. 79*a*, and elsewhere) of three distinguishing virtues of Israel, it is said that they are ' doers of kindnesses ' (*gōmĕlē hasadim*), and the proof text quoted is (Gen. xviii. 19), ' For I know him . . . that they may keep the way of the Lord, to do justice and judgment,' where the word for ' justice ' (*tzedakah*) is taken in its later meaning of ' almsgiving '. Yet ' gemiluth hasadim ' was not the same as ' tzedakah '. Almsgiving was called ' tzedakah ' because it was giving to the poor what the poor had a right to, while ' the doing of kindnesses ' was a free act of goodwill. The difference between them is clearly brought out in a passage (T. Peah. iv. 19) which runs as follows: ' Almsgiving [*tzedakah*] and the doing of kindnesses [*gem. hasadim*] are equivalent to all the mitzvoth in the Torah; but almsgiving has to do with the living, doing of kindnesses with the living and the dead. Almsgiving has to do with the poor, doing of kindnesses with the poor and the rich. Almsgiving is the spending of money, the doing of kindnesses is the spending of self and money'. And in the next following clause of this passage it is proved that a man who refuses to give alms (and therefore presumably one who refuses to do kindnesses) is as bad as an idolater. An indication of the kind of action which comes under the head of ' gemiluth hasadim ' is given (b. Sot. 14*a*) in connexion with a haggadah on the burial of Moses, as follows: ' R. Hama b. Hanina said What is that which is written (Deut. xiii. 5) '' After the Lord your God ye shall walk ''? Is it possible for a man to walk after the Shechinah? And has it not been said already (Deut. iv. 24): '' For the Lord thy God is a consuming fire ''? But (it means) to walk after the ways of the Lord. As he clothes the naked (Gen. iii. 21, And the Lord God made, etc.), so do thou clothe the naked. The Holy One, blessed be He, visited the sick (Gen. xviii. 1), so do thou visit the sick. The Holy One, b.H., comforts the mourners (Gen. xxv. 11) so do thou comfort the mourners. The Holy One, b.H., buries the dead, as it is written (Deut. xxxiv. 6): '' And he buried him '', etc., so do thou bury the dead. . . .' ' R. Simlai expounded (*darash*) '' The Torah begins with the doing of kindnesses and ends with it,'' ' and the examples are given of the clothing of Adam and Eve, and the burial of Moses, as in the first part of the passage. These are the typical examples of what is meant by ' gemiluth hasadim ', and it should be noted that kindness after this manner is to be shown alike to Jews and Gentiles. Thus it is said (b. Gitt. 61a), ' Our Rabbis have taught: They feed the poor of the Gentiles along with the poor of Israel; they visit the sick of the Gentiles along with the sick of Israel; they bury the dead of the Gentiles along with the dead of Israel, because of " the ways of peace ".' This passage is a *baraitha*, i.e. it belongs to the period of the Mishnah, and is, in fact, found in substance, though not in the same words, in T. Gitt. v. 4, 5 (p. 328, 19, Zl.). For ' the ways of peace ', see above (p. 120). It is there shown that the halachah was developed in certain directions on the principle of ' ways of peace ', but this does not imply that everything done in view of this principle was defined by a halachah. It means that the same desire to promote peace and goodwill which led to the defining of certain halachahs was also a motive for ' gemiluth hasadim ', and found therein its most natural and spontaneous expression.

(2) LOVE TO ONE'S NEIGHBOUR. This follows naturally upon the ' doing of kindnesses '; but it calls for special treatment, because of the difference of opinion amongst scholars, or rather amongst theologians, as to the precise meaning of ' neighbour ' in the text (Lev. xix. 18): ' Thou shalt love thy neighbour as thyself', the text, of course, which governs the whole subject. The reason why theologians are referred to, as distinguished from scholars, is that theologians, at all events Christian theologians, have usually tried to establish a difference between the meaning of ' neighbour ' in the text of Leviticus and its meaning in the teaching of Jesus, the difference being, as it is alleged, that in Leviticus ' neighbour ' means ' fellow Israelite ', and in the teaching of Jesus it means ' fellow-*man* ', and that he was the first to give this wider meaning to the word. Considering that the text in Leviticus was written many centuries before the time of Jesus, the question of its exact meaning ought to be answered without any reference to the teaching of Jesus. It is a question of scholarship, not of theology; and to bring in the alleged contrast between the original meaning and that which Jesus gave to the word ' neighbour '

ETHICAL TEACHING ON THE RABBINICAL LINE

is simply irrelevant, quite apart from the truth of the allegation. In a later chapter the comparison between the teaching of Jesus and that of the Rabbis will be made in detail. For the present it is, as it obviously should be, left entirely out of account. We have, then, to deal with the text (Lev. xix. 18), 'Thou shalt love thy neighbour as thyself'. The word translated 'neighbour' is *re'a*, and the question is What did 're'a' mean to the writer of the passage? The natural way in which to find the answer is to examine other instances in which the same word is used, and to look for the common thought in them. 'Re'a' is used in connexion with things as well as with persons. Thus (Gen. xv. 10) there is a description of an elaborate sacrifice which Abraham was directed to offer, consisting of several animals and birds. The account then goes on to say: 'And he took him all these and divided them in the midst, and laid each half over against his "re'a"'. The meaning can only be his 'fellow', the corresponding piece. The idea is that of some kind of relation between two objects (or persons) such that each is the 'fellow' of the other. In the text in Leviticus the 're'a' is a person; we have therefore to inquire in what sense it is used of personal relationships? We read, in the story of the building of the Tower of Babel (Gen. xi. 3): 'And they said, each man to his "re'a" (*lĕrēēhū*)', etc. This is rightly translated (R.V.) 'one to another', man to his fellow-man. On the lines of the story, there were then no separate nations. 'The whole earth was of one language and one speech.' A man of that multitude spoke to his 'fellow-man' because there was no one else to whom he could speak. Again, we read in the story of Jonah how the prophet took ship for Tarshish, and how a storm arose so that the ship was in danger. Then (Jon. i. 7): 'And they [the sailors] said, every one to his "re'a",' rightly translated (R.V.) 'his fellow'. That 're'a' in this passage cannot mean 'man of the same religion', or 'of the same race', is shown by verse 5 of the same chapter, where it is said: 'And the mariners were afraid and cried every man unto his god', which surely implies that several different gods were addressed by persons of different religions. Again, it is told (Exod. xi. 2) how Moses was commanded: 'Speak now in the ears of the people and let them ask, every man of his "re'a" and every woman of her "re'a" jewels of silver,' etc. Here 're'a'

L

obviously means 'neighbour', and no less obviously cannot mean 'fellow-Israelite', because the 'neighbours' who were to be 'spoiled' were Egyptians. If 're'a' carried the meaning of 'member of the same race', 'adherent of the same religion' it would be quite unsuitable in such a case as the last, or, indeed, in any of the others that have been cited. It is applied, in human affairs, to denote one who shares any relationship, *whatever it may be*, and the point lies in the fact of relationship not in the nature of it. A priest would presumably speak of a fellow priest as his 're'a', but that would not indicate that 're'a' implied the office of a priest. And that it can be applied to the widest of all relationships, that of common human nature, is shown by (Job xvi. 21): 'That he would maintain the right of a man with God, and of a son of man with his "re'a".' 'Fellow-man' is the natural meaning here; for, even if the immediate reference is to Job's three friends, there is nothing which limits the meaning of 're'a' to 'friend'. From the examination of these various instances, the conclusion seems to be justified that 're'a' always means the person (or thing) with whom some relationship is shared, whatever that relationship may be; 're'a' does not indicate what the relationship is, it denotes the person who is one's 'fellow' in that relationship.

We have now to inquire What does 're'a' mean in (Lev. xix. 18) 'Thou shalt love thy "re'a" as thyself'? It is fair to assume that it can hardly mean something which would be contradicted by the immediate context. It is said in the same chapter (vv. 33, 34): 'And if a stranger sojourn with thee in your land, ye shall not do him wrong. The stranger that sojourneth with you shall be unto you as the home born among you, *and thou shalt love him as thyself*; for ye were strangers in the land of Egypt. I am the Lord your God'. The word translated 'stranger' is 'gēr', not 're'a'; but precisely the same commandment is given in respect of both, viz., 'Thou shalt love . . . as thyself'. Evidently 're'a' cannot in this passage be more restricted in meaning than 'ger'. If it were, if it meant 'thou shalt love thy fellow Israelite as thyself', and no one else, then it would be a contradiction to add 'thou shalt love the "ger" as thyself'. Moreover, if it be insisted on that 're'a' means 'fellow Israelite and no one else', then 'thou shalt love the *stranger* as thyself' would have been the more inclusive commandment, and therefore the one naturally singled out as the supreme commandment of its kind. It is accordingly clear that in the text 'Thou shalt love thy "re'a" as thyself', 're'a' cannot mean less than what 'ger' means; and 'ger' means one who lives among people not of his own race or language or religion, as the Israelite himself was a 'ger' in the land of Egypt. What constituted the Egyptian a 'ger', would constitute a man of any other nation a 'ger', and thus 're'a' would be properly used of any and every such person; in other words, 're'a' (in Lev. xix. 18) means 'fellow-man', and nothing more restricted in range.

If this be admitted, then it follows that whatever any later teachers may have said on the subject they had before them the declaration of the Torah enjoining love to one's fellow-man in the widest sense of the term, so that if they narrowed its range and impoverished its meaning, they did so deliberately. There is not the slightest evidence that they ever did so. They were quite familiar with the idea of 'fellow-man' meaning any human being, and nothing would have been easier for them than to say that 're'a' in the text of Leviticus did not mean fellow-man. They never said that. The example of Hillel is much to the point. He said (Aboth i. 12): 'Be of the disciples of Aaron, one that loves peace, that loves *mankind* and brings them nigh to the Torah'. The word translated 'mankind' is *berioth*, which means all created beings, though usually only human beings are thought of. But it certainly includes *all* human beings, without any barrier or restriction of race or religion. It cannot be, and never was, restricted to Israelites, let alone Jews. If Hillel wanted to bring a man 'nigh to the Torah', that was precisely because he did not already know the Torah, which he would have done if he had been a Jew. Hillel wanted that all mankind should come to the knowledge of God, and he expressed this in the terms most natural to him, by saying 'bring them nigh to Torah'. Hillel did not refer to the text in Leviticus, but his saying is an emphatic endorsement of it, in its widest sense, and without any hint that a narrower meaning might be, still less that it was, read into it.

The text is referred to in a well-known passage (Siphra, 89*a*, j. Nedar. 41*c*, and more fully Ber. R. xxiv. 7) in which Akiba declares it to be the greatest general principle (*kelāl*) in the Torah. His younger contemporary, Simeon b. Azai, declared that there was another even greater, viz.: ' This is the book of the generations of man, in the day in which God created man in the likeness of God created he him ' (Gen. v. 1). Akiba and Ben Azai were not disputing whether the one text or the other enjoined love to one's fellow-man, but which text expressed it better. Akiba read the text, as it always had been read, in the sense of loving one's fellow-man whoever he might be, and declared that the general principle could not be, or had not been, better expressed. But it was pointed out that ' to love thy fellow-man as *thyself* ' brought in an element of uncertainty, because it opened the way for the wish that the fellow-man might be as oneself, suffering the same adversity, or reproach or what not. Ben Azai held that the real ground for love of one's fellow-man was that he, and all men, are made in the likeness of God. This, therefore, as expressed in Gen. v. 1 was the really greatest general principle in the Torah. A later teacher, R. Tanhuma, referring to the objection that a man might say ' I have been despised, therefore may my fellow-man be despised; I have been cursed, therefore may he be cursed ', remarks ' If thou hast acted so, know who it is whom thou despisest; in the likeness of God made he him ' (Ber. R. xxiv. 7). The objection is somewhat far-fetched, because a man who uttered such a wish would not be loving his fellow-man at all. But it was a true insight which saw the reason for love of one's fellow-man in the fact that all men are made in the likeness of God.

So far the consideration of ' love to one's fellow-man ' has been based on the great text in Leviticus. A word must be added about the saying of Hillel, to which there are so many parallels earlier and later, ' What is hateful to thee do not to thy fellow'. It is not necessary, for the present purpose, to examine all the parallels, whether in the negative or the positive form. A good survey of them may be found in Abrahams, *Studies*, i, 18-29, and in an essay by Kohler on 'Nächstenliebe in Judentum ' (Cohen, *Festschrift*, pp. 469-480). The saying quoted from Hillel as above is found in b. Shabb. 31*a*, and A. d. R.N[B]. 26, p. 27*b*. In the latter passage it is ascribed to Akiba, which would seem to show that Akiba had Hillel's saying in his mind. The fact that there are earlier forms of the saying may indicate that alike for Hillel and for Akiba it was already a current maxim. However that may be, it only confirms the position already taken up that the idea of love to one's fellow-man, in the most inclusive sense, was quite familiar in the time of Hillel, and is rightly placed amongst the leading principles of the Rabbinical ethics.

This conclusion I hold to be justified, on the grounds already given; but it may be well to remark on one or two points where misunderstanding is possible and not unlikely. Although the fellow-man, ' re‘a ', is any fellow-man without distinction of race or religion, yet in practice it would very often be the case that the fellow-man was a Jew. Indeed, it may be said that in ordinary usage a Jew would most often be thinking of his fellow Jew, being at the moment not specially led to think of men in general. He would thus use the term ' re‘a ' in a sense more restricted than that of fellow-man, merely for the convenience of the moment. But this does not imply that he would deny the wider meaning if he were challenged on the point.

Moreover, the command to ' love thy neighbour as thyself' is primarily ethical, whereas many of the commandments were defined by halachah into strict law regulating the community of Israel. The law, so defined, did not treat all men alike. It prescribed the rights and duties of those who were members of the community, and distinguished clearly between those who were members and those who were not. So it is, of course, under the law of every civilised country. The alien does not share all the rights and privileges of the national. If to make such a distinction be an infringement of the principle ' thou shalt love thy neighbour as thyself', then it is so under Christian law no less than under Jewish law. It will not be contended that it is so under any law. Therefore, when regulations are laid down in the Mishnah having special reference to the treatment of Gentiles, or Samaritans, by way of restricting intercourse with them in various ways, these are not to be taken as evidence that the principle of ' thou shalt love thy neighbour as thyself' was ignored or denied. The treatment of those who were not of the Jewish community was regulated by such general rules as ' thou shalt not oppress the stranger'. He was never to be wronged nor ill treated; he must always receive what was just, and what was due to him as a human being. But the law had to take account of questions of status and nationality as well as of common humanity; and precisely in so far as it was just to all and each, it did not treat them all alike.

Finally, there are, in various passages in the Rabbinical literature, expressions of strong condemnation of Gentiles, or of ill will towards them, even amounting to violent hatred, which contradict the idea of love to all mankind. Considering what the Jews had to suffer at the hands of the Romans and later at the hands of the Christian Church, it is not surprising that such bitter and angry words should have been flung out under the stress of persecution. They *were* bitter and angry words, and it is better to recognise them as such than to try and explain them away. But they do not express the normal mind of those whose teaching is set forth in the Rabbinical literature. The settled and deliberate judgment of those who in all ages, from at least Hillel downwards, have given expression to the ethics of Judaism is that the fellow-man, whatever be his race or religion, whatever be his moral character, is one who was made in the likeness of God, and that to seek less than his good is to dishonour that likeness and commit a wrong against God.

(3) TRUTHFULNESS AND SINCERITY*. The virtue indicated by these names is more inclusive than either. It involves singleness of mind, simple directness of purpose, all that can afford a firm ground of trust. It concerns not merely the relation of man to his fellow-man, but also the relation of man to God; for it was felt, and taught, that no deceit could stand before him, and no dissembler approach him. Truth was in some way inherent in the very nature of God, so that an offence against truth, in any form, was an offence against him. This is clearly to be seen in the Old Testament, and it is insisted on with no less clearness and with even greater emphasis in the Rabbinical ethics as will be shown presently. It is therefore reasonable to conclude that in the Ezra-Hillel period it was no less fundamental in the ethics of the Sopherim and the later teachers of Torah.

It is especially important to consider the Old Testament sources of the teaching about truth and truthfulness, because,

* On this section see Hamburger, *Realencykl. I. s.v. Wahrhaftigkeit*, and Perles, *Critique of Bousset*, pp. 72-74.

as every reader of the Bible knows, there are passages in the Old Testament which do not by any means show a high regard for that virtue. Jacob's deliberate lie to Isaac (Gen. xxvi. 19, 24), and the statement that God himself sent a lying spirit to deceive a prophet (1 Kings xxii. 19-22), are gross contradictions of the teaching that truth is of God and must be revered accordingly. Of course, these instances only show that the moral standard rose very considerably between the earlier and the later periods covered by the Old Testament; but they show also, as was pointed out above (p. 10), that the greater stress was laid by the later teachers on the nobler ethical elements in the older Scriptures, and not upon the baser. This is true of the Old Testament itself, and it is no less true of the Rabbinical teachers.

Within the Old Testament are to be found, e.g., such a passage as Ps. xv. in its entirety, and especially v. 2: 'He that walketh uprightly and worketh righteousness and speaketh truth in his heart'. Again, Ps. li. 6: 'Behold, thou desirest truth in the inward parts'. And, more emphatically, Zech. viii. 16: 'These are the things that ye shall do: Speak ye every man the truth with his neighbour; execute the judgment of truth and peace in your gates; and let none of you imagine evil in your hearts against his neighbour; and love no false oath; for all these are things that I hate, saith the Lord'. Other texts speak of truth as an attribute of God. Thus, Ps. xxxi. 5: 'Thou hast redeemed me, O Lord, thou God of truth'. Ps. xci. 4: 'His truth shall be thy shield and buckler'. Ps. c. 5: 'His truth endureth to all generations'. Ps. xix. 9: 'The judgments of the Lord are true and righteous altogether'. The underlying thought in all these passages, and similar ones that might be quoted, is that he in whom is truth is trustworthy, whether 'he' denote God or man. In other words, truth is not an intellectual correspondence of assertion with fact, but a moral quality in virtue of which he who trusts is not put to confusion. The recognition of truth in God and the requirement of truth in man are the divine and the human side of the same spiritual perception, and both have their source in the prophetic teaching of the sole Unity of God. The great prophets were not concerned to declare that God was numerically one, or even the only one; they proclaimed him as the only one because he alone was true and all other supposed gods were false. He was *the* holy, righteous, and just God, and therefore there could not be any other beside him. Neither could there be in him anything which contradicted his own nature. He, like his judgments, must be 'true and righteous altogether'. Therefore man as made in his likeness could be, and ought to be, true to his divine origin, single-minded, entirely sincere, free from any slightest trace of falsehood in his character, his word, and his act. The increased emphasis laid upon truth, in reference both to God and man, is a marked feature of the later portions of the Old Testament, and is clearly due to the influence of the prophets.

Upon the foundation laid in the Old Testament the ethics of the Rabbis was built, in regard both to other virtues and to the special one of truth, truthfulness, and sincerity. The Rabbis did not reach a greater height than the Prophets had done in their teaching about God, as indeed there was little or nothing else to be said. But they developed the human implications of the demand for truthfulness in much fuller measure than the older Scriptures had done; and they did so because, as has been insisted on repeatedly in the earlier chapters of this book, they were before everything else practical teachers whose object was to train up good men and women. They were not theologians, philosophers, or even moralists.

A direct link between the teaching of the Old Testament (especially the prophetic teaching) and that of the Rabbis is contained in the saying of R. Simeon b. Gamliel (Aboth i. 18): 'Upon three things the world stands, on truth, on judgment, and on peace'. This is clearly a generalisation of the text (Zech. viii. 16) quoted above, and this text is actually included in the passage in Aboth as part of the saying of R. Simeon. But it shows how naturally the Rabbi took up and enlarged the teaching of the prophet. And another link may be the inclusion in the liturgy, at the end of the Shemoneh Esreh, of words which are taken almost verbatim from Ps. xxxiv. 13: 'Keep thy tongue from evil and thy lips from speaking guile'; but though the Shemoneh Esreh had its origin in the period of the Sopherim, the inclusion of the verse from the Psalm cannot be shown to have been made until a much later date. What the Rabbis taught concerning truthfulness and sincerity may be seen from the following passages. It is said: 'Three doth the

[152]

Holy One b.H. hate, him that says one thing with his mouth and another in his heart ', etc. (b. Pes. 113*a*), thus condemning explicitly all mental reservation. With this may be compared the saying of R. Gamliel: ' Let no one enter the B. ha-Midrash whose outward [action] is not as his inward [nature] ' (b. Berach. 28*a*). The phrase *tōchō kĕbārō*, ' his outward as his inward ', became a popular proverb, and has remained so to the present day. ' The seal of God is truth ' (b. Shabb. 55*a*, and parallels). ' Four classes [of men] behold not the Shechinah; the class of the mockers, the class of the hypocrites, the class of the liars and the class of the slanderers ' (b. Sot. 42*a*) in all of whom is falsehood in some form. Hypocrisy is singled out for special condemnation, in the same context as the passage just quoted. Thus, ' Every man in whom is hypocrisy brings wrath upon the world, as it is said (Job xxxvi. 13): They that are hypocrites in heart lay up anger. And not only so, but his prayer is not heard '. ' The man in whom is hypocrisy, the unborn children in their mothers' womb curse him.' ' Every man in whom is hypocrisy falls into Gehinnom.' And the reason for the condemnation is given in the saying: ' They unmask hypocrites because of profanation of the Name ' (T. Joma, v. 12). How serious is the sin of *Hillul ha-Shem* has already been shown (see above, p. 132). ' He who changes his word is as an idolator ' (b. Sanh. 92*a*).

From the above passages it is clear that the Rabbis laid the greatest stress on the virtue of truthfulness and the sin of falsehood and hypocrisy, and it is hard on them that that particular sin should have been laid to their charge, and have been accepted ever since as a matter of course. It must suffice to record their own emphatic teaching about truth and falsehood, which is confirmed by the whole tenor of their literature, not merely in the Talmud and the Midrash, but in the ethical writings of the Middle Ages and down to the present time, and to leave the matter to the judgment of the fair-minded reader.

Two remarks may be made before leaving the subject. Reference has been made (p. 151) to passages in the Old Testament which show a complete disregard of the virtue of truthfulness, and therefore flatly contradict the later teaching, of which illustrations have just been given. The Rabbis could not pick and choose between the various contents of the Scriptures, nor had they any idea of criticism as it is now understood, so that they could distinguish successive stages of ethical development. For them, the Scriptures contained what God had caused to be written; but none the less they felt the difficulty caused by the passages such as those referred to, Jacob's lie to Isaac and the lying spirit sent on purpose to deceive, and sent by God himself. As these things were recorded in Scripture, and Jacob's lie even in the Torah itself, they could not be rejected. Therefore the Rabbis took refuge in fantastic and far-fetched special pleading in order to remove the ethical contradiction. Their explanations in themselves are worthless, and probably did not satisfy anyone; what is really valuable about them is that they show how sensitive the conscience of the Rabbis had become since the ancient time in which, e.g., the Jacob story had been told. They felt keenly the outrage to the divine majesty of truth implied in those old stories, and they showed it by the efforts they made, at all cost of reason or probability, to vindicate the truth in those flagrant instances. The means they used were poor indeed, but from their point of view they could use no others; what really matters is that they maintained the higher standard against the lower. They did not justify a lie, in the case of Jacob; they tried to make out that he could not really have told a lie, he must have meant so-and-so. (See Rashi on Gen. xxvi. 19, 24.)

The other remark that needs to be made is to remind the reader of what has been said above (p. 121) about supposed evasions of the law. If it were true that the practices there mentioned, under the general term *erub*, were evasions of the law, there would be ground for charging the Rabbis with violating the principle of strict truthfulness on which they laid so much stress. But the *erub* was no evasion of the law; it was the application to the written word of the principle of the Unwritten Torah, by which a departure from the letter was deliberately made for the purpose of maintaining the spirit of what was enjoined in the Torah. And the same is true of all alleged evasions of the law. The Rabbis doubtless had their faults; but what they did they did with their eyes open, and what they taught, they taught with deliberate intention as being, for them at all events, the truth as God had granted them to see it.

[154]

(4) HONESTY. This is so closely allied to truthfulness and sincerity, already discussed, that little more need be said about it. The ground on which honesty rests as a virtue is much the same as that on which truthfulness rests; and both have their roots in the recognition of truth as inherent in the nature of God, and therefore as one of the attributes in respect of which man, being made in the image of God, can be like him (see above, p. 130 ff.). But the implications of honesty in the relation between man and his fellow-men were worked out by the Rabbinical teachers with remarkable fineness of perception, and form a very characteristic feature of Rabbinical ethics.

It is said (Lev. xxv. 14, and again v. 17): 'Ye shall not wrong one another'. The words so translated, *lō thōnu*, are quite general, and imply some kind of wrong not specified. In v. 14 the reference is to buying and selling, and the particular wrong is presumably some form of cheating. The Talmud understands it so, and comprises such offences under the head of *ōnāath mammon*, 'injury in respect of money value'. But, from the repetition of the words 'ye shall not wrong', etc., in v. 17, it infers that the prohibition extends to other forms of wrong which it classes under the head of *onaath debarim*, 'injury by words,' and thereby designates much more subtle kinds of wrong. The general idea underlying these is that of 'exploiting' a man, trading on his disadvantage or his defenceless position, or his ignorance. It is *onaath debarim* to say to a man who wishes to buy corn: Go to so-and-so, when you know that so-and-so does not sell corn. The man is wronged by the pretence of offering helpful advice, and by the vexation and disappointment inflicted on him. It is *onaath debarim* when a man asks the price of something in a shop when he does not mean to buy it, or has not the money to pay for it. It is a more serious form of the same offence to say anything which will cause suffering to a man, as by slander, or even by recalling to him his own past misdeeds or those of his forefathers. To put a man to open shame is a sin severely condemned in the Talmud; and though this does not necessarily involve falsehood, it does involve exploitation, because the offensive words are meant to discredit the man and to lead him to do what he otherwise would not do. *Onaath debarim* is a graver sin than *onaath mammon*, because the latter can be legally dealt with, by compensation, restoration, or penalty; the former is left to the conscience, as a *dabar masur laleb* (see above, p. 137 f.).*

Closely allied to the phrase just considered is another, *genibuth da'ah*, ' stealing of knowledge ' (or opinion). As a form of stealing it is of course an extension of the eighth commandment in the decalogue, an extension made in order to reach various offences more subtle though no less evil than ordinary theft. The general idea of *genibuth da'ah* is that of ' false pretences', the misrepresentation of the truth by word or act in order to influence a man against what would have been his better judgment. It is stealing because it is wrongfully depriving him of the knowledge which would have enabled him to judge truly. Seven classes of thieves are enumerated (Mech. 89*b*), and the first (and worst) are ' those who steal the knowledge of men', while the other six classes are of men who in various ways practise deceit, make false representations, give wrong impressions, among them being those who use false weights and measures and those who adulterate food offered for sale. Of all these it is said (*ibid.*): 'And not only so, but they regard him [the thief] as if he tried to "steal the knowledge " of the Most High'. And then follows the curious remark: 'And so we find in the case of our fathers, when they stood before Mount Sinai they sought to "steal the knowledge" of the Most High, as it is said (Exod. xxiv. 7): " All that the Lord hath spoken we will do and hear". Can it be that the heart of the Beth Din was " stolen " by them, as it is said (Deut. v. 29): " O that there were such an heart in them", etc. [implying that there was not such a heart]. And if thou sayest " Is not the whole revealed and known to Him "? learn to say (Ps. lxxviii. 36) "And they deceived him with their mouth", and (*ib*. v. 37) " their heart was not right with Him". And although (*ib*. v. 38) "he being merciful forgave their sin ", still it says (Prov. xxvi. 23): " Fervent lips and a wicked heart are an earthen vessel covered with silver dross ".' This passage was worth quoting because it throws much light on the ideas of the Rabbis in the matter of honesty, and also because it shows the same sensitiveness towards lower ethical standards which has been noticed above

* For a full discussion of the development of the idea of *onaah*, see Lazarus, *Ethik des Judentums*, i, 295-310; also Perles, *Critique of Bousset*, pp. 75-76. For the Talmudic treatment see b. B. Mez. 58*b*, and references in Perles.

(p.153 f.). Little more need be added, but it should be noticed that mental reservation is definitely condemned (b. Shebu 39a; and see Perles, *Critique*, p. 77). There can be no question that this is the settled judgment of all the ethical teachers represented in the Rabbinical literature. There is, so far as I know, only one passage which might be (and no doubt has often been) quoted to show that the Rabbis approved mental reservation. It is b. Kallah 51a, and it is there told, in a rather disagreeable story, that ' R. Akiba said to a certain woman, "My daughter, if thou wilt tell me what I ask of thee, I will bring thee to the life hereafter". She said "Swear it to me". R. Akiba swore with his mouth but annulled it in his heart'. The tractate Kallah is one of the so-called small tractates, and is later than the Talmud proper. The alleged prevarication is out of all keeping with the very well-known character of R. Akiba, and is nowhere referred to in the earlier texts. I regard the passage in Kallah as a stupid invention, of no authority whatever against the consensus of all Jewish moralists both in the Talmud and out of it, or against the character of Akiba, the great teacher, saint, and martyr to whom his own and all succeeding generations have looked up with reverence.

(5) FORGIVENESS*. This would admit of treatment under the two heads of God's forgiveness and man's forgiveness, and in fact has been so treated by Schechter and Abrahams. I shall consider here only the second term, man's forgiveness of his fellow-man. The former belongs rather to theology than to ethics in the strict sense; and although as explained at the outset (see above, p. 2) the term ethical is used in the present book in a wide sense to cover all teaching directed to the right conduct of life, yet the divine forgiveness is a condition under which life ought to be lived, while human forgiveness is an exercise of will immediately concerned in the right conduct of life.

In Rabbinical ethics man's forgiveness of his fellow-man is one of the essential virtues, insisted upon times without number, and emphasised in a manner which leaves no doubt of its importance. In so treating it, the Rabbis were only following the lead of the Old Testament Scriptures, interpreting and

* For the subject of this section see Abrahams, *Studies*, i, pp. 150-167, an essay to which I am much indebted for what I say about Forgiveness.

developing these by the help of their own moral discernment. Yet it is perhaps true to say that they regarded forgiveness not so much as a virtue on its own account as, rather, a corollary of other virtues. They would say that a man should be forgiving towards those who had injured him, not that he should cultivate and practise ' forgiveness ', as he would practise ' gemiluth hasadim ', or do good deeds. The reason why a man should be forgiving is to be found in the principles already discussed of the Imitation of God (*Kedushah*, above, p. 129 f.), and Love to one's neighbour (above, p. 144 ff.). If the ideal for man is to be like God, in whose likeness he and all his fellow-men were made, then clearly the unforgiving temper is a denial of that likeness and an offence against the law of holiness implied in it. The essence of forgiveness is the renewal of right relations between a man and his fellow-man, when these relations have been interrupted by wrong done by one against the other. The right relations are such as should exist between those who have God as the father of them all, and who are therefore brothers in his sight, to be treated accordingly. This thought is implied, though not expressed, in the Old Testament teaching about forgiveness, such as love thy ' neighbour as thyself ', ' hate not thy brother in thy heart', 'avenge not', 'bear no grudge', and many other texts referred to by Abrahams (*Studies*, i, p. 150). These are given as instances to show how a man should realise his likeness to God in the matter of injury inflicted on him. To be forgiving, merciful, unvindictive and the like, is to fulfil the two precepts, ' Thou shalt love the Lord thy God ' and ' Thou shalt love thy neighbour as thyself ', in the special circumstances of suffering under injury. The specific virtue of forgiveness is a particular case of the supreme and inclusive duty.

The Rabbinical teaching about forgiveness is plainly based on the Old Testament Scriptures, and is beyond question true to the main spirit of them. But to that main spirit a contradiction is presented by certain passages in the Psalms, and especially by the two imprecatory Psalms lix and cix. The forgiving spirit is conspicuously absent from these Psalms, and they offend every conscience which is not dulled by custom or warped by specious arguments. It has been suggested that the imprecations in Ps. cix are quotations by the Psalmist of what his enemies said against him; but even if this were so, and there is little to show that it is so, the Psalmist need not have repeated all the bitter words. If he had been of a really forgiving spirit he would have been silent about them. It is hard, and perhaps impossible*, to make out a case which would save the moral credit of these Psalms. The present writer can only frankly regard them as blots on the ethical record of the Book of Psalms. It is not known by whom they were written, nor under what circumstances, nor for what reason they were included in the final collection. Two remarks, however, may usefully be made. The first is that occasionally, as in Ps. cxxxix. 19-22, the objects of the Psalmist's hatred are those whom he regards as the enemies of God, not his own personal enemies. ' Do I not hate them, O Lord, which hate thee. . . . I hate them with a perfect hatred.' Presumably the Psalmist meant to say that he was ' on the Lord's side ' as regarded all wickedness, and all doers of wrong, and to that extent his unforgiving temper was not personal vindictiveness. But the history of every persecution shows how easily the assumed ' Enemies of God ' come to be regarded as personal enemies, and the Psalmist has furnished a weapon which intolerance has never been slow to use. The Rabbis themselves used it in their denunciation of those whom they regarded as traitors within the camp, such as ' Minim ' (usually Jewish Christians) informers, apostates (T. Shabb. xiii. 5, Siphré, ii. §331; and see the present writer's *Christianity in Talmud and Midrash*, pp. 155-7, pp. 325-6). Of course it is true that forgiveness only has its right place in regard to wrongs done to the individual. It is not for him to forgive social wrongs, simply because he is an individual and not collective society. Wrongs against society can only be dealt with by social methods, expressed in laws and public pronouncements; and the individual usurps a function to which he has no right when he takes on himself to forgive a social wrong. And no less does he usurp a function to which he has no right when he expresses his condemnation of social wrong by hatred against those who so offend. By failure to recognise this distinction the Psalmist

* Nothing seems to be gained, ethically, by interpreting these Psalms collectively instead of individually. If the imprecations are uttered by (or in the name of) the community they are of the wrong kind when offences against the community are involved. Social indignation does not justify itself by personal abuse, and its would-be spokesman only betrays his cause by vindictive hatred, such as that uttered in these Psalms.

spoiled a fine lesson and left an evil legacy to posterity. So, in greater degree and without the excuse just given, did the authors of Ps. lix and Ps. cix; and that these should have been included in the Book of Psalms and in the whole collection of the Old Testament Scriptures can only be deplored.

The second remark which needs to be made is simply this, that the two worst Psalms just mentioned were never used in the Synagogue liturgy. There is very little reference to them in the Rabbinical literature; and when commentators on the Book of Psalms had to deal with them in the regular sequence, they found makeshift explanations, which are only valuable as showing how the conscience of the commentator was offended by the plain meaning of the passages before him. (Cp. what has been said above in regard to Truthfulness, p. 154.)

Having thus dealt with the case of the imprecatory Psalms, we may go on to study the general Rabbinical teaching about forgiveness. The difference, so far as there was a difference, between the Biblical and the Rabbinical teaching in this matter was not in principle, but in detail. Substantially there was no difference, so far as the duty of forgiveness was concerned. But the Rabbis drew out some of the implications of forgiveness for the purpose of enforcing the duty. Thus, they taught that the man who refused to forgive was cruel (M. B. Kamma, viii. 7) and a sinner (b. Ber. 12b), which may seem a rather severe judgment on the man who had already been wronged. But when it is considered that forgiveness is essentially (see above, p. 158) the restoring of right relations between man and his fellow-man, and that these right relations represent the ideal state of human social life in the sight of God, then it is seen that to refuse forgiveness is wilfully to obstruct the carrying out of the divine will, when the occasion for doing so presents itself. To forgive the man who has injured his fellow-man is primarily the fulfilling of a duty towards God, and is therefore required even if the injurer does not repent and seek to be forgiven. In such a case to forgive would mean that the person wronged would not harm the wrong-doer or wish ill to him, would even do him good if he had the opportunity. It would not mean that he could treat him as if nothing had happened. If, however, the wrong-doer repented and asked to be forgiven, then forgiveness would mean the restoring of personal relations between the two, as nearly as may be to what they had been before; not, however, without the memory on both sides of the wrong that had been done. That can be forgiven, but it cannot always be forgotten.

Forgiveness was the duty of the person wronged. But the wrong-doer had also his duty, which was to repent and ask forgiveness from the man whom he had wronged. And the reason in each case was the same, viz., the need of restoring the right relations of social life as it appears in the sight of God. The wrong done is a breach made in the divine order of human life; and, as it concerns two persons, both must do their part in healing the breach. It must not be left to one only, although only one has caused the mischief. This I believe to be the real meaning of the Rabbinical teaching about forgiveness; and if this explanation be correct, the reason becomes plain why the Rabbis deduced the duty of forgiveness from the wider principles of the Imitation of God and Love to one's neighbour, and did not regard it as a virtue on its own account. To fail in regard to the duty of forgiveness by showing hard-heartedness or hatred was to do a wrong against God and not only against one's fellow-man (or fellow-*men*, for all suffer through the vindictiveness of one), and thus it is said: ' Whoso hates any man hates Him who spake and the world was ' (Pesik. Zut. on Num. viii, quoted by Abrahams, *Studies*, i, 160). Observe that the hatred denounced is hatred against *any* man, not the fellow-Jew alone.

(6) HONOUR TO FATHER AND MOTHER. It would be impossible for even the most severe critic of Rabbinical ethics to deny that the duty of honouring parents is everywhere insisted on by the Rabbis. Although theoretically all the precepts in the Torah are equally binding, since they are the commands of God, yet practically they were distinguished as being weighty or light. And the command ' Honour thy father and thy mother ' was singled out as the weightiest of all. This is stated in j. Kidd, 61*b*, as follows: ' R. Abba b. Cahana said: Scripture puts on an equality the most weighty of the precepts and the lightest. The lightest is that of sending away the bird from the nest (Deut. xxii. 6, 7) and the weightiest is that of honouring father and mother, and in regard to both it is written " Thou shalt prolong thy days ".' This is a comparatively late haggadah, but it only expresses in a fresh form the ancient thought about

M

the precept. There was never a time when the duty of honouring father and mother was lightly regarded; and what is said
about it in the Rabbinical literature is merely by way of
dwelling upon a duty owned by all and taken very seriously.

Unlike some of the virtues hitherto examined, this one of
honour to parents cannot be brought under the principle of
Imitatio Dei, nor perhaps under any other of the principles
reviewed in the early part of this chapter. No doubt the ground
on which this virtue was exalted into a duty was that it was
included in the Decalogue, and distinguished there by the
promise attached to it, 'that thou mayest prolong thy days'.
But its inclusion in the Decalogue surely implies that it was
recognised as supremely important by Moses, or whoever it
may have been who formulated the Decalogue. And the
importance thus assigned to it shows how deeply it was rooted
in the moral consciousness of Israel during all the ages of its
history. There is nothing to show that there was ever any
decline in the strength with which it has asserted itself in
Jewish hearts. In itself it is a natural instinct, and Jewish
ethical insight was quick to perceive the divine aspect of it.
A medieval commentator, Nahmanides, finds the source of it
in the likeness between the relation of a man to God and the
relation of a man to his parents. As God is the father, the
source of a man's being and the original in whose likeness he is
made, so, under God, a man's father is the source of his being
and reproduces in his son some likeness of himself. As honour
is due to God, so honour is due to the earthly parents; and
therefore, in the Decalogue, the first four Commandments
which enjoin duties towards God are followed by that which
enjoins honour to parents (see Ramban on Exod. xx. 12). The
classic passage in the Talmud which deals with this precept is
(b. Kidd 31a, b) where are given various examples to show the
length to which some eminent Rabbis had gone in showing
honour to father and mother, and one Gentile who had
exceeded them all. The not unnatural comment is added that
a man might be called happy who had never known his parents,
if the duty of honouring them were so exacting. The instances
given are indeed extravagances of filial piety, but they show
how deeply rooted the feeling was which expressed itself in
honouring father and mother. The Rabbinical literature adds

nothing to the development of that feeling, but accepts it in its full strength, and only lets the imagination play upon it in order to realise its strength and its beauty. Perhaps the crowning instance of this is that of the Rabbi who, when he heard his mother approaching, said, ' I will arise before the Shechinah which draweth near' (b. Kidd 31*b*), the Shechinah being the visible manifestation of God.

(7) CHASTITY. The Jewish moral consciousness has always been very sensitive on the subject of the right relations between the sexes and of offences connected therewith; and nowhere is that sensitiveness more conspicuous than in the Rabbinical ethics. The Old Testament gave a strong and unfaltering lead in the direction of sexual purity, continence, modesty, chastity, and the Rabbis followed that lead—or, rather, they built on that foundation a structure of their own, more elaborate in its details and more severe in its lines than that sketched in the older Scriptures. The commandment in the Decalogue was extended to include every kind of sexual offence, or even irregularity; and the breach of this commandment, so extended, was made one of the three deadly sins which the Jew must die rather than commit. The other two were idolatry and bloodshed.

As in the case of veracity, and forgiveness, the older Scriptures presented instances of sexual laxness (to call it no more) which by no means came up to the high moral standard of the Prophets and the Rabbis; and these were dealt with in much the same way, viz., by far-fetched devices to show that there could not really have been the moral offences which the story as recorded would seem to indicate. In other words, the moral standard of the later ethical teachers was far higher than that of the original authors or recorders of the stories in question. The reason why so great stress was laid on chastity, and so severe a condemnation passed on the sins against it, is probably to be found in the principle of *Kedushah* discussed above (p. 130), and especially in that of *Kiddush ha-Shem* (p. 132). Both of these imply the Imitatio Dei, the realisation of the likeness in man to the nature of God. Man was to do such things as God did, acts of kindness, mercy, and the like, and to be what God was, forgiving, loving, and holy. The likeness was, and could only be, in respect of the spiritual nature of God and man. Bodily

[163]

likeness there could be none. In proportion as this was realised, the more clearly it was seen that there could be no real likeness if the bodily nature was left uncontrolled, to indulge its appetites without restraint. The body was, indeed, the work of the Creator, and all its functions were intended to serve the purpose with which he appointed them. Nevertheless, the body was that in which man resembled the animals; and if the true likeness of man to God was ever to be attained, it could only be by establishing the control of the spiritual nature over the physical. There could be no *Kedushah* (holiness) until this was done; and every act or resolve in this direction was a *Kiddush ha-Shem*, every temptation resisted, every self-restraint endured, every assertion of the true self on the side of the higher life as a loyalty to God. This is probably the reason why the word *Kadosh* (holy), along with its more general connotation, was often applied in a special sense to a man who was especially virtuous in the matter of sex. R. Judah, the Prince (Rabbi), was known as Judah ha Kadosh by reason of his habitual conduct in this respect.

Reflections of this kind, on the incompatibility of holiness (with its implication of likeness to God) and unrestrained physical appetite, were no doubt in the minds of the Old Testament writers who held up the ideal of chastity, even of writers like those in the Wisdom books, who were mainly concerned with pointing out the folly of the ' immoral ' life. But the Rabbis were profoundly convinced of that incompatibility, and did their utmost to establish in their followers the same conviction. They followed the lead of the Old Testament in recognising that sexual offences were not confined to physical acts, but included thoughts and desires tending thereto; and they worked out this principle in warnings and safeguards against sin which may be thought to be over-elaborated, and not unlikely to provoke the very evil against which they were directed. Yet it is not difficult to understand why the Rabbis took this line, and pursued it to the length which in fact they did, perhaps farther than was really necessary or wise. They were confronted by the fact that the Gentile world, in the midst of which they lived, was under little or no restraint in regard to sexual relations, either from public opinion or force of law. The Jew, wherever he turned, was liable to come in

[164]

contact with what he felt to be abomination. Unless he retired from the world altogether, like the Essenes, he must guard himself somehow from moral contamination, from a danger that was not merely a matter of ritual purity, but a source of grave social corruption. The Essenes avoided the danger and fled for safety. The Rabbis and their followers did not flee, but strove to maintain the rights of purity in the midst of uncleanness, to be a holy people in a foul world. In every respect the moral standard of life which the Rabbinical ethics upheld was far higher than any which was recognised in the Gentile world, and nowhere higher than in regard to the relations of the sexes. The difficulty of maintaining that standard was great in proportion, and is perhaps reflected in the anxious multiplication of safeguards in warnings and prohibitions characteristic of the Rabbinical teaching on the subject.

Moreover, the Rabbis could not, any more than their forerunners in the Old Testament, take the line that the sexual instinct from which all the mischief proceeded was in itself evil. The command to ' increase and multiply ' could not be fulfilled without it, and that was an express command, mitzvah, which has never been disregarded or set aside in Judaism from the time when it was first formulated. The Rabbis never took the line of asceticism in regard to this or any other practice where indulgence might lead to evil results. They held to the belief that what the Creator had ordained or provided was good and not evil, and that it was for man to make use of it only for its proper purpose, and not to abuse it. What they condemned and loathed in the Gentile world was the reckless abuse of a function implanted in the nature of man by the Creator; and they condemned it because its result was to efface the likeness between God and man by emphasising the animal nature in man at the expense of the spiritual.

We have surveyed in this chapter the main elements in the ethical teaching of the Rabbis as it was expressed chiefly in the haggadah, not indeed setting forth every minute detail, but presenting, it is hoped, enough to give a clear and true account of its leading ideas and principles. It only remains to apply the results of what has been learned to the answering of the question raised above (p. 110), What was the character of the ethical teaching given during the period from Ezra to Hillel? The answer there briefly suggested was that it is possible to infer from the ethical teaching given respectively before and after that period what it probably was during the period. The material with which to support such an inference has now been presented, in the present chapter. When the haggadah emerges into view, as illustrated in the passages quoted from the Talmud and the various Midrashim, it is seen that what is taught is always rooted in the older Scriptures. This was indeed only likely; for the whole structure of the Rabbinical teaching, ethical and other, was built up by the method of interpretation, the development of something already taught, the drawing forth into clearer form what was, or was thought to be, implied in the older teaching, and, above all, in the Torah. We have, therefore, at one end the ethical teaching contained in the Scriptures, and at the other end that contained in the haggadah, and the difference between them is not in principle but in elaboration of detail. The inference therefore seems to be justified that in the Ezra-Hillel period the ethical teaching was the same in principle as it was before and after. If it was not, then there must have been a breach at some point, an interruption or a decline followed by a recovery; and neither of interruption nor of recovery is there the slightest trace. If there had been, then some indication of it might be fairly expected in the later literature, from men who were quite aware of the fact that Ezra had made a new beginning in regard to the Torah, and that Hillel had introduced a new method into its halachic interpretation. If, in the period between them, there had been teachers who had departed in any marked degree from the ethical teaching of the Old Testament, and again other teachers who had returned to it, that would be a double change of sufficient importance to call for explanation. In the absence of any slightest hint of such a double change, or of any change at all, in general ethical principle, it is reasonable to suppose that no such change occurred, and that the line of ethical development through the Ezra-Hillel period was continuous both with the Old Testament at one end and with the haggadah at the other. That the contents of the ethical teaching given in the Old Testament are not identical with those of the later teaching disclosed in the Talmud and Midrash only means that

[166]

the later teachers were diligent students of the Scriptures, and also of the teaching of their own predecessors, and drew out more and more of its implicit meaning. It is not possible to show the actual process of development of detail in the Ezra-Hillel period, so as to prove that such and such an application of ethical principle was made at such and such a time, or by this or that teacher; but there is now no reason to doubt, and good ground for asserting, that the ethical teaching given in that period was all of a piece with what went before and came after it, and with that assertion the account of the ethical teaching along the Rabbinical line given in the preceding chapters, and more particularly in the last two, may be brought to a conclusion.

Before proceeding, however, to the next main division of the subject, the ethical teaching contained in the non-Rabbinical literature, a few final remarks may be made upon the body of teaching which has hitherto engaged our attention. We have traced the progress, from the time of Ezra, of the development of a certain conception of the Torah, along clearly marked lines both of theory and practice. The object in view was to make the authority of the Torah supreme in the life of Israel, both as means of guidance and a source of instruction; and the end in view was not fully attained except by the conscious acceptance, on the part of the members of the community, of the duty enjoined and by their deliberate intention to carry it out in actual conduct. The whole movement initiated by Ezra was a discipline, a training of men and women in the right conduct of life as the true service of God. It was not merely a body of teaching, given forth to be taken or left as the chance hearer might think fit.

Moreover, it was a collective effort on the part of many teachers, and was continued through many centuries. The effort was made through the three agencies of the Synagogue, the Beth ha-Midrash, and the Great Beth Din, working together in the manner explained in a former chapter, and engaging the thought and energy and devotion of many men for generation after generation. It stands to reason that the men who gave their best years and strength to such a work were men who took their religion in deadly earnest; and even if it were thought, as some seem to think, that the line they took was a mistaken

[167]

one, yet the energy which they put into the work could not fail to produce very substantial results. Those who carried on this work, the Sopherim, the Pharisees, and the Rabbis, were indeed only a minority in actual numbers of the whole community. They were not the only thinkers; there were other movements and other types of Judaism beside the one which they represented, as will be seen when we come to study the non-Rabbinical literature. But in all the varied life and thought of the Jewish community in the centuries with which we are concerned there was no movement so strong, so carefully thought out, so resolutely led, so persistently carried on, and all for the promotion of the higher life of the Jewish people, as this which we have been studying. And for this reason it outlived every other, and carried with it the vitality which enabled Judaism to endure through the centuries down to the present day. Other movements of thought and other types of Judaism were represented in the non-Rabbinical literature, and in the age when they were active they were, no doubt, of great importance. There was ethical teaching equal to that given in the Rabbinical schools and learned in the synagogues, some of it perhaps superior; but there was not behind any of the movements of thought the driving power of the Rabbinic movement, simply because no other movement was due to the combined effort of hundreds of teachers and workers over a period to be measured by centuries.

And this is the explanation of the fact, well known to every student of Rabbinics, that at all events down to the close of the Talmudic period there is a remarkable likeness of style in all the literary works of the period. There were no books which could be assigned to this author or to that. It is a mistake to speak of the ' writers ' of the Talmud or of any of the Midrashim. The Rabbinical literature properly so called is the literary precipitate of the collective movement of thought which went on during the centuries since the time of Ezra. What was finally put into writing was so much as had been handed down from the countless teachers in the earlier times, of what they had taught in the Synagogue or debated in the Beth ha-Midrash; and it was recorded at last as the joint effort of them all, from great masters like Akiba to the obscurest teacher whose name is mentioned only once or not at all. This immense mass of recorded teaching was arranged in separate groups according as its subject-matter was mainly halachah or haggadah; distinctive names such as Mishnah, Tosephta, Talmud, or again Siphra, Siphré, Mechilta, were given to collections made for special purposes. But within these collections is found not the work of an individual author but the contributions of many teachers, who, because they were all engaged on the same great task, and were using the same means in dealing with the same general principles, expressed their thoughts—within limits—in much the same style. The Rabbinical literature bears witness, not merely by its enormous extent but by its comparatively uniform style, to the manner of its origin, which was not in the minds of a few thinkers but in the united wisdom, energy, and devotion of a host of the most faithful and devoted sons of Israel and servants of God during at least a thousand years. So it has continued to be since the close of the Talmud down to the present day, but with this later period we are not concerned. For the purpose of this book it is enough to have shown that the movement which began with Ezra grew stronger with each succeeding age; and that the stream of ethical teaching, such as has been described in the preceding chapter, flowed on in ever greater volume and strength right through the period with which in this book we are concerned, and pursued its way down the centuries of Israel's history.

Book III

THE NON-RABBINICAL LITERATURE

Division I
THE APOCRYPHA AND PSEUDEPIGRAPHA

Chapter I
THE APOCRYPHAL AND PSEUDEPIGRAPHIC LITERATURE IN GENERAL

The title prefixed to this chapter is used to denote certain books of Jewish origin, composed at various times during the two centuries before and the century after the Christian era. They are, so far as is known, the only extant productions of Jewish literary activity during that period; and for that reason, if there were no other, they would deserve to be closely studied. On examination they prove to have marked affinities with other expressions of Jewish thought, and no less marked differences of treatment. For the purposes of this book they are important because in all, or nearly all, of them the ethical element is present, while, at the same time, that ethical element is combined with other matter of a kind seldom found and never in so great an amount in any other Jewish literary works. It is the presence of the ethical element which makes possible that comparison between this literature and the Rabbinical literature which it is the main object of this book to present. The link between them is the fact that importance was attached by each of them to ethical ideas; and that link holds them together, although the books at present under consideration never made the slightest approach to halachah, nor even to haggadah properly so called, and the Rabbinical literature contains only a trifling amount of the Apocalyptic matter which is so prominent in the Apocryphal and cognate literature.

It has been shown in the preceding chapters how the Sopherim and their successors gradually developed a theory and a system of ethical teaching on the lines of the interpretation of the Torah; and the object of describing the development of that system was to bring out the real meaning and intention of the teaching to which it led up. Merely to state that the Rabbinical teaching on this or that point was so-and-so would have been of little or no use. And in like manner it would be of little or no use to offer a summary of the Apocryphal ethics under separate heads*, without some explanation of the reasons why they were taught in that way and not in the Rabbinical or some other way. However the Apocryphal books came to be written, the purpose and importance of their contents, ethical or any other, cannot be properly understood and appreciated without a careful study of the origin and development of the literature which comprises those books. This literature is different in form from the Rabbinical, perhaps also in intention; but it is no less a product and partial expression of Judaism, and therefore worthy of study on its own account. Whatever importance may be ascribed to the Apocryphal literature by reason of its influence on the development of Christianity, that literature can only be fairly estimated when it has been studied for its own sake, and its real nature ascertained as it was in itself. Whether it ever has been studied, or ever would have been studied, without a side-glance at Christianity, is a question not to be hastily answered. Yet it ought to be possible to study it simply for its own sake and on its own merits, as exhibiting a type or types of Judaism nowhere else so clearly presented; and to make such a study will be the purpose of this and succeeding chapters.

The literature thus to be studied includes books of varying character and origin, and it may be well at the outset to give a list of their names, so that the reader may know what will be the object to which his attention is to be directed.† They are usually divided under the two heads of Apocrypha and Pseudepigrapha. The Apocrypha are those books which were included in the Greek Old Testament, but not in the Hebrew. They are often printed separately as the Apocrypha of the Old Testament. The Pseudepigrapha are certain books which were never included in the Canon of Scripture at all, but never-

* Dr. Maldwyn Hughes' book, *The Ethics of the Apocrypha*, offers hardly more than such a summary. Moreover, it is laid out on the lines of a treatment of ethics which is not Jewish, and shows little, if any, acquaintance with the Jewish background.

† They are all collected, with translation, critical apparatus, introduction and notes, in Charles' great edition of the Apocrypha and Pseudepigrapha, Oxford, 1913, to which constant reference will be made.

theless had a close affinity with the Canonical books. The books comprised under the two heads just mentioned might be arranged in some other order, according to the nature of their subject-matter, or their date or country of origin; but the main object at the moment is to state which are the several books at present under consideration. The following list, taken from the Oxford edition, includes certainly all the important ones:*

Apocrypha:
  Historical:
    1 Esdras
    1, 2, 3 Maccabees
  Historical Romances:
    Tobit
    Judith
  Wisdom Books:
    Sirach (Ecclesiasticus, Ben Sira)
    Wisdom of Solomon
  Additions to Canonical books:
    1 Baruch
    Epistle of Jeremy
    Prayer of Manasses
  Additions to Daniel:
    Prayer of Azariah
    Song of the three Children
    Susanna
    Bel and the Dragon
  Additions to Esther
Pseudepigrapha:
  Jubilees
  Sacred Legends:
    Letter of Aristeas
    Book of Adam and Eve
    Martyrdom of Isaiah
  Apocalypses:
    1 Enoch
    Testaments of the Twelve Patriarchs

* For detailed surveys of the Apocryphal and Apocalyptic literature see the *Jewish Encyclopedia* and the *Encyclopædia Biblica*, under those heads. The views expressed in the latter work, as to authorship and origin, are open to serious objection, as will be shown below.

Sibylline Oracles
Assumption of Moses
2 Enoch
2, 3 Baruch
4 Ezra
Psalms:
    The Psalms of Solomon
Wisdom Books:
    4 Maccabees

The Oxford edition adds the Story of Ahikar, which is not specifically Jewish, and Pirke Aboth, which belongs to the Rabbinical literature, and ought not have been included in Charles' work*; also the Zadokite Fragment, which it is convenient to have along with the others.

The books included in the above list were written during a period of some three centuries or thereabouts, beginning with Ben Sira (Sirach, Ecclesiasticus) and ending with 4 Ezra. The lower limit does not indeed mark a total cessation of pseudepigraphic literature; but later works of that nature are not of sufficient importance for the purpose of this book to be taken into consideration.

The fact that all of these books were excluded from the Canon of the Hebrew Old Testament, and many of them from that of the Greek Old Testament also, might naturally suggest that there was a clearly marked division between the Canonical and the non-canonical books in order of time, in the sense that all of the former were written and the Canon definitely closed before any of the non-canonical books appeared. But there was no such division in order of time. Ben Sira wrote his book apparently about 180 B.C., and the book of Daniel came out just before the Maccabean Revolt, ten or fifteen years later. Moreover, some of the Psalms are Maccabean or even later. On the other hand, there is clear evidence that literary activity of some sort went on before the Canon was closed, and that the books so written were not included in the Canon. It is agreed that the book of Koheleth is one of the latest of the Canonical books,

* The present writer did the Pirke Aboth at the request of the General Editor, but was so little satisfied with the task or his accomplishment of it that he has since published a separate edition of Aboth (New York, 1925; second edition, 1930).

and the writer, or editor, of that book says in the Epilogue (xii. 12): 'Moreover, my son, be warned; of making many books there is no end, and much study is a weariness of the flesh'. What the books were to which the writer here alludes there is nothing to show. The remark is a curious one, coming from a writer who had himself just finished composing or editing a book; but at least it shows that in his time books were being written in considerable numbers. It would indeed be strange if literary activity had entirely ceased at any time during the period which includes the latest of the Canonical and the earliest of the non-canonical books. For, whatever other reasons there may have been why books should be written, there was one strong inducement in the presence of the Canon of Scripture itself, complete in regard to the Torah and the prophetical literature, and containing certainly most of the hagiographa. That this great collection of Scripture should be studied was only natural; thoughtful readers could hardly fail to be influenced by it, and if those readers also wrote books, they may well have been prompted to do so as the result of their study. There must have been men in Jerusalem, at the time indicated, of sufficient learning to be able to study the Scriptures, and to write about them if inclined to do so. Yet it is a remarkable fact that Ben Sira, who certainly wrote a book himself and who lived just about the time indicated, does not mention the writing of books as one of the natural pursuits of a man of leisure and learning, such as he describes under the title of 'Sopher'. He never advises his pupils to read books (except by implication the Scriptures) in order to become wise. He tells them to listen to wise men, frequent their company, sit at their feet so to speak; he does not tell them to study their books or any books. There was probably no very long interval of time between Koheleth and Ben Sira, yet the latter gives no hint of that 'making of many books' which troubled the former. Ben Sira himself would seem to have given his own teaching orally, as he mentions (li. 23) his 'Beth ha-Midrash' or 'house of study', and (*ib.* 30) his 'yeshibah' or 'class-room', and presumably his book contains the substance of what he taught to those who met there. But he said nothing to them about books; in short, books other than the Scriptures do not seem to have entered into his scheme of culture. If, nevertheless, there were books being written in his time, and in view of the dictum of Koheleth there must have been, then it becomes evident that no complete picture of the culture of his time is to be found in his book, nor even one approximately complete. The bearing of this remark will be seen later.

The appearance of the non-canonical literature was not the mark of a new beginning of literary activity, there was no breach of continuity between the literature which was finally canonised and that which was not. The stream of literary production never ran dry, though at times perhaps it was reduced to a slender trickle, at all events so far as strictly Jewish authorship was concerned. Under the influence of Hellenism it is to be supposed that Greek books were well known and widely read, perhaps frequently written, and it is possible that the caution of Koheleth was directed against these; but purely Greek books do not come within the range of present consideration, because the Apocryphal and cognate literature was fundamentally Jewish in thought, and, for the most part, originally written in Hebrew.

That the literature in question was fundamentally Jewish in thought is of course admitted on all hands; and this would not need to be even mentioned if it were not for the fact that the implications of that statement are not always, if at all, clearly seen and taken into account. If the Apocryphal books had not been fundamentally Jewish there would never have been any question of including them in the Canon, as they were included in the Greek Old Testament, nor would the Pseudepigrapha have been able to claim so much attention as was actually paid to them, at all events by Hellenistic Jews. The slightest glance at the contents of any one of these books shows that they are concerned with subjects of Jewish interest, and more particularly that there are clearly marked affinities of thought, and sometimes even of style and treatment, between them and the Canonical Scriptures. The later literature is obviously the descendant of the earlier.

Now the influence of the Maccabean Revolt and its successful issue made itself felt not only in the politics, but also in the literature of the time. As has been shown above (p. 80 ff.) the struggle was waged in defence of the Torah, and the result was to establish the authority of the Torah as supreme, acknowledged by everyone, openly challenged by no one. That supremacy of the Torah was thenceforward a constant factor in the development of Judaism, but it would be a great mistake to suppose that everyone who acknowledged the authority of the Torah meant the same thing by it. Sadducees and Pharisees alike acknowledged the Torah, and were even devotedly loyal to it; but they certainly did not mean the same thing by it, and they came into violent opposition to each other for precisely that reason. The Pharisees made of the Torah as much as they possibly could, the Sadducees made of it as little as they could, but were not at all inclined to abandon it altogether. They were Jews as truly as the Pharisees were, and the Torah belonged to both, as the chief factor in their common Judaism.

If this is true of Sadducees and Pharisees, as it obviously is, then it is true for all others, whether groups or individuals, who in various ways expressed the Judaism of the time. All were united in allegiance to the Torah, but not all meant the same thing by it, not all attached the same importance to it, nor interpreted it in the same way. The Torah may be compared to a ring-fence within which the whole of Jewish thought and literary activity was enclosed; but within that ring-fence there was room for all degrees of difference and variety, from the position of the Sadducees who stood at the circumference to the Pharisees who stood at the centre. Or better, lest the figure should be misunderstood, the Sadducees regarded the Torah as the outer limit of their Judaism within which they found room for much that was not specifically Jewish, while the Pharisees regarded the Torah as the centre and focus of their Judaism, the point of reference for everything which could claim that name. If there were any other types of Judaism beside those represented by Sadducees and Pharisees, as there certainly were, it follows that the representatives of these other varieties must have acknowledged the authority of the Torah, and it follows also that one who had much to say about the Torah was not on that account necessarily a Pharisee. If his attitude towards the Torah and his method of dealing with it was not that of the Pharisees, then he was not a Pharisee at all. Whether any of the authors of the Apocryphal and cognate literature were Pharisees is a question which will have to be answered on other grounds than that of their homage to the

N

Torah. So far as this ground is concerned, the assertion is a pure assumption without any foundation. ' Pharisee ' is a well-known and convenient name, as are also Sadducee, Zealot, Essene, and Amhaaretz; and there are no generally known names for other types of Judaism which undoubtedly were present. To class together the Apocryphal and Pseudepigraphical books, or most of them, as the work of Pharisees, is a mere makeshift, which would not be adopted if it were recognised that the Judaism of the period was much more complex than such a simple classification would indicate. It is much nearer the truth to say that these writers represent other types of Judaism to which indeed no specific names can be attached, unless perhaps in the case of the Apocalyptists, but which all united to make up, along with those whose names are known, the complex whole of Judaism as it was in the period before us.

An examination of the contents of the non-canonical books shows that two main elements are to be found in them, viz. the Ethical and the Apocalyptic. Not, indeed, that both these elements are present in every book, but that these are the characteristic features of the literature as a whole. There is little or nothing of the Apocalyptic element in the book of Ben Sira, nor in 1 Maccabees, which latter, indeed, is a history pure and simple. On the other hand, in books like Enoch, where the Apocalyptic element is very conspicuous, the ethical element is by no means wanting, and is certainly not put in as a sort of after-thought by a writer whose main interest was in Apocalyptic. Whatever was the real intention of the Apocalyptic writers in developing this particular element as strongly as they did, they included the ethical element as a matter of course. It was abundantly represented in the Canonical Scriptures, and had been a factor in the development of the religion of Israel and of the Judaism which succeeded it during well-nigh all the centuries of its history. A Jew at any time, and most of all in the period with which we are concerned, would, if he had anything to say for the instruction of his countrymen, naturally and instinctively say it in terms which implied the ethical consciousness, and assumed that as existing in the minds of his people. His book would necessarily have an ethical basis, on which would be built up whatever particular ideas, such

as Apocalyptic, might be the occasion of his writing at all.
The non-canonical books were obviously written under the
influence of the Canonical Scriptures, and by writers who
closely studied those Scriptures. It is not surprising that, in the
ethical teaching which they set forth in their books, there should
be a good deal of likeness, as between one and another, nor
that a high standard should be reached which is more or less
the same for all. It is also natural that this standard should be
in some respects higher, at all events more developed, than the
standard set in the Canonical books. This is very noticeable in
the Twelve Patriarchs, where the height reached is the greatest
that apparently ever was reached, at all events in regard to the
specific points which are dealt with. Now we have seen, in
studying the Rabbinical literature, that the ethical standard
there also was a high one, and that it was reached through the
study of the Canonical Scriptures, for all that it was developed especially in terms of Torah. We are justified in concluding
that, on the whole, there was a high ethical standard for all who
came under the influence of the Canonical Scriptures, and that
it was much the same alike for those who followed the highly
specialised line of the Pharisees, and for those who gave their
teaching in more general terms. Whether the leaders of the
Pharisaic development ever came in close contact with the
writers of the non-canonical literature, or read their books, is
a question upon which more will be said later on; but so far as
the ethical standard is concerned, there is nothing to show
that it was appreciably different in the one case from what it
was in the other. That there were clearly marked differences
between the Rabbinical teachers and the Apocryphal writers
goes without saying, and is one main reason for studying both;
but in regard to the quality of their ethical teaching they stood,
broadly speaking, upon common ground, along with everyone
else, if there was anyone else who concerned himself with
ethical questions. The Apocryphal writers, so far as they gave
ethical teaching, had as it would seem no special reason for
writing, as if they had some wholly new truth to proclaim.
They wrote ethically, we may say, because it would not occur
to them to write otherwise, either by implication or explicitly.
In the outstanding case of Ben Sira, he wrote avowedly as the
result of his meditation upon those who had gone before him,

especially in the field of the Wisdom literature. And even in the other cases of ethical teaching in the non-canonical books, it may be said that the writers were reflective students of the Canonical Scriptures in the light of their own ethical discernment.

The really new element in the non-canonical books is that of Apocalyptic, even though it be freely admitted that the first traces of Apocalyptic are to be found in the Canonical prophets. The hints there given were not followed up until the writer of the book of Daniel called emphatic attention to them, and opened a way of advance in a direction wholly new and along which many followed him. The Apocalyptic writers were not, of course, the first to study the prophetical books. We have seen that the Sopherim and their successors did the same, and presumably so did every Jewish thinker and teacher and writer in the period since the Canon of the Prophets was closed. But the Rabbinical teachers laid the chief stress on the ethical element in the prophetical books. The prophets were for the Rabbis, before everything else, preachers of righteousness; and the whole Rabbinic system of halachah and haggadah was mainly the result of applying to the Torah the ethical teaching of the prophets. The Rabbis did not lay any special stress on the predictive element in the prophetic books; the Apocalyptic writers took the predictive element as their starting point. This would be evident, even if the writer of Daniel had not said in so many words that this was what he did (Dan. ix. 2). But all the Apocalyptic writers deliver their message in the form of prediction, usually describing what has been shown them in a vision, and usually also writing in the person and under the name of some famous man of old, Enoch, Solomon, or even Ezra*. The source of Apocalyptic writing in the prophets is not

* The choice of Ezra for a pseudonym is curious in view of all that has been said above of his importance as the founder of the Rabbinical line of development on the basis of Torah, which did not follow the line of Apocalyptic. Does the choice of Ezra for the hero of the 4 Ezra Apocalypse indicate that he was owned even in non-Rabbinic circles as a great man and one of the chief figures in Judaism? Or did the author wish to connect the apparent breakdown in the religion of Torah with the man who was mainly responsible for that form of religion? He asks the question (4 Ezra vii. 118): O Adam, what hast thou done? Had he perhaps in his mind also the question: O Ezra, what hast thou done?

open to question, and the form of it is based on indications contained in some, at all events, of their writings. But it is not merely imitative. If the writers, or at all events the earlier ones, had not felt that they had something to say which the older prophets had not said, there is no obvious reason why they should have written at all. The author of Daniel certainly had something to say which to him was of great importance, and the later Apocalyptists, who followed him so closely, can hardly have been without some special reason for saying what they said, even though it seems little more than a repetition of the former thoughts with only a change of imagery. The writer of 4 Ezra certainly had something very special to say.

If we can pass behind the veil of imagery, and regard this and also the device of an assumed name as merely a literary artifice, then we shall perhaps find the clue to the meaning and intention of the Apocalyptic type of writing in a strong belief that the God who had spoken through the prophets was watching over his chosen people still, that what he had spoken through the prophets had not been spoken in vain, that what he had promised must come to pass, and that he who had spoken of old must have a word for the present time, if only some wise and holy man could discern what it was and make it known to his countrymen. The Apocalyptic message almost always implies a contrast between the evil of the writer's own time and the future when the evil shall be done away, and probably every Apocalypse was the product of persecution or other form of national calamity. In the centuries during which the Apocalyptic literature was mainly produced such reasons for writing in this manner were unfortunately never long absent; and Apocalyptic may be regarded as the reaction of a certain type of Jewish mind to the sufferings of his own time. The message of Apocalyptic was, or was intended to be, always one of hope and encouragement, though not without an undertone of anxiety in spite of the brave and confident words. This seems, to the present writer, at all events, a truer explanation of the meaning and purpose of Apocalyptic than to say that it is, or includes, an attempt at ' a philosophy of history '. The writer of Daniel certainly did survey the past, and review the succession of great empires as one after another they rose and fell; and he did so presumably in order to show how the God of

Israel had caused them to fall, and how he would again defend his people against the tyrant of the writer's own day. That was something to tell his oppressed and tortured countrymen, and something which might well, and apparently did, inspire them with new courage. But what had he, or they, in that time of agony to do with a ' philosophy of history', even if they knew what it meant? And so of all the other Apocalyptic writings, the motive was religion, deeply felt and strongly held, and not intellectual reflection, philosophical or other. It is this underlying ground of religion which gave to the Apocalyptic writings their strongest power of appeal, and enabled them to carry the weight of fantastic imagery in which the writers chose to clothe their deeper thoughts.

Yet the ' fantastic imagery ' cannot be dismissed as unimportant. For whatever reason, one Apocalyptic writer after another followed the lead of the author of Daniel in descriptions of visions, strange beasts and elaborate symbols, veiled allusions and figurative representation of contemporary history as he saw it. Why did they use this method, and why did they write under an assumed name? Charles' explanation is well known: ' Apocalyptic is the true child of prophecy, and became its true representative to the Jews from the unhappy moment when the Law won an absolute autocracy in Judaism and made the utterance of God-sent prophetic men impossible except through the medium of pseudepigraphs, some of which, like Daniel, gained an entrance, despite the Law, into the Old Testament Canon ' (Preface to Charles' edition of Enoch, 1912*). Dr. Charles seems to imagine that there was a sort of ' censorship of the press ', if the term may be allowed; at all events some kind of control, either by an official body or by public opinion, over the publication of books. If there had not been such control, what was there to ' make the utterance of God-sent prophetic men impossible '? The ' absolute autocracy of the Law ' was doubtless the ideal of the Sopherim and the Pharisees, but it was very far from being a reality except in the circle of their own adherents. They could not compel anyone to accept their ideas and adopt their practices, even though their authority as religious teachers was very great. If they could

* Repeated with no variation of meaning in the edition of Enoch in the Oxford Apocrypha, ii, 163, Introd. § 1.

have enforced any censorship, they would presumably have exercised it against all outside their own ranks. They had no power to exercise any kind of censorship in the matter of publication, and there is not the slightest evidence that they ever even tried to do so. Neither is there the slightest evidence that anyone else ever tried to do so. It may be safely asserted, against Dr. Charles, that there was no outward constraint of any kind, whether by public opinion or official act, which would make it impossible for anyone, God-sent or otherwise, to say what he had to say, in the form of a book. And even if there had been such constraint, the prestige of the Torah, however great, would certainly not have been cast on the side of repression.

The Apocalyptic writers had nothing to fear from the censure or restraint of anyone, and could write whatever they liked, and publish it if they could find some way of awakening interest in their work. There was nothing to prevent them from writing in their own names, as Ben Sira had done, though apparently he was the only one who had done so. Yet most of the later Scriptures, since the Canon of the Prophets was closed, were the works of authors whose names were unknown or not recorded, or else were ascribed to famous men of old, like David and Solomon. The Apocalyptic writers quite evidently founded themselves upon the prophets, and presumably their intention was to do in their own time something like what the prophets had done of old, out of a faith in God no less fervent and sincere. And if they had really been prophets, like their forerunners, if they had felt themselves impelled to speak or write the word of the Lord at his bidding, they would have done so, and done it in their own name. Those whom he sends on his errand do not wait for the permission of men before saying it; nor do they conceal the fact that it was they to whom the word of the Lord came. To conceal it would have been disloyal to him who sent them. The Apocalyptic writers lived in an age when it was admitted that there were no more any prophets; and only the appearance of another prophet, speaking in his own name as the messenger of God, could have proved the contrary. None such appeared, and no one could make himself such by merely wishing. The name of some unknown person would carry no weight, unless that unknown person had such

[183]

real prophetic power as that which once compelled men to listen to an Amos or a Hosea. There was nothing to be done, by the Apocalyptic writers, except to put their message into the mouth of someone already famous, in order to gain attention. And if it be said that such a proceeding is of doubtful honesty, this would be true if the standard of modern literary usage were applied, but it cannot be said with any confidence in the case of writers in the time with which we are concerned. There can be no doubt of their sincerity in saying what they had to say, nor of the warmth of religious faith which impelled them to say it; and that was, presumably, for them a much more important matter than the rather curious literary form in which they chose to clothe it. What they did was to say, as well as they could, what they supposed the older prophets would have said if they had been living in the later time. They took up especially the predictive and of course also the ethical side of prophecy; and although they had no difficulty with the ethical element, they could only supply prediction by imagination. Hence the use of visions, and all the elaborate machinery of symbols and riddles, which are found in all the Apocalyptic books, and which sometimes seem to draw attention away from the poverty of the thought in order to fix it on the ingenious devices through which it is presented. These writers, earnest and pious as they doubtless were—or, let us say, as they certainly were—having something to say which they greatly desired to say, were yet over-weighted with their task; and, while they did their honest best to fulfil it, hardly rose above the level of mediocrity in their well-meant attempt. At least, it is true that no one else in that age succeeded any better; no one else, in fact, produced anything at all of the kind and for the purpose which the Apocalyptists had in view. In their way they were unique, and on that account rather than for any outstanding excellence in their work they deserve to be studied. They belonged to Judaism, and they illustrate one aspect of it; but it does not follow that they represented the main element in Judaism, or exercised any considerable influence upon its development. All that has been ascertained so far is that the non-canonical literature appeared at a certain time, and possessed certain characteristic features indicating the purpose of the writers. But who those writers were, and what their relation was to the history of their time and to other contemporary movements of thought, where their books were written and where they were circulated, are questions which need to be more closely studied, and are of sufficient importance to be discussed in a separate chapter. To this discussion we now proceed.

CHAPTER II

THE ORIGIN AND AUTHORSHIP OF THE NON-CANONICAL BOOKS

IT is well to bear in mind that the non-canonical literature, so far as it falls within the period with which we are concerned, comprises only a small number of separate works, and these not all of one kind. The list given above (pp. 173-4) contains twenty-eight, and these are spread over a period of three centuries. That they may be the relics of a much more extensive literature is possible but by no means self-evident. Nor, on the face of it, is it even likely. That the book of Enoch represents the successive deposits of an extensive Enoch literature is probable enough; but that there were other parallel and more or less independent attempts to do what was finally done in the compilation and editing of the book which has come down under that name, there is nothing to show. The book of Tobit is a very beautiful religious romance, and must have been read with delight by all into whose hands it found its way; but that is not enough to show that there must have been a number of other religious romances, now unfortunately lost. So of all the rest. All that we actually know about them in this respect is that there they are, of such and such contents and so many in number, and so far no evidence has been brought forward to show that once there were many more of a similar kind. That the non-canonical literature is in its way very interesting and important is one thing; that it was ever very extensive and, on that account, representative of a considerable factor in the Judaism of its time is quite another thing.

It is generally agreed that most of these books, if not all, were written in Hebrew; and that is taken to imply that they were written in Palestine. The argument from language is, however, not decisive. No doubt an author living in Palestine would naturally write in Hebrew, and one living in Alexandria would only be doing what many did if he wrote in Greek. But if he, living in Alexandria, were writing with any special reference to the Judaism of Palestine or to the conditions prevailing there, then he might quite naturally write in Hebrew. A knowledge

of Hebrew, at all events on the part of some persons, is implied
in the existence and use of the Scriptures. For though for most
purposes and by most people the Scriptures were read in
Greek, it is hard to believe that there was no one at all in
Alexandria who could read Hebrew, and, on occasion, write in
it. I am not contending that the non-canonical books were
actually written in Alexandria; I am only arguing that the use
of Hebrew does not by itself prove the country of the writer
to have been Palestine. It leaves Egypt as a possibility.

Very little attention has been given to the inquiry into the
actual facts of the writing, publication, and circulation of books
in Palestine during our period. It has generally been assumed
that the literature at present under discussion had a wide
circulation in Palestine as well as elsewhere; some of it is said
to have been extremely popular, and it has been imagined that
there were actually libraries more or less public where books
of supposed general interest could be read. It is true that very
little is known of the facts in regard to the publication and
circulation of books in Palestine, but that little does not lend
much support to the alleged existence of a large reading public
or a considerable demand for books, other than copies of the
Scriptures. There were men whose business it was to write
copies of these; they could be bought and sold, and probably
there was always some demand for them. But of a bookseller,
in the sense in which the word would be understood in Rome
or Alexandria, viz. a man who dealt in books generally, not
sacred books especially, there is not a trace in Palestine. The
Rabbinical literature gives a fairly inclusive picture of Jewish
life in the period which it covers, and it does not record—so far
as I know—a single case of a person who sold books, or of one
who says that he went and bought a book, or that he kept books
in his house for his own private reading, or that he ever wrote
a book, or knew anyone else who had written one. And if I am
reminded that the Rabbinical literature is later than our
period, then it is all the more strange that there should be
such a silence in the later literature as to the existence of a book
trade and book circulation, if these had been considerable at
the earlier period, and when there could be no reason for
keeping silence about the fact.

Of course there were books, not counting the Scriptures,

which in the present discussion must be left out of account as they only confuse the issue. But the fact that a book was written does not imply that it was widely read; and there was, so far as is known, nothing in the usage of Palestine at all like publication as the term is understood now, or even as it was understood in Rome or Alexandria in our period. If a man in Palestine wrote a book, what would he do in order to find readers for it? The only thing he could do, apart from reading it aloud to his friends, was to write one or more copies of it or get someone else to write copies, as they might be asked for. There was no one to act as publisher to make his book known and to put it on the market; and there was no market on which to put it. And who was there to read it? What did the ' reading public ' amount to? Of course, there must have been some who could read Hebrew, apart from Scripture; but of anything like a regular reading habit amongst the people in general there is not a trace. Persons of leisure and wealth would be the only ones in a position to buy books, and such persons were not numerous in Palestine in the times of the later Maccabean princes and that of Herod. Most of the people were poor and oppressed, and could have but little if anything to do with books. So far as the contents of books became known at all, it would for the most part be the result of oral transmission; the possessor of a copy of the book would read it aloud if he had an opportunity, or repeat the substance in his own words as something that he had read or heard of. Even so much as this is not certain; but unless there were so much as this, it is hard to see how books could become known at all. But more than this is mere matter of conjecture, resting on no ground of known fact. To assume that what was certainly true of Rome, and probably true of Alexandria, in the matter of the circulation of books, was also true of Palestine or even of Jerusalem, is wholly without warrant. So far as the very scanty evidence goes, the probability is entirely the other way.

Now the non-canonical books, being written in Hebrew, were presumably meant to be read in Palestine; if they had been meant for Alexandrian readers, it would have been easier to have written them in Greek. Whether written in Egypt or in Palestine, they were written, we must suppose, for the instruction of persons in the latter country; and they would have to make their way into public knowledge and favour by some such very imperfect method as that described above, with the result that so far as appears they had no great circulation in Palestine, or rather were not widely known. It is a highly significant fact that these books have become known only through translations of them, at first into Greek and then into other languages. Even Ben Sira, though he wrote in Hebrew and apparently in Jerusalem, left so little mark on the literature of his time that his work first became generally accessible when his grandson took the Hebrew text to Egypt and translated it there into Greek. It is true that the Hebrew text was not wholly lost sight of; the Rabbis knew the book and read it, and several quotations from it and allusions to it are contained in the Talmud. And in recent years a large part of the Hebrew text has been recovered. But if it had not been for the fact that his book was translated into Greek and included in the Alexandrine Canon of the Old Testament, practically nothing would have been known of him. It might well be expected that 1 Maccabees, a book of serious historical purpose, written, as it would seem, by someone who could speak with authority of public affairs, would have kept its place in Palestinian literature as an authentic and valuable document; but it also has only survived in a Greek translation, and even Josephus does not seem to have read it in Hebrew. So of all the other non-canonical books. Wherever they were written, and whoever were the writers, the only real evidence of wide circulation and interest taken in them is the fact of their translation into the various languages of the Diaspora. It would not be far from the truth to say that they never came into their own till they got to Alexandria, whence they could pass out through translation into a larger realm of thought. That to some extent they were known and read in Palestine is likely enough, but to what extent is mere matter of conjecture with nothing to go on.

If the above considerations had been present to the minds of those who have been rightly regarded as leading authorities on the subject of the non-canonical literature, notably Schürer, Charles, and Bousset, they would not have so readily committed themselves to the theory that most of the books in question were written by Pharisees. And still less would they have done so if they had understood who the Pharisees really were and what they stood for. Devotion to Torah proves nothing, because Torah was the common element in all Jewish thought and all Jewish writing of the period. The likeness between the Pharisaic ethics and the Apocryphal ethics also proves nothing, for the ethical standard was much the same for both, being mainly that of the Canonical Scriptures somewhat more fully developed. To pitch on the Pharisees as the authors of the non-canonical books is to make the most unhappy choice of which the case admits; for they, of all the various types of Jews living in that period, were the least fitted for the part assigned to them. To write books at all was entirely off their line. They built up their whole system on oral teaching; and there is not, so far as I know, a single case on record of a Pharisee having written a book, at all events in the period with which we are concerned*. The Megillath Taanith is a possible exception, but that was only a sort of calendar of notable days. And if R. Jehudah b. Illai wrote the original of the Seder Olam, he lived after the close of our period, and was a rare exception even then. To speak of ' a writer of the school of R. Akiba ' (Charles, vol. ii, pp. xii and xiii) is simply a contradiction in terms. Akiba certainly had a Beth ha-Midrash, like any other Rabbi, and that might loosely be called a school; but neither he nor his pupils wrote in his ' school '. And if ' school ' be intended to describe a group of (alleged) writers, whose opinions were more or less founded on those of Akiba, the ' opinions ' may be allowed, but the ' writers ' are a mere creation of fancy. There were no schools of writers among the Pharisees, and to ascribe to them the composition of the Apocryphal and Apocalyptic books, any or all, is merely to beg the question.

It has been shown in the preceding Book that the whole system elaborated by the Pharisees was a discipline, and not merely a body of instruction. It was a definite training, having for its object the doing of good actions and the avoiding of bad ones by those who came under the discipline. The great instrument which the Pharisees used for this purpose was the

* In the edition of Sirach in the Oxford Apocrypha, i, p. 316, note on v. 4 (' by speaking and writing ') it is said ' The literary activity of the earlier Scribes, as well as the later, is also implied in a number of references in the Rabbinical literature; see Strack, *Einleitung in den Talmud* (4th edition), p. 12 ff.' The earlier Scribes are not here mentioned at all. The references are to the period of the Amoraim, i.e. after the Mishnah.

interpretation of Torah, under the two forms of halachah and haggadah, an interpretation which took into account the whole of the Canonical Scriptures. The Pharisees were out to give actual and practical guidance for the right conduct of life to all whom they could influence; and they brought that influence to bear in the synagogues, by personal address to those whom they could gather there. To write books would not have helped their object. Anyone could write books, but not everyone could wield the powerful instruments of the Synagogue and the Beth ha-Midrash. The Pharisees were certainly not the only type of Jews in the period before us, but in their way they were unique. They did what no one else was doing; and, whether they were right or wrong, they would not be in the least likely to give up their peculiar way in order to go and write books. If there were some, like the Apocryphal writers, who expressed in their books opinions such as the Pharisees held, that was all to the good. Much of it was common stock of all the Judaism of the time. But that does not prove that those writers, or any of them, were Pharisees; and the only thing which would prove that would be if the writers in question expressed their views in the form of an interpretation of Torah along the two lines of halachah and haggadah. No single writer fulfils that condition. The books are in no case interpretations of Torah, or even of Scripture generally. The word halachah is never mentioned, nor even implied. There is no haggadah properly so called. For haggadah does not mean merely fanciful discourse on sacred themes; it is definitely a technical term, and is only rightly applied to exposition of what the Torah declares on its non-preceptive side, the Torah being illustrated from the rest of Scripture. The kind of thing abundantly found in the Apocryphal books, in the form of discourse or narrative based more or less on Scripture, is not haggadah at all and ought not to be called by that name. It is not even Midrash. If, by a stretch of imagination, we could suppose that a Pharisee had set out to write one of those books, he would necessarily have written it quite differently; more probably he would have given up the attempt, as being entirely off his line. Whoever wrote those books, the last place in which to look for their authors is amongst the Pharisees.

It does not seem to have occurred to those who have assigned these books to Pharisaic authors that the exclusion of them from the Canon of Scripture becomes, on that hypothesis, all the more difficult to understand. If they were written by Pharisees, presumably Pharisees in general would approve of them, even value them; and, though it might be impossible to include them in the Canon of Scripture, it does not seem likely that Pharisees would allow them to be wholly forgotten. Why should they deprive themselves of such excellent teaching, written down by men of their own way of thinking? Since, however, they were not included in the Canon, and were, with the exception of Ben Sira, never so much as mentioned in the Pharisaic literature, it does not look as if the Pharisees knew or cared much about them, let alone wrote them. Instead of assigning these books to Pharisees, presumably because these were the most conspicuous party at the time and were known to have held strong views about the Torah, it is simpler to recognise that there were other types in the Judaism of the time, and that especially the Apocalyptists, but more or less all the other Apocryphal writers, represent some of those separate types. They ought, in fairness, to be taken at their own valuation, so to speak, and not to be identified with other types merely because these other types happen to be better known by name, though indeed little known in their real significance.

I have elsewhere* suggested that at all events the Apocalyptic books were written by Zealots, or at least by persons who held the Zealot point of view; and perhaps in making that suggestion I have myself been guilty of too hasty identification with a known type of contemporary Judaism. I would hardly now go so far as to say that the Apocalyptic literature was Zealot literature, for the Zealots were revolutionaries, in theory and—when they could find the opportunity—in practice also. It is not among such men that one would naturally expect to find writers of books, nor, for that matter, readers of books either. But there was a good deal in the Apocalyptic writings which would strongly appeal to minds of the Zealot type, such as fierce national pride and hatred against the enemies of Israel; also, and much more significant, the thought, running through all the Apocalypses, of despair of ordinary human means of setting right the cruel wrongs under which Israel groaned, and the passionate longing that God himself would interfere and

* See my *Pharisees*, p. 188.

bring deliverance. The Zealots were those who had become desperate under oppression, and would not wait for the slow working of Providence; they would fight, if they could get the chance, and God must surely come to the rescue of his people. The Apocalyptic books gave a stimulus to such ideas; and it is not at all necessary to suppose that they were widely read for them to produce that effect. The views expressed in them were such as could easily be passed on in speech and repeated, until they spread far and wide through the people.

The relation of the Apocalyptic books to the Zealot movement may perhaps be most truly stated by saying that the writers were men who pondered deeply the past history and the present condition of Israel, in the light of the divine promises, and who sought to encourage their countrymen by showing them that there must be a bright future. They wrote as men of reflection, having something to teach, but not themselves concerned with the application of what they taught. The Zealots were those who most eagerly caught up their teaching, and made it the inspiration of their policy of violence. Whether these writers lived in Palestine or Egypt can hardly be decided, but is of no great importance. In either country they must know what was going on which concerned the Jewish people, could reflect upon what they knew and could offer the result of their reflections for the encouragement of all whom it might concern, and of any who might happen to read their words. If the considerations put forward above be well founded, then these writers found their readers mostly outside Palestine, and found them only when their books were translated into Greek and thence into other languages. Whatever connexion the non-canonical literature may have had with Palestine, its real centre of gravity was in Egypt; and if in that country it did not actually breathe its native air, as it may well have done, it certainly found there a more congenial mental climate in which it could flourish and exert all the influence for good of which it was capable.

Reasons have been given above for saying that the Pharisees had nothing to do with the production of this literature. The question remains: Had they anything to do with it at all? It was certainly not included in the Canon of the Hebrew Scriptures, which was arranged under Pharisaic control in the deliberations of the teachers of Torah in the Beth ha-Midrash.

Were the Apocryphal books deliberately excluded, or were they left out because no one ever suggested that they should be put in? If the Rabbinical literature be searched for evidence upon which to base an answer to these questions, only a very few passages can be found which throw even a faint light upon the subject. In the Mishnah, Sanh. x. (xi.) 1, it is stated that ' all Israel have a part in the world to come ', and then follow various exceptions, e.g. he who says that the Torah is not from heaven; then ' R. Akiba says, " He who reads in external books " ' (*sepharim ḥitzonim*). In the Palestinian Gemara on this passage (j. Sanh. 28a) this is amplified into the following: ' R. Akiba says " he who reads in external books ", such as the books [*sic*] of Ben Sira and the books of Ben Laanah. But [as for] the books of Homeros* and all books which were written from that time onwards, he who reads them is as he who reads a letter '. And this is supported by a reference to Koheleth xii. 12, ' of making many books ', etc. The Babylonian Gemara (b. Sanh. 100b) explains ' external books ' by ' books of the Minim '. One authority adds ' also Ben Sira ', an opinion which met with some criticism. In Koh. R. on xii. 12, in place of the name Ben Laanah is the name Ben Tagla. Neither of these names is mentioned elsewhere.

The important words in the above passages are ' external books ', and, as the texts are unpointed, it is uncertain whether the words should be ' in *the* external books ', with a reference to some definite class of books. The word ' external ', however, can hardly imply any other meaning than ' outside the canon ', i.e. books which were not recognised as holy Scripture, and this would apply to all non-canonical books whatever, to anything which could be read. That R. Akiba meant to forbid all reading of general literature other than Scripture seems hardly likely, but his dictum was open to that interpretation, and the Gemara in both Talmuds seeks to qualify his words and give them a more particular reference, by specifying the kind of book which Akiba must have meant to proscribe. Both mention Ben Sira as an example, and the Pal. Gemara carefully distinguishes

---

* Various explanations have been suggested of this name, but Krauss decides in favour of the traditional, and also natural, view that the reference is to Homer, the poet (see Krauss, *Lehnworter*, i, Einl. p. xiv). The same name occurs (M. Jad. iv. 6) in a somewhat different connexion.

between books of this kind and secular literature generally, such as the poems of Homer. Now secular literature, in the nature of the case, lay entirely out of the range of any possible comparison with Scripture, let alone of inclusion within it. To call it external would be unnecessary because self-evident. The only need for the word would arise in the case of books which could be brought into comparison with Scripture, and which could suggest the question Might these not be allowed to be read? Ben Sira* was evidently regarded as such a book, and was in fact read and quoted in the Talmud and Midrash. Ben Sira is one of the group of Apocryphal books, and the mention of him as a specimen *may* imply that the reference was to the whole group which included him. This is by no means certain, but, admitting the possibility of such wider reference, the fact remains that Ben Sira and all the rest designated as ' external ' were outside the Canon of Scripture. The only question was, How should they be dealt with as matter for reading? Akiba's dictum is given as his opinion only, not as an accepted judgment, like the two previous exclusions in the Mishnah. In the time of Akiba it was recognised that Ben Sira and the rest (whoever they may have been) were outside the Canon. This is stated in T. Jad. ii. 13, where it says: ' The " gilionim " and the books of the Minim do not defile the hands. The books of Ben Sira and all books which were written from then onwards do not defile the hands'. In other words, these books were not holy Scripture. This is the only hint, so far as I know, in the Rabbinical literature of the reason why these books (including though not specifying the Apocryphal and cognate literature) were regarded as uncanonical. There is no mention of any deliberate act of exclusion on the part of those who were

* It is worth noting that the Pal. Gemara speaks of ' the *books* of Ben Sira ', as if there were more than one. It is also worth noting that the Pal. Gemara groups together ' the books of Homeros and all which have been written since his time'. This would apply to a large part of the Canonical Scriptures, and can hardly have been meant. The real intention is surely expressed in the statement (T. Jad. ii. 13): ' the books of Ben Sira and all books that have been written from then onwards, do not defile the hands'. The Tosephta was earlier than the Pal. Gemara, and the latter presumably misread the statement of the former. This passage is quoted in the Oxford Apocrypha (Sirach) i, 271, n. 3), and is there wrongly translated. The words which signify ' from then onwards ' are rendered ' after the prophetic period'. This is to beg a very large question, and to corrupt a plain text.

responsible for the definition of the Canon of the Hebrew Scriptures. And it is worth noticing that when objection was raised to the canonicity of Ezekiel (b. Shabb. 13*b*), Koheleth, and Shir ha-Shirim (M. Jad. iii. 5), the question was not whether they should be now included or excluded, but whether they ought to have been included when they were? There was no suggestion of reopening the Canon. If there had been, then would have been the natural opportunity for a decision against the Apocryphal books. But there is no record that this latter question was decided or even discussed.

From the above very scanty material no certain conclusion can be drawn as to the facts and the reasons for the non-inclusion of the Apocryphal and cognate literature from the Canon. So far as it goes, and it goes only a very little way, it rather supports than contradicts the view expressed above that the Pharisaic leaders neither knew nor cared very much about this literature. They went their own way without paying attention to it; and if they knew in a general way of its existence, that was about as much as they knew. There was room in the Judaism of the time for many different types of thought, and we shall make more progress towards a right understanding of what that Judaism really was if we refrain from hasty identifications with some well-known type, such as the Pharisees, and are prepared to recognise that the existence of writers such as those of the Apocryphal books points rather to complexity than simplicity in the literary activities of the time. Also, that the presence of many elements in the contemporary Judaism by no means implies that there was close interaction and mutual influence between them. We need to widen our whole conception of Judaism, as it was then, before generalising about it.

Having now surveyed the Apocryphal and cognate literature in its main features, it will be convenient to say what further seems needful to be said under the heads of the several books or the more important of them. To this further study we now proceed, and the first to engage our attention will be the book of Ben Sira.

CHAPTER III

THE BOOK OF BEN SIRA (SIRACH, ECCLESIASTICUS)

IT is generally accepted by scholars that the author of this book was living in 180 B.C. or thereabouts, the date being inferred from the statement of his grandson in the Prologue to his translation of the original Hebrew book into Greek. The book itself may well have been the outcome of many years of thought and research on the part of the author, the fruit both of his own meditation and his gleaning in the field of the older teachers of wisdom, as he says himself (ch. xxxiii. 16-18). This, together with the whole form and contents of the book, clearly indicates that he stands in the succession of those writers who produced the so-called Wisdom literature. The affinity between his book and the book of Proverbs is unmistakable even by the most casual reader of the two; probably most readers would agree that the book of Ben Sira stands higher in the quality of its ethical teaching than Proverbs, and will regret that the later book did not find a place in the Canon, even to the exclusion of the earlier. There is also some likeness of form between the book of Ben Sira and Koheleth, although the two books differ widely in the spirit of their teaching. Ben Sira rises to a height which Koheleth never reached, and seldom if ever sinks so low as his predecessor. How far Ben Sira was acquainted with Koheleth or made use of the book is a matter of conjecture; but it is hardly likely that a professed student of Wisdom, such as Ben Sira obviously was, would neglect to study a book so remarkable, especially as it was included in the Canon. Ben Sira, in a famous passage (xxxviii. 24—xxxix. 11), enlarges on the qualities and accomplishments which distinguish the ' Sopher', or Scribe, by contrast with those of the manual worker, several types of whom he vividly describes. There can be no reasonable doubt that he regarded himself as a Sopher, and would call himself by that title, and the description in xxxix. 1-11 may be taken to indicate both his aims and his practice. It shows clearly what he meant by a Sopher. Now we have already met with the term Sopher (Sopherim) as the designation of those who followed the lead of Ezra and developed the interpretation of Torah on his lines (see above, Bk. II, Ch. II, p. 43 f.). The Sopherim described in that chapter, and identified with the men of the Great Synagogue, belonged to an age considerably earlier than that of Ben Sira, and ceased to function under that name in or about 270 B.C. (see above, p. 45). Moreover, the earlier Sopherim do not by any means fit into the description which Ben Sira gives of what he understands by a Sopher. The use of the same term in reference to two apparently very different types of men has led to much confusion; and we shall not get to a right understanding of Ben Sira and his relation to the Judaism of his time, until that confusion has been reduced to order.

In the edition of Sirach in the Oxford Apocrypha (i, 292) it is said: ' As a scribe [he is described in the Prologue as *anaginōskōn* = "Sopher"]—for by this time "scribe" and "wise" had become amalgamated—he imparted instruction to young members of the Jerusalem aristocracy, who assembled in his " house of instruction " (Beth ha-Midrash, ch. li. 23), and there doubtless he lectured on matters of jurisprudence, as well as ethics, in the manner congenial to the Teachers of the Law (cp. xxiii. 11, 23). Ben Sira, however, belonged to the earlier *Sopherim* in whom the spirit pervading the Wisdom-Literature was still strong'. Here we find an instance of the confusion above referred to. The earlier Sopherim, the only known persons bearing that name before the time of Ben Sira, were the followers of Ezra who studied the Torah and interpreted it on the lines of halachah and haggadah, as shown already. It is quite clear from the evidence of his own book, the only evidence available, that Ben Sira was not in the line of succession of the early Sopherim, that he had indeed nothing more in common with them than with any other learned and thoughtful man of his time. He was not in any special way a teacher of Torah, certainly not in the way which the earlier Sopherim had made their own. Of their leading principles and methods there is not the faintest trace in his book. When it is said, in the passage quoted, that he ' doubtless lectured on matters of jurisprudence, as well as ethics, in the manner congenial to the Teachers of the Law (cp. xxiii. 11, 23) ', it may be remarked that if he lectured on jurisprudence at all, and there is nothing to show that he did, he certainly did not do so ' in the manner congenial to the Teachers of the Law* ', either the earlier Sopherim or their later successors in the Rabbinical line. The fact that he had a ' Beth ha-Midrash ' and a ' yeshibah ' proves nothing whatever in this respect. He was a teacher, and naturally needed some place in which to collect and address his pupils; but that is no evidence of any likeness between him and other teachers in regard to the manner of their teaching. The passage quoted on li. 29 n., from *Jew. Encycl.* xii. 595*d*, refers to the period after the close of the Mishnah, third century A.D. onwards, and has no relevance to the period of Ben Sira.

In the confusion arising from the use of the word Sopher is to be seen another case of the danger of hasty identification on the strength of names not fully understood (see above, p. 193). The succession of earlier teachers were known, in their own circle at all events, by the name Sopherim, and it meant something quite definite when it was applied to them. Ben Sira called himself (or implied that he was) a Sopher, and left no doubt what he meant by it. The conclusion to be drawn is not that Ben Sira is to be identified with the earlier Sopherim as being in that line of succession, but that he was entirely independent of them; and not merely of the Sopherim properly so called, who had ceased to function under that name a century before his time, but also of their successors contemporary with himself. The Teachers of Torah on the lines of the older Sopherim were certainly active in his time, and carried on their work in the Beth ha-Midrash and the Synagogue, as already explained at length. But there is nothing to show that Ben Sira had anything to do with them or knew anything about them. He never refers to them in his book, and never mentions synagogues. Which only goes to show that there was room in the social life of that time, and even in Jerusalem where Ben Sira lived, for activities and movements of thought to be carried on side by side without coming into contact, and that the Judaism in which Ben Sira and the Teachers of Torah, his contemporaries, alike shared, was more complex and many-sided than it is usually supposed to have been. Ben Sira described the social

* The reference to ch. xxiii. 11, 23, does not support the statement in the text, and is perhaps intended for some other passage.

life as he saw it around him in Jerusalem, but only as he saw it, and so much as he saw. It is well to recognise that there were aspects of it which he did not see, and, in particular, that the activity of the Teachers of Torah did not come within his observation. This gives the simplest explanation of the fact, so often remarked on and puzzled over by scholars, that Ben Sira did not mention Ezra in his review of the heroes of Israel. It was only among those who followed on his lines and developed his principles that Ezra was regarded as of any importance, perhaps even that his name was known, except as that of a man of an earlier time mentioned in Scripture. There was nothing to make Ezra of any importance in the eyes of Ben Sira; and the surprise that has so often been expressed at the omission of Ezra's name is only due to the fact that the Judaism which finally prevailed over the many other types was that one which was developed on the lines which Ezra had laid down. But in Ben Sira's time it was not so. Even the cleavage indicated by the names Pharisee and Sadducee had not yet disclosed itself; and while it is true that in a few years after Ben Sira's time the Maccabean Revolt was to show how powerful the influence of the Teachers of Torah was and had long been, yet that influence was exerted mainly beneath the surface, so to speak. To which may be added that it was stronger outside Jerusalem than inside the city, as was clearly shown by the course of the Revolt. Jerusalem was the natural headquarters of the Hellenising party, and though the Torah party was no doubt well represented there, it was certainly not at its full strength. There is nothing at all surprising in the fact (if it is a fact) that Ben Sira knew nothing about it.

In this connexion a further passage from the Introduction to Sirach in the Oxford edition (i, p. 282) calls for remark. It is there said: ' Dr. Taylor, in his edition of *Pirqe Aboth* (1897), p. 115, says in reference to the books of the Sadducees: We have no authentic remains of Sadducee literature, but it has been suggested with a certain plausibility that the book Ecclesiasticus approximates to the standpoint of the primitive Çaduqin as regards its theology, its sacerdotalism, and its want of sympathy with the *modern* Soferim '. Then (omitting a remark by Kuenen as to the reason why Ezra was not mentioned in the list of worthies), ' The modern *Scribe* was to Ben Sirach an unworthy descendant of the primitive *Wise*, in accordance with Eliezer ha-Gadol's lament over the degeneracy of a later age ' (Hebrew given, and then a translation quoted from Surenhusius' edition of the Mishnah, Sotah ix. 5, which ought to be ix. 15, as follows): ' Ex quo Templum devastatum est coepere *Sapientes* similes esse *Scribis*, Scribae aedituis, Aeditui vulgo hominum ', etc. The reference to Eliezer ha-Gadol is quite irrelevant; he was describing the state of things after the fall of Jerusalem in A.D. 70, and what he said was: ' The Wise came down to be like *teachers of children* ', etc. There is no reference to Scribes in the sense in which Ben Sira uses the word, nor in the sense in which it was applied to the Sopherim. Also it is not said that the Wise *began* to be like Scribes, after the fall of Jerusalem, but that they could not maintain their old position, by reason of the hardship of the time. If, for any reason, this contrast or comparison between ' Wise ' and ' Scribe ' is justified, then what becomes of the assertion quoted above (p. 200): ' For by this time Scribe and Wise had become amalgamated', i.e. in the time of Ben Sira?

The Sadducean tendency of Ben Sira, if it existed, is not made more evident by this hardly successful appeal to the Mishnah. Nor is it helped by calling in Dr. Taylor's remark about the books of the Sadducees: ' Dr. Taylor points out further the important fact that in the Babylonian Talmud (Sanhedrin, 100*b*) the *Books of the Sadducees* and the *Book of Ben Sira* are placed side by side on the " Index Expurgatorius " '. Then follows the Hebrew of the passage, which is wrongly printed, i.e. according to the censored text, and which ought to be rendered, 'One has taught (i.e. in the Mishnah) "the books of the *Minim*" (are forbidden to be read). Rab Joseph said, In the book of Ben Sira also it is forbidden to read '. This passage has been referred to above (p. 195), and is only quoted here in order to point out that it has no bearing on the question whether Ben Sira was inclined to Sadducean views*. The Minim whose books are forbidden to be read were not Sadducees; in most of

* The reading ' Minim ' in place of ' Tzaddukim ' is vouched for by Rabbinowicz, *Dikd. Soph., ad loc.* This only shows the need of care in using Talmudic material. The Rabbinical references and translations in the Oxford Sirach—and, indeed, in the whole work—need to be carefully checked by the original texts, and often corrected. They cannot be accepted as reliable as they stand.

the passages* where the word occurs the reference is to Jewish Christians.

To raise the question whether Ben Sira showed Sadducean tendencies is only another instance of the temptation to make hasty identifications on the strength of well-known names. That the Sadducees as a party only became prominent nearly a century after Ben Sira's time is, of course, true, and affords no reason for saying that he might not have been an early forerunner of them. But the indications alleged by Dr. Taylor, as quoted above, are not in themselves distinctively Sadducean. The real line of cleavage between Sadducee and Pharisee was, as has been often repeated in this book, their respective attitude towards the Unwritten Torah, and Ben Sira gives no hint of his views on that question—if, indeed, he had any views at all. ' The prominence given to the Law in Sirach may therefore well indicate the Sadducean attitude' (Sirach, Oxford, p. 283). This remark is beside the point, because if a Sadducee *qua* Sadducee gave prominence to the Torah, he would necessarily do so by emphasising the written as against the unwritten. Merely to exalt the Torah is what every pious and thoughtful Jew would do if he had occasion to mention the Torah. For that was the heritage of all Israel, and the chief element in the Canon of Scripture, however it might be interpreted; and a devout student of Scripture, as Ben Sira certainly was, did not need to be of a Sadducean tendency in order to accord a high place, even a very high place, to the Torah.

It is hardly necessary to pursue further the ' mirage ' of Sadduceanism in Ben Sira. Instead of trying to identify him, even though only in part, with this or that sect of later times, it is safer and more reasonable to take him for what he was on the showing of his own book; in other words, to recognise him as a teacher on his own account, having such and such things to say, on which other men in later times may, or may not, have thought as he did, or may not have thought at all. Ben Sira was beyond any question a careful student of the Scriptures, which included in his time the Pentateuch, the prophetical and historical books, and probably the greater

* On the Minim, see the present writer's *Christianity in Talmud and Midrash*, the second division of the book, where all (or most of) the passages referring to Minim are collected and analysed.

part of the Psalms and the Proverbs. The form of his book shows that he was especially drawn to the Wisdom literature, and that he considered himself to be in the succession of those who in earlier times had sought and imparted wisdom. His purpose was apparently to do in his time something like what they had done in theirs. But the contents of his book show that he was well acquainted with the other Canonical literature, so far as it was extant in his time. And, whatever his originality as a thinker may have been, the main lines of his belief and his teaching were laid down for him in and by his study of the Scriptures. So they would have been, and presumably were, in the case of other devout and careful students of Scripture in his time. No doubt there were such, quite apart from the Sopherim (properly so called) and their later successors, with whom, as we have seen reason to believe, Ben Sira had nothing to do. Indeed, if we ask how anyone at that time came by his religious beliefs, the only answer is that he got them from the Scriptures either by his own reading or by the teaching of others; but in the last resort, all was derived from the Scriptures, partly as a body of teaching on its own account and partly as the natural stimulus of pious meditation. Neither Ben Sira nor anyone else set out to fashion a set of religious beliefs *de novo*. There was a common stock (using the word in a general sense) which was the inheritance of all Jews, and whose contents were mainly derived from or shaped by the teaching of the Scriptures. Where teachers and thinkers of various types differed from each other was in what they severally added to this common stock, or modified it in this point or in that, or laid a special stress on some particular feature of it. All were Jews, and their religion was Judaism; and this was so in virtue of the common stock which belonged to them all. Therefore, when we find that some specific belief was held, e.g. by Ben Sira and by the Pharisees, or by the Pharisees and the Zealots, or by Ben Sira and the Sadducees, or by the Pharisees and the Apocalyptists, that does not prove that Ben Sira was either a Pharisee or a Sadducee, or that the Pharisees were Zealots or Apocalyptists. It only proves that all shared in the common stock, and leaves their respective differences exactly where they were and what they were.

Now the particular importance of Ben Sira is that he represents, on the whole, the common stock at an earlier stage than it is to be found in any of the other Apocryphal books, and also that he affords a basis of comparison with the common stock as it was represented in the teachers (earlier than and contemporary with himself) of the Rabbinical line.

The common stock, as represented by Ben Sira, included first and foremost a strong, clear, and deep belief in God, as Creator of the world and of mankind, as the Ruler and Judge, the Merciful and Just, a God such as the prophets had made known. God, moreover, as being in a special degree the God of Israel, to whom he had revealed himself as to no other people, though all were his.

The Torah was the revelation which he had made to Israel by the agency of Moses, for the guidance and instruction of his people. It was the chief among the books which were accounted sacred, and what it contained was the highest truth which was accessible to man. To live in accordance with its teaching was to serve God in the way which he desired.

Worship was the natural and right response of man to God, and it found its fullest public expression in the services of the Temple in Jerusalem. What was done there was done in accordance with the express directions given in the Torah, and the priests who carried out those directions were a sacred band deriving their authority from God himself, who had caused Aaron to be consecrated the first High Priest. The outcome of all the past history of Israel, as recorded in the Scriptures, was the establishment of the Temple as the supreme expression of religion in public worship, and thus as in some sense the counterpart of the Torah.

God, Torah, and Temple were the three foci of Judaism as it was gradually developed under the influence of the Scriptures, by devout men closely studying those Scriptures; and all else that Judaism contained was associated with one or other of those foci. Prophecy had been, in a former age, also one of the great spiritual forces, even the greatest of all, in the religion of Israel. But prophecy came to an end, as was admitted by all, and its influence as sublime teaching was preserved in the beliefs about God. The Rabbinical teachers applied the prophetic teaching to the Torah, as already explained at length; and the Apocalyptists, as we shall see presently, developed the predictive side of prophecy. These were special developments;

and so far as the common stock is concerned the prophetic element in the older religion is represented mainly by the exalted conception of God. Wisdom had also been a prominent factor in the older religion, though its connexion with religion was not always very close. The Wisdom books, especially Proverbs, illustrated wisdom both as divine and worldly, as a gift imparted by God and also as a faculty of acute judgment in purely human affairs. Both these conceptions of wisdom have their place in the common stock; and whatever doubts there might be as to the validity of the claim of worldly wisdom to hold that place, were resolved by the identification of wisdom with Torah. Ben Sira makes this identification in the most explicit manner, and that is presumably why he felt himself able to follow the lead of the older Wisdom teachers so closely as he did, and to give along with noble and lofty teaching about life as the true service of God, counsels of by no means lofty worldly prudence. The earlier chapters of the book of Proverbs had prepared the way for the identification of Wisdom with Torah; and the fact that it already appears completed in the book of Ben Sira explains, in part at least, why in his book there is so much more of clear and conscious utterance of personal religion than is to be found in Proverbs.

That there is in the common stock no reference to a belief in a future existence after death, other than the ancient one of Sheol, is due to the fact that in all but the very latest of the Canonical Scriptures there is no other conception of future existence than that of Sheol, apart from a very few scattered hints and suggestions. The study of the Scriptures, so far as the Canon was complete, would naturally lead to a result which did not include a belief in a future life after death. The Rabbinical teachers may have been feeling their way to it; but we can safely say that it did not form part of the common stock.

The expectation of a Messiah probably did form part of the common stock, because no one could read the prophets without noticing that expectation. But it was not a prominent element in the common stock, at least Ben Sira hardly mentions it; and when it did become prominent it was as a feature of the Apocalyptic development which was obviously an addition to the common stock.

The above may, it is hoped, be taken as a fairly true account of what were the main features of Judaism in the time of Ben Sira; and it should be observed that he was by no means a creative thinker. It is not as if he were setting forth a theology, or even an ethical system in the narrower sense of the word. He was a thoughtful and God-fearing man of his time, having something to offer for the guidance of his countrymen, and in saying it he spoke from the standpoint of a religion such as has been described; and did so not because that was in any way peculiar to himself, but because it was in a general way the religion of his time and his people.

If we ask what is there in Ben Sira's book which can be regarded as characteristic of himself, we shall find it perhaps in the way in which he enlarges on the various subjects of his discourse. Especially is this the case with the ethical maxims, which illustrate both the likeness and the difference between his book and Proverbs. He says that he was a gleaner after the older teachers of wisdom, and no doubt intended by that to indicate especially the book of Proverbs. And as the author, or final editor, of Proverbs had done, so Ben Sira collected maxims from many sources as he found opportunity. But he was not content with merely collecting them, he took them as subjects for his own reflection, and his book is mainly, as it would seem, the outcome of such reflections. If he lectured to young men in his Beth ha-Midrash, as he seems to indicate that he did (li. 23, 29), though perhaps ' lectured ' is too modern a word, then his book probably contains what he taught them, and, in its practical counsels, what he most desired to teach them. It is in these personal reflections that we come nearest to the thought of Ben Sira, and to such originality as he possessed; and it is perhaps because of this impress of his personality upon a subject otherwise mainly conventional that his book made so deep an impression as it did upon later generations of readers. As is well known, his book was read and quoted in Rabbinical circles for centuries after his time, although it was not included in the Canon of Holy Scripture; and it passed into Christian use through its inclusion in the Alexandrine Canon, and acquired in the Church such high regard that it was called Ecclesiasticus, as being the Church book *par excellence*. In both cases the ground of approbation was the general quality of its teaching, but perhaps also the unconscious effect upon the readers of the influence of the man behind the book.

On the whole, Ben Sira may be taken as the representative of the common stock of Judaism on its ethical side, both in the wider and the stricter sense of the term. For him, Judaism meant the right conduct of life in obedience to God, and in his service. What was needed was not a speculative theory about God, but practical teaching how men should live as in the sight of God, men being such as he made them, and God being he who made them. Such teaching Ben Sira made it his purpose in life to give, and his book shows how he carried out his purpose. There is not much that is new or striking* in the teaching he gave, and he did not claim to be one who opened out new paths. In the main, what may be called the theology and ethics of his book are such as are implied in the Canonical Scriptures on their higher side, such as would be naturally drawn from those scriptures by a reader to whom they were in their several ways the means of imparting divine truth. That everyone in his time would find there exactly what he found is not likely and is not here asserted; but that few would question or deny any important feature in his presentation of Judaism may be affirmed with reasonable certainty. But it should be remembered, especially by Christian scholars who usually are unaware of the fact, that there was not for Ben Sira or anyone else then any question of a creed meaning an authoritative statement of belief. To speak of the ' orthodox belief' of Ben Sira, as is done in the Oxford Sirach, is to present the whole subject from a wrong point of view. Ben Sira, if the above considerations are well founded, was in accord with the best thought of his time in regard to religion and its application to life; but the whole conception of a creed and of an orthodoxy lay outside the range of his thought, as it has lain outside the range of Judaism ever since, with only a few temporary exceptions.

On the strictly ethical side, Ben Sira's teaching on the main virtues and vices is in general accordance with that of the older Scriptures. He lays, no doubt, his own emphasis on particular points; but in its main features his ethics represent the common

---

* It is remarkable that in li. 10 he calls God ' my Father ', and does so with no hint that it was unusual to apply that term to God in a directly personal sense.

stock; and whatever considerable differences are presented by the contents of the various Apocryphal and Apocalyptic books in regard to other features, there is but little in regard to the specifically ethical teaching. Ben Sira may be said, with a good deal of truth, to represent Judaism as it was before the parting of the ways, the ways being those of Apocalyptic on the one hand and Rabbinic on the other. As the Rabbinical development, with its characteristic feature of halachah and haggadah, has been studied and set forth at length in the earlier part of this book, we shall how proceed to the study of the Apocalyptic development, as represented in the non-canonical literature.

CHAPTER IV

THE BOOK OF ENOCH

No better representative of the Apocalyptic literature could be found than the book of Enoch, in its complete form. It includes every type of Apocalyptic matter, and is, moreover, laid out on a larger scale than any other work of its kind. With the exception of Daniel it is, at all events in its earlier portions, the oldest Apocalyptic book now extant; and if Daniel gave the first vivid flash of the Apocalyptic illumination, Enoch showed how powerful and how far-reaching that illumination was, and to how much of what was dark and mysterious it could be applied. If Apocalyptic, for good and for evil, played a great part in the Judaism of its time, a considerable share in the influence which it exerted may fairly be claimed for the book of Enoch.

With the appearance of Apocalyptic we have the second main divergence from the common stock of the Jewish religion. The first was that indicated by the development of the interpretation of Torah along the Ezra-Pharisaic-Rabbinical line, and having for its most characteristic expression halachah and haggadah. This has been treated at length in Book II. We have, in Apocalyptic, a new divergence from the common stock in a quite different direction and leading to quite different results. But both developments are included within the range of Judaism, properly so called, and both have in common the ethical element, which is really fundamental in every type of Judaism. The two divergences did not take place at the same time. The one was made by Ezra and his successors, and had been going on for nearly three centuries before Apocalyptic appeared— except, of course, so far as there are traces and even broad hints of it in the later prophets. Of these, more will be said presently. Ben Sira may be said to stand at the parting of the ways, not merely because he wrote only a short time before the appearance of the book of Daniel, but because he represents what has been called the common stock, and shows hardly a trace of the divergence along the Ezra line, and none at all of that along the

Apocalyptic line. After his time the two divergent developments are clearly discernible, side by side and hardly, if ever, coming into contact, while both retain a connexion, through the ethical element, with the common stock. Such being the general state of the case, we have now to study Apocalyptic, and that in its most notable representative the book of Enoch.

The edition of the book, in the Oxford Pseudepigrapha, gives an elaborate analysis of its composite structure and varied contents, and leaves nothing undone to give the reader the means of understanding its teaching and significance. The present writer is quite incompetent to challenge the accuracy of the general exposition, even if he wished to do so, though he cannot agree with some of the conclusions which Dr. Charles draws from his study. He gratefully accepts Enoch as Dr. Charles has presented the book, and takes it as the basis of what he has himself to say.

Whatever the original Enoch may have contained, the book as finally edited may be regarded as a sort of compendium of Apocalyptic, in all its various types. Along with predictions, as of the final judgment, the overthrow of the Gentiles, and the like, it contains speculations of a quasi-scientific nature, relating to the heavenly bodies, thunder and lightning, winds and other physical phenomena. Also, descriptions of wonderful sights shown to Enoch, and strange places to which he was led by one or other of his angelic guides. The ethical element is by no means absent, and perhaps the whole purpose of the book is ethical, after a fashion; but the main interest of the writer, or writers, seems to be in the various mysteries which he is commissioned to disclose. Without these, his book would have lost most of its substance and nearly all its power to draw and hold the attention of the reader, as it certainly did.

Indeed, the sense of mystery is one of the main roots of Apocalyptic, as the prophetic literature is another. The study of the prophets would not of itself have produced Apocalyptic, although it was clearly an indispensable factor in that production. Other men had studied the prophets without arriving at anything like Apocalyptic. But the prophets had said many things hard to understand, and had foretold much that had not come to pass; while yet they had spoken in the name of the Lord, and his word could not have been without meaning:

' My word, which goeth forth out of my mouth shall not return unto me void, it shall accomplish that which I please ' (Isa. lv. 11). What could be the real meaning of that which the prophets had said? Evidently they had not spoken for their own time alone, if at all, but for some future time. When was that future time to be? And what would be the signs of it? Moreover, they had foretold a glorious future for Israel, and Israel had suffered and was still suffering various calamities, which were in sharp contrast with the glowing pictures of the prophets. But the prophets were dead and gone, and had left no explanation of what they had meant. Men of a later age must seek that explanation for themselves. The mystery of the prophets presented a challenge, as all mystery does; and Apocalyptic is the reaction to that challenge, the attempt to solve that mystery, on the lines and within the range of Jewish thought and speculation.

To approach a mystery with the purpose of discovering its meaning is to enter a region where thought is not controlled by reference to ascertained fact, and where statements can be made but cannot be verified. The inquirer in such a field may be fully convinced that he really has seen what he describes, in vision or symbol, and be fully assured that it shadows forth some divine reality; but he has no safeguard against his own power of imagination, no objective proof that he has not himself conjured up what he believes that he has seen. Moreover, when once he has got it into his mind that he is on the track of finding some deeper meaning than appears on the surface of the subject before him, he is at the mercy of the temptation to find clues even where they do not exist, and to read in the most innocent and trivial words the signs of a hidden truth. He may be quite aware of the danger, but he is powerless against it, and will not even know when he is yielding to it. Also, he may not be aware of the danger, and may in all good faith suppose that he is unravelling the mystery, while yet he is being carried along by his own imagination whithersoever it will.

Further, when he comes to put into words the substance of what he wishes to make known, to declare the meaning of the mystery, he has no standard by which to control his statements, or to regulate his expression of the truths he wishes to disclose. He is here again, and perhaps even more than before, at the

[213]

mercy of his imagination, for his task now is not to find what he shall say, but to devise the means of saying it. As he has learned what he has now to teach through mysterious hints, or, as he believes, through being shown what ordinary human intelligence could never have discerned, so it is natural and perhaps inevitable that he should set forth these things in symbols and figures, in forms which themselves are mysteries needing to be explained. All this can go along with the most complete sincerity on the part of the writer of Apocalpytic, and there is no need to impute conscious deception to any of them, certainly not to the various authors of Enoch. But it had one result, or, at all events, it probably had. Such a writer would not write in his own name, for if he did he would introduce a jarring note into his work. The whole of what he puts before his readers is, as he regards it, a disclosure of what is hidden from the ordinary man, and can only be presented in a form congenial to its nature. If the writer were to give his own name, and thus proclaim himself an ordinary man, living in such a place and known to his neighbours, he would lay himself open to the questions, 'How did he come to know all these things?' What is the evidence for them? Who is he to set himself up for a revealer? To such questions there could be no reply, while yet the writer could be quite convinced of the truth of what he had written. It was therefore entirely in keeping with his subject and his treatment of it that he should present it under the name of some ancient seer or sage, as containing what had been revealed to him in some superhuman manner. And thus we get to such a book as Enoch, and all the other later Apocalyptic books.

If the foregoing gives a correct account of what may be called the psychology of an Apocalyptic writer, it may throw some light on the psychology of the reader of Apocalypse, and may explain how the effect of such reading continued through long periods of time. The reader of Apocalypse had before him not the mystery at first hand, but a book which purported to disclose the mystery, a book which appealed to his sense of curiosity, which offered a challenge to his understanding, and, much more important, which purported to make known to him some of the divine realities, ' the deep things of God,' those things 'which eye hath not seen, nor ear heard, neither have entered into the heart of man to conceive'. A book which could offer so much, and offer it under the sanction of some revered name, made a powerful appeal, which to some types of mind was irresistible. It was not Canonical Scripture, certainly, but it was very far from being just ordinary literature. It is not strange that Apocalyptic in general, and Enoch in particular, as its most splendid representative, should have exercised a powerful influence upon many Jewish readers, nor that that influence should be so plainly traceable as it is in the earlier Christian writings.

The appeal of Apocalyptic was fundamentally an appeal to the sense of mystery, and especially of mystery in religion. But that was not by any means its only appeal. The religion in question was the Jewish religion, and the Jewish religion included what had been revealed to the prophets and declared by them as the word of the Lord. And the prophets had foretold a glorious future for Israel, had spoken of a great day of the Lord, of a victory over all the powers of evil, a final overthrow of all who at present oppressed the chosen people, of a Messiah whom God would send, of a kingdom which should be set up, of a new heaven and earth where only righteousness should dwell. Apocalyptic offered an answer to the question: What had become of all these?

If this was the task of Apocalyptic in general, it certainly was so in the case of Enoch. That book offers an answer which applied to all the subjects just named. It had much to say about the ' last things ' and about the Messiah who was to be the divine agent in bringing them to pass. It could describe the heavenly and the infernal regions in great detail, and give the names and explain the functions of many of the angels. It elaborates the story of how the angels fell, and brought evil into the world. It is never weary of contrasting the righteous with the wicked, and of denouncing woe on the latter while promising bliss to the former. It sketches the history of the chosen people under the figures of white bulls and other animals, whose actions as described it is very hard to take seriously, but which presumably the writer meant to be taken so. It contains a long excursus on astronomy, of great interest in itself apart from its relevance to Apocalyptic, but which would not have been included unless it had been in accordance with the writer's purpose.

It is evident that the writers of Enoch were concerned to lay stress on one aspect of Judaism which differed widely from that represented in the Wisdom literature and no less from that represented in the teaching of the Ezra line. They emphasised the sovereignty of God, his glory and splendour and almighty power, and connected closely with that the hope of deliverance from the evil of the world. The problem was urgent because the evil was great, and there seemed no remedy through human agency. The way of escape from its crushing weight was by dwelling on the thought of God who was not only above all evil, but who alone could, and surely would, put an end to it. It is this underlying conviction which gives deep and serious meaning to the book of Enoch, in spite of all its extravagance of expression, its often grotesque and trivial symbolism. Or to put it more accurately, it is when we understand that this underlying conviction was in the minds of the writers, and that they had a deep and serious meaning in writing what they did, however little they succeeded in expressing it, it is only then that we can do justice to their work, and refrain from throwing it aside, as the natural man is tempted to do.

Recognising then to the full what the writers of Enoch aimed at, the necessity which they felt of making known the faith that was in them, we can understand that the book should have great influence upon religious thought, in some developments at all events of the Judaism of their own time and later. Yet it is remarkable that their work, elaborate as it was, accomplished so little of the kind which might fairly be expected from a revelation of hidden truth. The writers of Enoch did not really know more than the prophets had known in regard to the 'last things'. They filled in the outline with a mass of detail, but the outline, the very bare outline, remained as the prophets had drawn it. The Enoch writers drew gorgeous pictures of the courts of heaven, spoke of the myriads of angels, the exceeding majesty of him who ruled them all, but they added nothing to the thought of God as the greatest of the prophets had left it. Certainly the prophets had had no glimpse, or no clear vision, of the future life, and certainly the writers of Enoch had much to say about it. But again, only by way of embellishing an idea already there, not by way of adding to it. That which is characteristic of the writers of Enoch is their elaboration of detail, whereby they persuaded themselves that they really were carrying on further what they had received from the prophets. But the prophets, so far as they had spoken of an ideal future, had done so out of the same glowing faith whereby they had become prophets at all. Their prediction was not on its own account, so to speak, but was one ray from the light which burned within them, and shone over the whole field of their thought and their work. The writers of Enoch were not prophets, and prediction in their hands became not a creative, but a merely imitative function. They attempted, in all good faith, to kindle again the light which had gone out when the prophets ceased to function. The will to do so was there, but not the power; and the difference between Isaiah and Enoch is apparent to everyone.

It has been said above that one main theme, if not the main theme, of Enoch is the sovereignty of God, his unapproachable majesty, his almighty power. Almost everything in the book eventually turns on that. But here again the subject is not really carried further than the prophets had carried it. And not only so, but the conception of God presented in Enoch differs considerably from that held by the prophets, and the difference marks a decline rather than an advance from the earlier to the later. Perhaps the highest point reached by the prophetic conception is that which is expressed in the words: ' For thus saith the high and lofty One that inhabiteth Eternity, whose name is Holy, I dwell in the high and holy place, with him also that is of a contrite and humble spirit, to revive the spirit of the humble and to revive the heart of the contrite ones ' (Isa. lvii. 15). The writers of Enoch may be said to have taken the first half of this utterance and left out the second; and not merely left it out, but made it impossible. They have piled up epithets and imagery to enhance the sublimeness of the thought of God, and in doing so they have put him at a further and further height above the range of human affairs, and sympathy with human needs. It is impossible to imagine the God of Enoch ' dwelling with him that is of a contrite spirit ', or with anyone else. He is surrounded by hosts of ministering angels, and by chosen archangels of highest rank; and it is the climax of Enoch's vision that he is led through these hosts who fill the splendid halls of heaven, into the presence-chamber itself and stands face to face with God. Whether all the elaborate description really serves its purpose better than the few words of Isaiah may well be questioned; but it leaves no room for the thought that God is near to every one of his children in personal sympathy. It is accordingly from Apocalyptic in general and Enoch in particular that Christians have usually drawn the conclusion that the God of Judaism was a lofty and distant Deity far removed from contact with mankind. A conclusion which by itself falsifies the claim made on behalf of Apocalyptic that it was in its time the true representative of Judaism. For all the other types of Judaism protest against it, and none more so than the type which finally survived.

As compared with the prophetic doctrine of God the Apocalyptic doctrine is not an advance towards a higher conception, but the exaggeration of one aspect at the expense and total loss of another. And even the aspect which is exaggerated loses rather than gains by the efforts made to indicate it by symbolic imagery. That perhaps is a matter of taste and feeling, in regard to which opinions may well differ. But the effect of the distortion and mutilation of the doctrine of God was not confined to that doctrine alone. It can be traced clearly in the ethics of Enoch, in more than one direction. By the exaltation of God, and the corresponding withdrawal of him from human contact, the ordinary distinctions of ethics between the several virtues and vices are lost sight of, as they are merged in the one broad distinction between the righteous and the wicked. Of ethics in the sense of the right conduct of life in the service of God, the writers of Enoch have hardly anything to say. They regard human life not in its duration, but at its conclusion. They do not offer counsel to men how they should live their lives from year to year; they tell what will happen when the ordinary course of life is suddenly brought to an end by the final judgment, and when it is too late to do whatever may have been neglected. If at that last hour a man is found among the righteous he is sure of future bliss. If he is among the wicked, he will be hurled to destruction. There is accordingly no place in Enoch for anything more than a general ethical basis, so far as specific conduct is concerned, though no doubt the writers of the book would accept the position already described in what has been called the common stock in its main features. But however that may be, it was not with the ethics of ordinary life that they were chiefly concerned. And if it be said that theirs were the ethics of a crisis, it would be truer to say that what they present is ethics as modified by a crisis. It is not that they teach what a man should do when the last judgment is at hand, it is that they assume that he will behave in a particular way when that time comes. The last judgment will involve, amongst other things, the overthrow of the wicked, amongst whom are included the Gentiles, also the kings and the mighty. The righteous will be saved, and will exult in the fate of the wicked. Thus, Enoch xcvi. 1: ' Be hopeful ye righteous; for suddenly shall the sinners perish before you; and ye shall have lordship over them according to your desires'. And again, xcviii. 12: ' Woe to you that love the deeds of unrighteousness. . . . Know that ye shall be delivered into the hands of the righteous, and they shall cut off your necks and slay you, and have no mercy on you '. And again, lxii. 11 (of the kings and the mighty): ' He will deliver them to the angels for punishment, to execute vengeance on them, because they have oppressed His children and His elect; and they shall be for a spectacle for the righteous and for His elect: they shall rejoice over them, because the wrath of the Lord of Spirits resteth on them, and his sword is drunk with their blood'. These passages are so far characteristic of Enoch that they are not decisively contradicted anywhere in the book; the writer indeed does not seem in any instance to realise that his words call for remark or excuse. They would be, no doubt, excusable, if not natural, in the case of a man driven to desperation by persecution and torture; but right and good they are not, by any ethical standard. They are the utterance of a perverted mind, and, what is much worse, they tend to rouse passionate hatred and thirst for vengeance in other minds. Ethically, they are rank poison, and a book which contains them, as an integral part of its teaching, carries its own condemnation with it. To attempt to justify them on the plea of extreme provocation is beside the mark. A better plea would be that the writers of Enoch could find, in the book of Psalms, Scripture warrant for hatred of enemies and thirst for vengeance. But two blacks do not make a white; and ethically the vindictive passages in the Psalms are

[219]

just as deserving of condemnation as those in Enoch. Judged by the ethical standard already reached in the time when Enoch was written, as shown in the Scripture teaching at its highest, the vindictiveness displayed in Enoch is a serious lapse, and the apparent unconsciousness of the writers that anything was wrong in this respect only shows how the ethical sense was blinded by passion.

Another feature of the ethics of Enoch, if there is anything left which can be called ethics, is the absence of any appeal to the sense of responsibility in the individual. He is not called upon to do anything, in regard to the great events described in the book. What is done is done by angels, or the Messiah, or God himself. Man's only part is to stand still and behold, and, if he is righteous, rejoice in the outcome of it all. It is taken for granted that the righteous have walked in the ways of the Lord, obeyed his commandments, etc., but even this more as a qualification for being on the right side in the day of judgment than as good for its own sake. Here, again, is a result of the distorted theology which laid all the stress on the sovereignty of God and left out all human contact with him. The victory over evil, with which the overthrow of the Gentiles, the kings, and the mighty was identified, was to be accomplished by the power of God and not by the ' patience in well doing ' of men who served him. To endure to the end was not to ' fight the good fight' by the present help of God, but to hold out till the wrath of God suddenly smote the enemy down and swept him away. The promises of victory of which Enoch, like almost every Apocalyptic book is full, were never fulfilled. And behind them all is the haunting note of despair, as if in truth God was not called in to save until there was no hope anywhere else.

Looking back on the whole book we can easily understand that it exerted a strong influence upon Jewish and, later, upon Christian minds. It appealed to the sense of mystery, it re-echoed and amplified the predictions of the prophets, it made no demands on the conscience and the will, it gratified the sense of curiosity, it gave the imagination plenty of diversion, and under colour of religion it opened the way for some of the worst passions of human nature. Whatever excuse may be pleaded, on the ground of the circumstances of the time and the weakness of human nature, may be readily accepted, but only as excuse, not as justification. Enoch is a great book in its way, but its way was not that of the prophets whom it professed to follow, nor of the Torah which it hardly mentions. It was a product of its time, embodying some of the worst along with some, very few, of the better elements of the Judaism in which it grew up; and the relation of Apocalyptic in general, and Enoch in particular, to the true essential Judaism can only be fitly compared to the relation of the diseased and misshapen branch to the sound trunk of the tree on which it grew.

CHAPTER V

THE BOOK OF JUBILEES

LIKE Enoch, the book entitled the Book of Jubilees was never included in the Canon, but nevertheless exercised considerable influence upon some types of Jewish mind. Certainly it is one of the most important of the Pseudepigrapha, not only because of its length, but because of its contents. It does not throw by any means as much light upon the post-exilic Judaism as Charles claims for it (Introd. to Oxford Jubilees, opening lines); indeed, it is very defective in that respect, but it does give some light which is hardly to be found in the Canonical Scripture, and still less in the Rabbinical literature. It is welcome, accordingly, as a means of enlarging the picture of the Judaism of the two pre-Christian centuries, and adding one more to its many colours. But it is easy to attribute an importance to Jubilees which may prove to be due more to its character, as a comparatively little-known book recently brought to the notice of scholars, than to any outstanding excellence of its own. There is not much in it which marks originality in the writer, though there is one feature at least, as will be shown presently; and its ethical teaching, though of a higher quality than that of Enoch, is mainly that of the common stock.

The date of the book is placed by Charles between the years 109 and 105 B.C. on the strength of allusions to events and persons in the reign of John Hyrcanus, who died in the latter year. It is seldom that a date can be defined within such narrow limits, but the present writer does not challenge it. Whether the author wrote in Palestine or Egypt there is nothing to show. If he lived and wrote in Palestine at the date assigned to the book, he might fairly be expected to show signs of a closer personal contact with the religious and political events of the time. His allusions to them, if they are allusions, seem rather to indicate an observer living at a distance, yet near enough, as he would be in Egypt, to know what was going on in Palestine.

[223]

He is usually said to have been a Pharisee. Charles says he was 'unquestionably a Pharisee' (Oxford Jubilees, *loc. cit.*), and most scholars have accepted that opinion. That this opinion is open to very serious question will at once appear from what has been already said as to the relation of the Pharisees to the non-canonical literature generally (see above, pp. 177 f., 191 f.). The considerations there put forward apply to Jubilees with the same force as they do to all the Apocrypha and Pseudepigrapha, and they need not be repeated. But there is one feature in Jubilees which does seem to give some little support to the view that it was the work of a Pharisee, though it really amounts to nothing after all. It was this, presumably, which led Charles to assert that the writer of Jubilees was 'unquestionably a Pharisee'. When compared with other non-canonical books, Jubilees has a great deal to say about Torah, being indeed a sort of enlargement of the book of Genesis. Whatever the intention of the author may have been, he could not have written his book at all unless Torah had meant a very great deal to him. So much is beyond dispute. But apart from that, there is no single trace of characteristic Pharisaic treatment of the subject. There is nothing about Halachah; from one end of the book to the other, the word is never mentioned. Charles refers in his notes (e.g. xv. 14, and Introd., pp. 6, 9) to the older Halachah and the younger; but the author does not. The only thing that he does is to refer to matters, e.g. Sabbath, Feast Days, etc., which in the Pharisaic schools were made the subject of halachic definition. The opinions, even the very decided opinions, which the writer expresses on these and kindred subjects, are not halachah; and, if he had been a Pharisee, he would have been quite aware of that, and would as a matter of course have expressed himself in a wholly different manner. He knew nothing about halachah or haggadah either, for his book is not haggadah and ought not be called so; and even if it were, no Pharisee would for a moment admit that haggadah by itself was sufficient for its purpose. Very possibly, if he had been a Pharisee, he would have taught, as haggadah, some of what appears in his book. But he would have changed the form, and he would not have written a line of it.

As for the prominence of Torah in Jubilees, that is no

argument at all for a Pharisaic author. Whatever may have been the case before the Maccabean Revolt, the result of that Revolt was the victory of Torah, and no one could do other than acknowledge the Torah, in speech or writing, if he had anything to say on religious matters. But while the Torah was thus the common property of the whole Jewish community, it was regarded differently by men of different types of mind, from the Pharisees at one extreme to the Sadducees at the other, including all between, and there were many in between, whom it is only confusing to identify with either the Pharisees or the Sadducees. The writer of Jubilees certainly had a deep veneration for the Torah, as the supreme revelation hitherto made to Israel; but that did not prevent him from trying to supplement the Torah, as if what it contained was not sufficient. The way in which he did this was not at all the way in which the Pharisees dealt with Torah, and they would have repudiated it; as in effect they did, since the book of Jubilees was never recognised by them, though probably they knew nothing about it.

It is in his treatment of Torah that the writer showed his originality; and he did so by applying to the ancient and venerable book the newly discovered method of Apocalyptic. He had before him the example of Enoch and, of course, Daniel. These two books are Apocalyptic in the full sense of the term, i.e. they profess to disclose the 'last things', the hidden future; and Jubilees has very little to say about the 'last things'. But, in both Daniel and Enoch, the hidden mysteries are revealed by angels at the command of God to some man commissioned to receive them. The essence of Apocalyptic is the disclosure of mystery by superhuman means, and its subsequent record by a human agent. The reference to future events is not an essential element in Apocalyptic, although it would be chiefly in regard to the 'last things' that the desire to know would be most strongly felt and the inducement to write Apocalypses would be greatest. Jubilees is rightly regarded as an Apocalyptic book because it professes to disclose by supernatural means mysteries which could not be, or had not been, made known to ordinary men; and it does this under the form of communications made by an angel to a man—in this case, Moses. As an example of Apocalyptic, Jubilees is so far an original book, and even a daring book, because it applies the Apocalyptic method

Q

in a new way, and to a subject which no writer till then had ventured to approach. In the case of Daniel and Enoch, the writers put what they had to say in the mouth of men of venerable antiquity but of whom nothing was known, except what was contained in the books bearing their names. But in Jubilees the revelations are made to Moses; and Moses, according to the common belief, had written the whole Torah, which was known more or less to everyone in the Jewish community. Here, therefore, was an attempt to add to what Moses had said, under the form of a new revelation, and to offer it to readers who were well aware of what he had said. This again shows that a Pharisee could not have written the book. For the Pharisees had their theory of the Oral Tradition, as fully explained above (Bk. II, Ch. III, p. 63 ff.); and by means of that theory they were able to supplement the written Torah in various ways. According to that theory the Oral Tradition had been handed down from the days of Moses, always from one human teacher (or group of teachers) to another. To suggest that a new disclosure had been made when Jubilees appeared, for that is what the appearance of the book implied, would be wholly out of keeping with the Pharisaic theory, apart from the certainty that the Pharisees would not admit the superhuman mechanism by which the alleged revelation was made. The author of Jubilees doubtless felt, as the Pharisees felt, that there was need to supplement the written Torah; but his method of doing so was quite different from theirs. He chose the method of Apocalyptic, by which he could declare what he wanted to declare as a message straight from heaven instead of deriving it as a conclusion from the ordinary working of human minds. That is the besetting sin of all Apocalyptic writing; and the saving of trouble which it thus affords to the reader is no doubt one reason why such writing has been so popular.

In Jubilees (i. 1) the disclosures are described as having been made to Moses, when he went up to Sinai to receive the Torah; certainly the most natural occasion and place for such communications to have been made. Moses is informed of many things which had taken place from the Creation to his own time, and also of things which were to happen later. Putting aside these latter for the moment, and admitting that the purpose of the writer was to tell at greater length what had already been written in Genesis, the question at once arises why, if Moses was told all these things on Sinai, did he not write them in his book? Why should he have written only what is contained in the Canonical Genesis, when he already knew all the other things? And if he did not write them then, why should it have been left to the author of Jubilees to disclose the fact that Moses had been aware of them all the time? Probably most readers to whom Apocalyptic is their favourite reading would not be troubled by such questions, for Apocalyptic appeals more to the imagination than to the reason. But the questions disclose one of the weaknesses of Apocalyptic, at all events as illustrated in Jubilees. That the author should not have written in his own name is, as has been shown (p. 214), a probable result of his writing in the Apocalyptic manner at all. But it is curious that in the case of Jubilees no reputed author is named. It is true that the titles ' Apocalypse of Moses ' and ' Testament of Moses ' are found in some late writers to indicate our book (see Oxford Jubilees, Introd., p. 2); but its oldest titles are either Jubilees or The Little Genesis, and Moses is not mentioned. After all, Moses is not as prominent in Jubilees as Enoch is in the book so called. He makes no journeys in heaven or hell, sees no wonderful sights, describes no strange beasts; all he has to do is to listen to the angel and write down his words, or else to receive what the angel has written out for him. The only reason for bringing him in at all would seem to be the writer's desire to put his own improved version of Genesis under the shelter of the name of the original author.

Another question which naturally occurs to the reader of Jubilees is: Why did the writer confine himself to the book of Genesis? If his purpose were to supplement the Torah, there was quite as much scope for doing so in the other four books of the Pentateuch, and what Charles calls his halachah would find a more suitable place in connexion with one or other of the legal passages. To re-write the whole of the Pentateuch on the same scale as that applied to Genesis in Jubilees would be a very serious undertaking, and the result would be a book so large that very few could be expected to read it. If the writer of Jubilees did not go beyond Genesis (and a small portion of Exodus) we may fairly take it that so much and no more was

[227]

sufficient for his purpose. Clearly he must have had some
purpose in view, but it is not at once apparent what his purpose was. His general point of view is that of one who wished
to mark the separation between Jew and Gentile very strongly,
and to bring out the fact that the former are under the special
favour of God while the Gentiles displease him by their evil
lives. Like all Apocalyptic writers he promises prosperity and
happiness to the former and denounces final destruction on
the latter. A writer who lived in the reign of John Hyrcanus
would not have to look far for material wherewith to illustrate
the contrast between Jew and Gentile; and there are plenty of
indications in his book that he knew a good deal of what
Gentiles, i.e. in his case Syrian or Egyptian Greeks, and the
Hellenisers who imitated them, were like when seen at close
quarters. Yet, if his purpose had been mainly controversial,
it would be reasonable to expect that he would have written
at greater length and with more severity upon the points of
greatest contrast between Jew and Gentile; also, that he would
hardly have taken up so much space in his book with matters
which were only of speculative interest. In the absence of any
explanation, for he gives none and, in fact, as an Apocalyptist
could not give one, we can only guess at the reasons which led
him to write his book. To the present writer his book gives the
impression that the author's purpose was more speculative than
practical, that what he set out to do in the first instance was
to try the experiment of applying the Apocalyptic method to
the Torah, that he found in the book of Genesis the best
subject for that treatment, and that in working out his plan he
could provide all the opportunity he needed for putting forth
his own views upon particular subjects. These particular
subjects would include those in regard to which he thought
that special warning ought to be given against laxity or disobedience, e.g. Sabbath, circumcision, festivals, mixed marriages and the like. On these points he could, and did, supplement the Canonical Torah as he thought the case required;
but at the same time he supplemented it by detailed information which was nothing more than the fruits of his own
speculation. Not only the name by which his book is known,
but the plan on which it is laid out shows the remarkable
interest which he took in the calendar. His whole book is

a record of the events from the Creation to the time of Moses arranged in periods of 49 years, i.e. successive Jubilees; and he rather rashly committed himself to a theory of the length of the year as a basis for the Calendar, which would have proved utterly impracticable. The year was to be 364 days, neither more nor less (vi. 32-35). On the whole, he may be perhaps not unfairly described as a man of no considerable force of character, and not much originality, holding rather pronounced opinions on religious subjects, strongly opposed to Hellenism, though less fierce than the writers of Enoch, and finding much mental satisfaction in the easy vagueness of Apocalypse.

It remains to describe the ethical teaching contained in Jubilees, a task which will not take long after what has already been said in regard to Enoch. Because in all Apocalyptic ethics there are certain common features, and the only difference between one Apocalypse and another is in regard to subsidiary matters.

Jubilees is ethical mainly because the Torah (including Genesis) is ethical, so far as it gives teaching concerning the right conduct of life in the sight of God. Practically all the commandments in Jubilees are the reinforcement or enlargement of what was already commanded in Genesis, or the other books of the Torah. Thus the motive, the duty of doing the will of God, is already supplied, though Jubilees expressly mentions it (xxi. 23). That the will is free to obey or disobey is indicated by saying (v. 13) that the way in which each man should go is written in the heavenly tablets, and judgment is also written there against any man who does not walk in the way prescribed for him. Temptation to depart from it, i.e. to sin, is mainly due to the agency of evil spirits under their prince Mastema. The whole duty of man is expressed generally in the requirement that he should be righteous as opposed to wicked; and righteousness includes, besides unspecified virtues, abstinence from fornication (and sexual impurity generally), from the eating of blood, and from strife between those who ought to love one another. It also includes strict observances of the times and seasons appointed for the festivals, of the manner of celebrating these and of the sacrifices which are to be brought. Worship of idols is, of course, strictly forbidden. Disobedience or disregard of all these things is the wickedness

[229]

of the Gentiles, and the writer draws the line between the righteous and the wicked with no faltering hand. He holds up to the righteous the promise of endless prosperity, and declares the doom of the wicked to go down into Sheol; but he does not gloat over their fate after the savage manner of Enoch.

Since Jubilees goes over the same ground as Genesis, the author is obliged to deal with incidents which are repulsive to the conscience, such as Jacob's deception of Isaac, and Reuben's sin with Bilhah, and that of Judah with Tamar. We have seen above (p. 151) that the Rabbis were faced with the same difficulty in reconciling such things with their own moral sense and their own higher ethical standard. They only saved the rights of the moral law by extravagant explaining away of the objectionable features of these stories. Their explanations were worthless, as they probably knew, but they would not condone the offences themselves. The author of Jubilees felt exactly the same difficulty. His moral sense would not allow him to justify the conduct of the offenders in the above cases, and he took refuge in special pleading just as the Rabbis did. The reason in each case was the same, viz., that these incidents were recorded in the Torah, by the direction of God. The most that Jubilees could do, by the help of the Apocalyptic method which was not at the command of the Rabbis, was to declare that the sin of Reuben and Judah was recorded in heaven and severely condemned there, though finally the wrongdoers were pardoned; and, in the case of Jacob and Isaac, to explain that what really made Isaac think that Jacob was Esau was a divine dispensation prompting him to that belief (xxvi. 18). Alike in the case of the Rabbis and that of Jubilees, the attempted explanation is worthless in itself, but it shows how the ethical standard of both was far higher than that implied in the original stories. For the present purpose that is what matters, and all that matters. On the whole, there is nothing of outstanding importance in the ethics of Jubilees, nor much of direct ethical teaching ; but, as compared with Enoch, the ethical basis or background of Jubilees is of a finer quality and shows a deeper insight. The common stock forms the substratum of both, but in Jubilees the author is more clearly aware of the common stock than can be said in the case of Enoch.

We shall consider next a work in which, along with the elements to be found in all Apocalyptic works, some ethical features are present in greater strength and purity than in any other of the non-canonical writings. This is the book known as the Testaments of the Twelve Patriarchs.

CHAPTER VI

THE TESTAMENTS OF THE TWELVE PATRIARCHS

As compared with Enoch and Jubilees, the book bearing the title of the Testaments of the Twelve Patriarchs contains very little that can be called Apocalyptic, only just enough to warrant its inclusion in that class of literature. The greater part of the book is purely ethical, and that of a very high order; so much so that it stands out from and above all the other non-canonical books at present under consideration. Whoever wrote it, and however it came to be written, it is a noble book.

For the purpose of the present study, the edition and commentary in the Oxford Apocrypha will be made use of. The analysis there given enables the reader to distinguish between the original book and later additions to it, partly Jewish and to some small extent Christian. Substantially the book is the work of one writer, who probably wrote in Hebrew, and seems to have been contemporary with the author of Jubilees, i.e. living at or near the end of the reign of John Hyrcanus. The assertion that he was a Pharisee may be at once dismissed, on the grounds given above in relation to the authors of Enoch and Jubilees, which need not be repeated. (See above, pp. 191-4, 224.)

That the chief purpose of the book was to give ethical teaching seems evident on the face of it. Not only would there be hardly anything left if the passages containing such teaching were removed, but it is in these passages that one seems to be most clearly aware of the personality of the writer. The Apocalyptic matter is, so to speak, common form, and hardly does more than provide a setting for the rest. If the Apocalyptic matter were left out, the absence of it would not detract from the value of the book any more than it does from the book of Ben Sira, nor would that absence be regarded in either case as an imperfection which would need to be explained.

The question why Apocalyptic is absent from Ben Sira and present in Testaments cannot be definitely answered, but is

worth considering nevertheless. In Ben Sira's time the Apocalyptic method had not, so far as is known, been made use of in
literature. Daniel is the earliest example of it, and Ben Sira
wrote before the appearance of Daniel. Whether he would have
used that method if he had known of it, is a question impossible
to answer. But the author of Testaments wrote at a time when
that method was known, and when two great examples of its
use had already been given, in Enoch and Jubilees. The writers
of Enoch had applied the method to the prophetical literature,
with very considerable effect. The author of Jubilees found that
it could be applied to the Torah, with effect no less remarkable.
It is conceivable, though it cannot be proved, that the writer of
Testaments wrote his book by way of trying whether the method
could also be applied to the Wisdom literature, the only
main division of the Canonical Scriptures not as yet brought
within its range. The Wisdom books were, on the face of them,
mainly concerned with ethical teaching; so are the Testaments.
These indeed carry forward the teaching of the Wisdom literature in direct succession, and carry it to a height never reached
before. The Apocalyptic method would not add anything to
the substance of the teaching to be given, but it would perhaps
afford a better means of presenting it, and increase its power of
persuasion, which, of course, was what the writer desired.

Instead of giving his teaching in his own name, as Ben Sira
had done, would it not have greater effect if it were given under
the names of men of ancient times, and were represented as
handed down from remote antiquity? If this thought were in
the mind of the writer, it was a happy inspiration to take as the
exponents of his teaching the twelve Patriarchs, and to make
each of them in turn discourse on the virtue or vice most
conspicuous in his own life. This is almost the only use which
the writer makes of the Apocalyptic method. The dying words of
the Patriarchs were supposed to have been treasured up by their
sons, and each of the Testaments begins with the words, ' The
copy of the words of, etc.', as if the writer of the book meant
to indicate that they were to be found in ancient writings, and,
presumably, that he had read them there. But it is worth noting
that no one is named as the person to whom this knowledge
was imparted. Apocalyptic is here reduced to its smallest
dimensions, and hardly extends beyond a few passages in which

one or another of the patriarchs foretells the future of his sons, especially the appearance of the Messiah in the tribe of Levi. These and similar details are interesting historically, but they have little bearing on the ethical quality of the book, and may be passed over for our present purpose. Yet one remark may perhaps be not unfairly made, that the Apocalyptic spirit and the ethical spirit do not get on well together. Where the Apocalyptic spirit is the dominant factor, as in Enoch, the ethical spirit is weak, and shows itself in perverted forms—hatred, thirst for vengeance, fierce national pride, and the like. Where the ethical spirit is strong, the Apocalyptic spirit is feeble and finds little to do. The meaning of which is that Apocalyptic in itself is not really ethical at all, however passionately in earnest its exponents were. To suppose that it is ethical is part of the self-deception to which all Apocalyptic writers and many of their readers are liable.

The writer of Testaments set out apparently to give a comprehensive view of the chief virtues and vices with which an ordinary man is concerned in the living of his life; and the ingenious device of connecting his teaching with no less than twelve conspicuous examples allowed him ample scope for his exposition. The following are the virtues and vices on which he chiefly dwells: Deceit; fornication (T. Reuben, and often); jealousy and envy (T. Simeon); sincerity and love of Torah (T. Levi); lust and drunkenness, love of money (T. Judah); singleness of heart, love to God and one's neighbour (T. Issachar); kindness to one's neighbour, compassion to all, including animals (T. Zebulon); lying and anger (T. Dan); prudence and order in doing the works of God (T. Naphtali); hatred and the spirit of love (T. Gad); the two ways (T. Asher); chastity and also brotherly love (T. Joseph); fear of God and love of one's neighbour (T. Benjamin).

It is probably true that the author of Testaments had closely studied the Canonical Scriptures; it would be only natural that he should do so. But he certainly went, in some directions, far beyond anything he could find there, and reached a height which none of the prophets or the Wisdom writers had ever attained to. The influence of the study of the Scriptures upon a devout and thoughtful mind is not confined to mere imitation, but is the means of stimulating such a mind so that with deeper insight and clearer vision it perceives truths (in this case ethical truths) which the older teachers had failed to discover or had been unable to express. The author of Testaments was in this respect original, a very notable man in his time, whose name posterity would have been glad to know and honour, if it had been possible. Why he should have his credit distributed amongst a supposed school of writers, as Charles suggests (Oxford Testaments, p. 293) is not apparent. ' The early school of the Hasidim ' (*ibid.*) is a fiction, so far as any positive evidence goes. And what is said in the same paragraph about Pharisaism is equally unfounded, if the considerations put forward in Book II of the present volume are accepted. It is not in the least certain that the author of Testaments was a Hasid at all; and it is surely fairer to take him simply on his own account, without going out of the way to make another hasty identification. He wrote his book, and gave in it a treasure of noble teaching, one conspicuous illustration of what Judaism could produce at its best. Whether there were other men like him in his time we do not know, certainly none who left such a mark as he has left. And he should be regarded as one who in himself and in his own right helped to make up the complex structure of Judaism as it was in the age to which he belonged.

If we compare the ethical teaching given in the Testaments with that contained in Proverbs and in Ben Sira we shall notice at once a striking difference. In the two older books there is a strong element of worldly wisdom in the counsels given, whether to avoid vice or to practise virtue. Ben Sira in this respect stands higher than Proverbs, but he has plenty of it. With both of them, vice is foolish, whatever else it may be. Virtue is a form of wisdom, and wisdom is intellectual quite as much as it is moral, or moral because fundamentally intellectual. In the Testaments there is hardly a trace of this view. Vice is condemned not because it is foolish, but because it is wrong; it is the fruit not of the misguided intellect, but of the corrupt heart. Virtue, in like manner, proceeds from a pure heart, one which is turned to God with the single desire to do his will. Whether it is prudent to be virtuous is a question which does not arise in the Testaments, and is never discussed there. The author does not lay out his teaching on the lines of a system of ethics, and his selection of particular virtues and vices for special treatment depended to some extent upon the need for connecting them with one or other of the Patriarchs. But, even within the lines of this rather artificial arrangement, he has managed to find room for a fairly wide survey of human nature in regard to virtue and vice. Though he laid down no general principle as the basis of his treatment, we shall perhaps not go far wrong if we assume that he started from the primary truth that man was created in the image and likeness of God, and drew from that truth the inference that the likeness must consist in spiritual qualities and in actions which are in harmony with the will of God. Thus, virtue would be such a condition of mind or such action as expresses the likeness between man and God, while vice would be such condition of mind or such action as distorts that likeness or denies it. In the case alike of virtue and vice the will is implicated, because man is free to choose between them, and knows that he ought to choose virtue that so he may realise in some degree his likeness to God.

If this was the real starting point of the author of the Testaments, it would account not only for his treatment of specific virtues and vices, but also for the broad humane spirit which pervades his book. If all men are made in the image of God, they are spiritually akin to each other, and for that reason virtue includes brotherly love, kindness, sympathy, pity, and forgiveness. Vice, in like manner, includes deceit, hatred, lying, cruelty, anger as well as lust. In all these, both virtues and vices, it is not merely a question of the individual realising (or denying) his own likeness to God, but also of respecting (or disregarding) that of his fellow men to God. Whether the foregoing be the true explanation of what was in the mind of our author, it is certain that in his teaching he strikes a far higher note than had been sounded before, except by those who were developing the Pharisaic ethics. To the teachers of the Rabbinic line the view taken by the author of the Testaments would have been entirely congenial; and, so far as this agreement goes, the author might well have been a Pharisee, if it were not that on other grounds, as already explained, a Pharisaic authorship of the Testaments is inadmissible. Whether our author knew anything about the teaching of the Pharisees, or they of his, it is impossible to say. But that he and they, starting as they did from the same fundamental principle of the likeness

[237]

between God and man (see above, p. 129 ff.), should have arrived independently at conclusions very similar to each other, is after all only to be expected. There is nothing to show that either borrowed from the other; and the author of the Testaments was none the less an original thinker, a man of deep spiritual discernment, although others in his time were seeing a good deal of what he saw and teaching lessons not dissimilar from his.

The general ethical position of the author of Testaments may be described by saying that what he taught belonged to the common stock but was presented with quite exceptional force and depth of insight. In other words, the ground which he covered was much the same, in its main features, as that covered by Proverbs or Ben Sira; but he understood far better than they did the psychological meaning and the religious connexion of both virtue and vice. No one whose words represented the common stock, whether inside or outside the Canon of Scripture, would dispute or deny any of the ethical teaching given in Testaments; they would only wish that they could have taught it so well. Our author touches upon practically everything which his predecessors had taught, at all events all the main subjects; but he has left his own personal mark upon each one, and in regard to one or two of them, his teaching is without parallel for depth of insight and nobility of expression. Nowhere is this more the case than in his teaching about forgiveness, and the closely allied subject of love to one's fellow man. A survey of the virtues and vices with which he specially deals will afford an opportunity for remark on the more important points. To such a survey we will now proceed.

It has been observed above that the order in which our author dealt with the various virtues and vices was regulated by the order of the Patriarchs with whose character they were severally connected. That order is only artificial, and there seems no reason why it should be followed here. What the order of the writer's own preference would have been can only be guessed at, but we shall do him no injustice if we begin with those which seem to rest on the principles of widest scope, and then go to the more specific virtues and vices.

In the foremost place must stand the remarkable combination of the two ancient commandments: Thou shalt love the Lord thy God (Deut. vi. 5) and Thou shalt love thy neighbour as thyself (Lev. xix. 18). These had, of course, long been known separately. The author of Testaments was, so far as is known, the first who linked them together. This he does in three passages, as follows: 'Love the Lord and your neighbour' (T. Iss. v. 2); 'I loved the Lord, likewise also every man with all my heart' (T. Iss. vii. 6); 'Love the Lord through all your life, and one another with a true heart' (T. Dan. v. 3). To these may be added: 'Fear ye the Lord and love your neighbour' (T. Benj. iii. 3). It is true that in the last passage the word is 'Fear' not 'Love'; but both are almost indiscriminately used in the Old Testament, and the present point is that the commandment to love your neighbour is linked to the commandment in regard to God.

It is usually supposed, at all events by Christians, that Jesus was the first who combined these two commandments; and not only so but that he was the first to extend the meaning of 'Love thy neighbour' so as to include all men. Neither of these assertions is true. The first obviously not, for here in the Testaments, a book written more than a century before the time of Jesus, the combination is already made, quite unmistakably though not so emphatically as Jesus made it. Whether Jesus learned it from the Testaments, or heard it in the Synagogue, or came to it independently, there it is in the passages cited above. Some have suggested that these and other passages in Testaments which are closely paralleled in the New Testament are interpolations by a Christian hand. That there are Christian interpolations in the book is admitted by all scholars; but they are dogmatic in character, and they break the context where they occur. The passages at present in question, and other alleged parallels, are of the same texture as the rest of the book; and if they were removed nearly all of the ethical teaching would have to be removed also. That the whole book was written by a Christian is out of the question. There is no getting away from the position that the author of Testaments was a Jew of very remarkable gifts, who wrote long before Jesus words which it has been thought could only be Christian, but which only show how much there was, in the Judaism of that time, of spiritual discernment and ethical nobility.

Further, the commandment, 'Thou shalt love thy neighbour

(as thyself),' is taken by our author to include all mankind. Jesus was not the first to give this wide extension to the ancient text. For that matter, neither was the writer of Testaments. In regard to this text Charles remarks (Oxford Patriarchs, p. 292): ' In the latter passage and possibly in our text (i.e. T. Iss. v. 2; vii. 6) the sphere of neighbourhood is limited to Israelites, but in our Lord's use there is no limit of race or country'. The last remark is true but irrelevant. Neither in the Testaments nor in Leviticus is there any limitation in the range of meaning of the word neighbour. This has been shown at length in regard to the original text in Leviticus (see above, pp. 144-149), and the argument need not be repeated. That the author of Testaments used the word neighbour in the same inclusive sense is shown partly by the fact that he would not be likely to make the word less inclusive than it always had been, and partly by the fact that in other passages he used it in a similarly inclusive sense. Thus: ' I bid you to keep the commandments of the Lord, and to show mercy to your neigh-bours, and to have compassion towards all, not towards men only but also towards beasts ' (T. Zeb. v. 1). ' Do you, there-fore, my children, from that which God bestoweth on you, show compassion and mercy without hesitation to all men, and give to every man with a good heart ' (*ib.* vii. 2). One who could write such words and think such thoughts was incapable of putting a narrow construction upon the words of the text in Leviticus. That narrow construction was unknown till Christians found a reason for it.

The broad humanity which inspired these passages and which may be traced through the whole book finds remarkable expres-sion in what the writer says about the Gentiles. One would expect that an Apocalyptic writer would show the usual abhorrence of those who were outside the community of Israel, even though he might not go as far as the savage thirst for vengeance which disgraces Enoch. Instead, he writes as follows: ' And there shall be given to thee a blessing, and to all thy seed, until the Lord shall visit all the Gentiles in his tender mercies for ever' (T. Levi iv. 4). And again: 'For through their tribes shall God appear on earth to save the race of Israel, and to gather together the righteous from among the Gentiles ' (T. Naph. viii. 3). ' He shall save Israel and all the Gentiles '

(T. Asher vii. 3). And ' Keep the commandments of God, until the Lord shall reveal his salvation to all Gentiles ' (T. Benj. x. 5). Comment on these words is needless. One is only inclined to wonder how many of those who read the book when it appeared would understand and sympathise with the world-wide charity of the writer.

He shows indeed a wonderful insight into the power of love in human relationships, whether realised in the virtues of kindness, goodwill, etc., and especially forgiveness, or defied in the vices of hatred, envy, anger, and vindictiveness. The often quoted passage about forgiveness is perhaps the most wonderful in the whole book: ' Love ye one another from the heart; and if a man sin against thee, speak peaceably to him, and in thy soul hold not guile; and if he repent forgive him. But if he deny it, do not get into a passion with him, lest catching the poison from thee he take to swearing, and so thou sin doubly. And though he deny it, and yet have a sense of shame when reproved, give over reproving him. For he who denieth may repent so as not again to wrong thee; yea, he may also honour thee and be at peace with thee. And if he be shameless and persist in his wrongdoing, even so forgive him from the heart and leave to God the avenging ' (T. Gad. vi. 3-7). Again comment is needless, and would be only an impertinence. In another passage we have a thought often echoed in later literature: ' Have therefore yourselves also my children compassion towards every man with mercy, that the Lord also may have compassion and mercy upon you. . . . For, in the degree in which a man hath compassion upon his neighbours, in the same degree hath the Lord also upon him ' (T. Zeb. viii. 3). Of the contrast between love and hatred the following is said: ' For hatred worketh with envy also against them that prosper; so long as it heareth of or seeth their success it always languisheth. For, as love would quicken even the dead, and would call back them that are condemned to die, so hatred would slay the living, and those that had sinned venially it would not suffer to live. For the spirit of hatred worketh together with Satan, through hastiness of spirit, in all things to men's death; but the spirit of love worketh together with the law of God in long-suffering unto the salvation of men ' (T. Gad. iv. 5-7). A few more passages may be quoted, in illustration of other

R [241]

points in the ethical teaching of Testaments, thus: 'Know, therefore, my children, that two spirits wait upon man—the spirit of truth and the spirit of deceit. And in the midst is the spirit of understanding of the mind, to which it belongeth to turn whithersoever it will. And the works of truth and the works of deceit are written upon the hearts of men, and each one of them the Lord knoweth. And there is no time at which the works of men can be hid, for on the heart itself have they been written down before the Lord. And the spirit of truth testifieth all things and accuseth all, and the sinner is burnt up by his own heart and cannot raise his face to the judge' (T. Jud. xx. 1-5). With this may be compared the following: 'There are two ways of good and evil, and with these are the two inclinations in our breasts discriminating them. Therefore if the soul take pleasure in the good (inclination) all its actions are in righteousness; and if it sin it straightway repenteth. For having its thoughts set upon righteousness, and casting away wickedness, it straightway overthroweth the evil and uprooteth the sin. But if it incline to the evil inclination, all its actions are in wickedness, and it driveth away the good and cleaveth to the evil, and is ruled by Beliar; even though it work what is good, he perverteth it to what is evil' (T. Asher i. 5-8).

This acute analysis of virtue and sin is illustrated in the succeeding sections, and forms the main subject of the Testament of Asher. It is too long to quote, but the concluding words, before the author sinks into Apocalyptic, may be given: 'For when the soul departs troubled, it is tormented by the evil spirit which also it served in lusts and evil works. But if he is peaceful, with joy he meeteth the angel of peace, and he leadeth him into eternal life'.

Fully to do justice to the author of Testaments it would be necessary to write out all the ethical passages of the book; but those which have been given above will show the rare quality of that teaching, and the wonderful insight of the author. Nothing is known of him apart from his book, and his book is only known through translations. It has left no trace in Jewish literature except in the Midrash of a later time. That it influenced some of the writers of the New Testament is fairly certain; that it influenced Jesus is possible. It remains an isolated witness to a nobility in the Judaism of its time which cannot be denied by those who look with least favour upon that Judaism; and the ray of its kindly light shines in the gloom of a dark and stormy age. Nowhere in the literature at present under consideration shall we find any writer who equals the author of Testaments in the purity and depth of his ethical teaching. We reverently salute him and pass on.

Chapter VII

THE REMAINING NON-CANONICAL BOOKS

THE above title is not meant to imply any disparagement of the books which have not so far been considered separately, or to deny that in their various ways they are interesting and important. It simply serves to indicate that, so far as their ethical contents are concerned, they do not add anything of importance to what has been already found in the four books which have been examined. But to pass them over altogether would be a great injustice to them; and not only so, but the fact that the ethical element in them is not their chief characteristic has a bearing on the main subject with which we are concerned, viz.: the Jewish ethical teaching in the period defined at the outset of our study. All these books have an ethical basis, in so far as the several writers assume certain ethical principles without discussion, and proceed at once to deal with the subject which specially interests them.

It is well to remember that the non-canonical literature is not a collection in the sense in which the Old Testament and the New Testament are collections. Each of these represents the result of an act of recognition on the part of some competent authority that the books respectively included in them were Holy Scripture. But the non-canonical books are only a collection in the sense that modern scholars have found it convenient to deal with them as a group. They were not, of course, produced as a group, any more than the writings of the Old Testament and of the New Testament were produced as a group. But they were not excluded as a group from the Canon, either Jewish or Christian. Whatever was done in this respect was done in reference to this or that book specified by name, or else was implied in a general reference to external ' books ' (see above, p. 197 f.), whatever they might be. The non-canonical books were simply such writings, of various date, authorship and character, as appeared from time to time, and were, so to speak, found lying about by any who were interested in them. They were not connected by any common purpose, nor do they form a unity in any sense; they were just what certain Jewish authors, for whatever reason, were moved to write. In the case of the Apocalyptic writers, indeed, a certain amount of dependence of the later upon the earlier can hardly be denied. The characteristic features of Apocalyptic recur over and over again in the various writings of that class, showing that there was an established form in this respect. But, within the limits of that form, even the Apocalyptic writers found room for very considerable differences of purpose and treatment. 4 Ezra is purely Apocalyptic in form, but what the writer had to say, and said with passionate earnestness, is not at all what had been said in Enoch or Jubilees. But, apart from the Apocalyptic books, the rest of the non-canonical literature consists of writings having no obvious connexion with each other; and it is only for convenience of treatment that they have been, of late years, gathered together for purposes of study. Certainly it was highly desirable that they should be so gathered together, and still more that they should be studied. Whatever else they are, they are products of the Judaism of their time; and any light they can throw on that Judaism is only to be welcomed.

To examine every one of them in a separate chapter, as has been done with Ben Sira, Enoch, Jubilees and Testaments, would involve a great deal of repetition, and is not necessary for the purpose of this volume. My object, as stated at the outset (see above, p. 3 *sq.*), is to place side by side for comparison the Rabbinical teaching and the non-Rabbinical, the link between them being the ethical principles more or less common to both. The character, other than ethical, of the non-canonical books can be indicated, with sufficient fullness to enable that comparison to be made, if they are briefly surveyed in order. Some will not need more than a few words; others will claim more extended treatment. To this survey we now proceed, and take the books in the order of the list given above (pp. 173-4), i.e. first the Apocrypha and then the Pseudepigrapha.

I. 1 ESDRAS

This book covers a good deal of the ground included in the Canonical books of Chronicles, Ezra, and Nehemiah. It may represent an independent version of the history therein contained. It contains one very notable addition to the canonical material, in the story about the three young men in the body-guard of Darius, who engaged in a friendly trial of wit in order to gain approval from the king. Each maintained a sort of thesis intended to show what was the strongest force in human affairs. One declared that wine was the strongest; the second that the king was the strongest; and the third, who was Zerub-babel, declared that women were the strongest, but that Truth was stronger than all (Es. iii-iv). The author turned that story to account by making it lead up to the permission given by the king to Zerubbabel to return to Jerusalem with a company of Jews. Whether he invented the story or found it in some source does not at present concern us. It is an outstanding ethical feature in the book, through its praise of Truth and the God of truth. There was indeed no reason why the author should include ethical teaching as such in his book, and the same remark will apply to many of the writings included in this survey. He wrote, as we may suppose, to give an account of the history of a certain period of Jewish history; and, so far as ethics is concerned, all that can be said is that he does not give any indication to show that his position was in any respect different from that which has been described above as the common stock.

2. 1 MACCABEES

Some idea of the nature of this book may have been gathered from the frequent use made of it in the earlier chapters of the present work. It relates the history of the Maccabean Revolt, and the rise of the victorious house to the rank of reigning princes. The author was evidently very well informed upon the subject of his history, and may have been himself an eye-witness of some of the scenes which he describes. He wrote a sober, straightforward narrative; and, considering how great had been the suffering which had led to the Revolt, he showed consider-able restraint of feeling. He was a cordial admirer of the Hasmonean princes; and, as he seems to have written, or at all events finished, his book after the end of the reign of John Hyrcanus (d. 105 B.C.) he must have witnessed the breach between the Pharisees and the Sadducees, and the adhesion of the prince to the latter party. He makes no allusion to this, and there is nothing to indicate whether he took sides, or which side, in that dispute. Of course he was not a Helleniser; but the victorious party who overthrew Hellenism in the name of the Torah included all the rest of the Jews, and, while some of these were Pharisees and some were Sadducees, there were many (probably the majority) who were not avowedly either one or the other. They were simply Jews, loyal to the Torah, and supporters of the leaders who had defeated the Gentile persecutor and delivered the chosen people. The author of our book was one of these Jews not otherwise described, and we can only judge of his religious position from the general tone of his book. It did not come within the scope of his history to say anything about ethics one way or the other, except so far as an ethical view is implied in faithfulness under persecution and sympathy with the sufferers, bravery in fighting the persecutor, a loyalty to the Torah which went to the length of considerable violence against renegades, and in general the virtues characteristic of a revolt in the name of religion.

3. 2 Maccabees

This is an independent attempt to cover some of the ground of 2 Macc. It is based upon extracts from the work of Jason of Cyrene; and as a history it is far inferior to the other Maccabean book. How much the author took over from Jason is a question for the critics, but he is clearly responsible for what now stands in his book. He there shows himself to be a religious partisan of a rather extreme type, and with much less reticence on sacred subjects than the author of 1 Macc. It is from this book that the story of the martyrdom of the mother and her seven sons gained currency, especially in Christian literature. Whether true or not, and it may well have been founded upon actual incidents of the persecution under Antiochus, the story is told with a vivid ghastliness which is not easily forgotten by the reader, and which no doubt was one element in its popularity. The belief in the resurrection, which does not appear in 1 Macc., is very prominent in 2 Macc.; and, while this is a theological rather than an ethical doctrine, yet it has a certain indirect bearing upon ethics in so far as it brings in an additional motive for right action, gives a new meaning to the thought of life as the service of God.

[248]

4. 3 MACCABEES

This was apparently written by an Alexandrian Jew in the late second century B.C. and was intended to show the excellence of Judaism as compared with Hellenism. It is a controversial pamphlet rather than a history; but its main feature is an alleged miraculous deliverance of the Jews in Alexandria from a cruel death decreed against them. The Judaism represented by the author is that of a strict adherence to the Torah, and the ethics apparently that of the common stock.

4 MACCABEES, see below, No. 26.

5. TOBIT

Whatever may have been the purpose of the author of this book, it is surely one of the most charming stories to be found in ancient literature. The critics have traced the influence of many earlier sources in its composition, and have found signs of acquaintance with it in many later writings, a proof of its well-deserved popularity*. It was almost certainly written in Egypt, perhaps about the end of the third or the beginning of the second century B.C. Nothing whatever is known of the author, and scholars are not wholly agreed as to whether he wrote in Hebrew (or Aramaic) or in Greek. Putting aside questions of criticism, we confine our attention to the ethical character of the book. This is shown not only in specific sentences, as when Tobit gives advice to his son, but in the whole setting of the story. The incidents described occur in the life of a Jewish family of humble station and simple piety. The writer may have had a controversial purpose here and there, and no doubt was careful to mark the contrast between what was Jewish and what was not; but the present writer cannot help feeling that the author of Tobit simply set out to write the story, as a story, and that in doing so he made his characters reflect and express his own religious and ethical ideas. The Judaism that is represented is that of a man who finds in it the best means of realising his own humane and kindly nature. The persons in his story are all devout and pious Jews, but they

* The story of Tobit has even been dramatised and presented in a London theatre under the title of *Tobias and the Angel*; the dramatist has introduced elements of comedy into his version of the story, and has failed to reproduce the delicate charm of the original. But even so the story is not entirely spoiled.

show little or none of the narrow, bitter spirit from which other representations of Jewish character are not always free. A spirit of kindness and cordiality runs right through the story; and the single evil element is provided by the demon Asmodeus, who is mentioned only as the occasion for the triumph over him of the power of the good. The particular virtues on which the writer lays stress are prayer, fasting, and almsgiving, though possibly the word rendered ' almsgiving ' may have the wider meaning of good deeds in general. The duty of burying the dead who would otherwise have none to bury them is made a special point; and one of the main lines of the story is to teach that a Jew should marry within the community and not seek a wife outside. Honour to father and mother is illustrated by the whole development of the story. Counsels against fornication, idleness, drunkenness, find a natural place in the book, being indeed only elements in the common stock of Jewish ethics. But in this book occurs for the first time, so far as is known, the prototype of what came to be known as the Golden Rule, in the form: 'What thou thyself hatest, do to no man' (T. iv. 15)*; and the story as a whole is in keeping with the spirit of that great saying. Tobit may well share with Testaments the honour of bearing witness to what Judaism at its best could produce.

6. Judith

Like Tobit, this book is a story, in form a historical novel, but one which is inspired throughout by a wholly different purpose. When or where it was written is not known. The situation described in the book does not correspond with any known event in Jewish history, in so far that the names, places, and persons mentioned cannot be consistently identified. The evident purpose of the story is to encourage the Jews in a time of great anxiety owing to the approach of a foreign oppressor, by showing how he was defeated by woman through her trust in God, also through her pious fraud. The writer can hardly have shaped the lines of his story without having in mind the story of Jael and Sisera; and, for the general intention, the book of Daniel sounded the same note which he wished to sound, of trust in the God of Israel, who was mighty to save and who could overthrow the greatest heathen kings. But Judith differs

* On the Golden Rule see Abrahams, I., *Studies*, First Series, p. 20 *sq.*

from Daniel by the complete absence of the Apocalyptic element. The deliverance is described as having been wrought entirely by human means without any of the Apocalyptic reference to the larger purposes of Heaven. Seeing that in Judith the means employed is the treachery of a woman, the substitution is of doubtful worth. Judith, the heroine, is described in terms of the strictest Jewish piety, in regard to observance of fasts and sabbaths, clean and unclean meats and the like; but the strictest Jewish piety, as elsewhere depicted, does not include prayer for the divine blessing upon a deliberate act of treachery, such as Judith offered. In the Oxford Judith, p. 247, the Editor of the book says: ' The objection which has been made to Judith's deceit (xi. 5) and approval of violence scarcely deserves notice. It could only be made in complete ignorance of the spirit of the time, and shows an utter inability to appreciate the position of a people struggling against overwhelming odds for their religion and their very existence'. If Judith had been a real person, and her exploit a historical event, there would be something in this remark. But the morality in question is that of the author of the story, who has chosen to give this particular form to it, apparently without misgiving. Jewish heroism in face of danger, persecution, martyrdom, has been shown in numberless instances; but it has seldom, if ever, stooped to deceit and treachery as one of its weapons. Severe temptation may have sometimes wrung a lie from Jewish lips, but never made it a thing to boast of or to pray over. Judith as a story is well told; but, from the point of view of the ethical teaching of Judaism, it counts for nothing.

7. THE WISDOM OF SOLOMON

To dismiss this book, one of the outstanding books of ancient literature in any language, in a few paragraphs would be a grave discourtesy if, as a whole, it were closely related to the subject of the present work. That there is a strongly ethical element in it goes almost without saying; but it is not primarily with ethics, even in the broad sense, that the writer was concerned. He was, to all appearance, an Alexandrian Jew; and, though he knew a good deal about Greek thought, he was under no doubt as to the greater excellence of the Jewish religion, and the Jewish way of expressing it.

[251]

There is no sublimer utterance of monotheism, as the belief in a personal God, than in the passages (xi. 21—xii. 2) and (xii. 12-18). They are in keeping with the spirit of the great prophets, with whose words the writer was doubtless familiar; but none of the prophets said anything quite like them. And though the later chapters of the book, in which the writer inveighs against idolatry in general and Egyptian idolatry in particular, seem to be animated by a very different spirit, yet there those loftiest passages are; and the book of Wisdom may well be compared in this respect with Ps. cxxxix, which begins with a meditation on the omnipresence of God like nothing else in the Old Testament, and ends with passionate words of hatred against the enemies of God (*ib.* 21, 22).

The title by which the book has generally been known, the Wisdom of Solomon (or simply Wisdom) is appropriate only to the first part of the book, which is usually considered to be cc. i-xi. 1. There is certainly a marked difference of thought and style between these chapters and the remainder of the book; but whether they are by two separate writers is a question which for the present purpose may be left undecided. We are concerned with the book as it stands. In the first half of the book the principal thought, one might almost say the principal figure, is that of wisdom, and the description of wisdom in vii. 22—viii. 1 is one of the marvels of the whole book. It is, of course, through the exaltation of wisdom that the book takes its place in the Wisdom literature, and beyond dispute at the head of that literature. The exaltation of wisdom began in Proverbs (viii. 1 *sq.*), which makes some approach to the personification of wisdom. Job and Koheleth show no noticeable advance on Proverbs in regard to their estimation of wisdom. Ben Sira, as we have seen (above, p. 207), identified wisdom with Torah, thus marking a considerable advance on the older thought. The author of our book probably knew that of Ben Sira, but he does not follow him in the identification of wisdom with Torah. Indeed, he says very little about Torah in his book. Yet it is not impossible that the difference between him and Ben Sira in this matter is really less than it appears to be. Our author went as far as he dared, i.e. as far as his monotheism would let him, in the direction of identifying wisdom with God. Certainly he stopped short of that identification, but he brought wisdom into the closest relation with God compatible with the subordinate position of a divine attribute. To identify wisdom with Torah, as Ben Sira had done, was certainly to bring wisdom into a very close relation with God, when it is remembered how the Torah itself was made to express a diviner meaning than that which it had had at first. The author of Wisdom shows no trace of knowledge of the Rabbinical development of the idea of Torah, and indeed his book is laid out on quite other lines; but may it not be that he aimed at saying, in a form moulded by Greek thought, much the same as that which the Rabbinical teachers were saying in terms of Torah? If this be so, then both he and they were witnesses to the spiritual development of Judaism in their time.

Wisdom, in our book, is the source of virtue. The good life is that which is based on wisdom; and vice and the evil life are the result of the neglect or defiance of wisdom. But the writer does not go into details of virtue and vice; he does not give specific precepts, as Ben Sira and Proverbs had done, but leaves the reader to draw conclusions from the general principles laid down. It is true that the first part of his book is an appeal to those upon whom chief authority is laid in human affairs to be guided in their actions by wisdom, and to this extent it does contain precepts; but even so it is more of a philosophical exposition than an ethical treatise. The writer himself was, beyond all question, a man of lofty character, ethically, and looked at his subject from that point of view; but his ethics appears in his pre-suppositions rather than his positive teaching, and his chief interest seems to be in wisdom as the highest gift of God to man. Through the gift of wisdom man comes nearest to the true knowledge of God, and therefore to the desire to worship him. Idolatry is in effect the negation of wisdom, the neglect or denial of the knowledge of God which wisdom would confer, and therefore the writer makes idolatry the special object of his attack. This may indicate the connexion between the first part of the book and the second, without assuming dual authorship, though it must be admitted that the book as it stands does not clearly explain the connexion. The second part, which is mainly a polemic against idolatry, leaves the Jewish animus of the author unmistakably clear; but it is worth noticing that, with all his severity, he does not express it in the Apocalyptic manner. He may have read Enoch, but he showed no desire to imitate that book.

The remaining writings included in the Apocrypha of the Old Testament take the form of additions to one or other of the Canonical books. These we will now survey in order.

8. I BARUCH

A short book, containing three distinct documents combined by an editor. According to the most probable view it was written after the fall of Jerusalem A.D. 70, the first two documents in Hebrew, the third probably in Greek. It perhaps reflects the sentiments of writers living at some distance from the seat of war; Jerusalem or its near neighbourhood was no place for the writing of books at the time. The author of the first document, who counsels submission to the conquerors, evidently agreed with the policy of the pacifists of whom Johanan b. Zaccai was the most eminent; which indeed was not difficult after the blow had fallen. The writers of all three documents show little, if any, originality. If all the quotations from and allusions to earlier writings, especially Daniel, were removed, very little would be left. The religious ideas expressed are mainly the commonplaces of Judaism, better expressed elsewhere. If the writers concerned in I Baruch had really come out of the furnace of the war, one might fairly expect them to have written something more passionate and more personal than the tame compilation from other sources which has come down under the name of Baruch. Of ethical teaching it has hardly any, though such teaching is hardly to be expected in a book written under such circumstances. What ethical ideas are implied are, like the religious ideas, merely common stock.

9. EPISTLE OF JEREMY
10. PRAYER OF MANASSES
11. PRAYER OF AZARIAH
12. SONG OF THE THREE CHILDREN
13. SUSANNA
14. BEL AND THE DRAGON
15. ADDITIONS TO THE BOOK OF ESTHER

The foregoing pieces, which never had any independent existence but were only additions to one or other of the

Canonical books in some Greek MSS., are of no importance for the purpose of the present work. They owe their preservation to Christian use; and, though some of them were perhaps originally written in Hebrew, there is no mention of them in Jewish literature unless traces of one or another can be found in some late Midrash. In themselves they are interesting and perhaps valuable from some points of view; but they contribute nothing beyond what has been already ascertained to the material for the study of Jewish ethical teaching. With these the list of Apocrypha of the Old Testament is ended. We now pass to the Pseudepigrapha, so far as these have not been already dealt with in the chapters on Enoch, Jubilees, and Testaments.

16. LETTER OF ARISTEAS

This book purports to describe the manner in which the Hebrew Pentateuch was translated into Greek by command of Ptolemy Philadelphus. The author, writing in the name of Aristeas, claims to have been an eye-witness of, and participator in, all that he describes. It is generally agreed that the book dates from a time long after the date implied in the narrative, and that its real purpose was to show the superiority of the Jewish religion over all others, especially that of the Greeks. The writer was an Alexandrian Jew, whose date is uncertain. Opinions vary between 200 B.C. and A.D. 40. In the course of his narrative the author describes how the seventy-two elders, who had been sent at the request of the king to translate the Torah, were entertained on successive days at a banquet over which the king presided. In the course of the feasting, the king proposed to each of the elders in succession a question on some religious, ethical, or philosophical topic. His guests in turn gave replies which delighted the king by the wisdom displayed in them. In this way the writer found a means of introducing into his book a specimen of Jewish ethical teaching to support his main argument. Whether he found questions and answers in some existing treatise and incorporated them in his own book, or whether he invented them all, is of no great importance. Such as they are, he showed his approval of them by adopting them. They thus furnish an illustration of Jewish ethics to be added to those which have been considered already. There is nothing very striking about these sayings; they are what commended themselves to a Jew of good sense and straight-forward piety, who did not trouble himself with deep questions of theology and philosophy. He was much more interested in practical and social problems, especially of government; though this is only natural, as the questions are supposed to be put by a king. The virtues and vices touched upon are mainly those specified in the ethics of the common stock, and do not call for remark. The other parts of the book have no relevance to the purpose of the present work.

17. THE BOOKS OF ADAM AND EVE

These are fragments of writings containing fantastic specula-tions upon subjects arising out of the story of the Garden of Eden. They are not Apocalyptic in form, since it is not said that the information contained in them was revealed to any person by superhuman means. But the style of the narrative is much like that of Apocalyptic description, and probably appealed to the same type of mind. That the writers were Jews is obvious from the contents of the books. That they were in some general agreement with the ethics of the common stock is probable, in the absence of anything to the contrary. More than that it is not necessary to say, for the present purpose.

18. THE MARTYRDOM OF ISAIAH

A Jewish fragment incorporated in a Christian work. Perhaps a kind of Midrash (not haggadah). There are traces of the story in the Talmud. The purpose of the fragment is to add detail to the tradition that Isaiah was put to death by King Manasseh. Such ethical value as the short piece possesses, which is very slight, arises from the fact that the story is that of a martyrdom. Neither the date nor place of authorship are known.

Of the Apocalyptic books which follow in the list of Pseu-depigrapha Enoch and Testaments have already been examined in previous chapters. The remaining books are more or less Apocalyptic in character; and thus, while important on that account, they are of much less value from the ethical point of view. Not because they are not ethical, but because the inten-tion of their writers was not to give ethical teaching as such. From this point of view they may be fairly dealt with in a brief notice.

[256]

19. THE SIBYLLINE BOOKS

Verses and collections of verses, containing predictions of future events and purporting to have been uttered by one or another of the Sibyls, were well known in the Near East during several centuries, including the period with which we are concerned. The Sibyls, of whom the Erythræan and the Cumæan were the most famous, were supposed to be inspired by some deity to utter prophecies; and although, or because, little was known about them, their reputed oracles were held in great respect and were widely known. It was the ingenious contrivance of some unknown Jew, or Jews, to use the form of the Sibylline verses in order to bring to a much larger public than could be reached in any other way a knowledge of the Jewish religion, and especially the knowledge of the one true God as contrasted with all Gentile deities. The whole of the extant Sibylline verses amounts to some twelve (fifteen) books, of which those of Jewish origin are found mainly in the third, fourth, and fifth. They are assigned by scholars to various dates, ranging from the second century B.C. to the second century A.D., perhaps later. Their Jewish character is shown in their assertion of strict monotheism and their polemic against all idolatry. There is no specifically ethical teaching in them, as indeed their purpose was not to teach but, in form, to prophesy. They therefore contribute nothing, beyond what has already been learned, to the knowledge of that teaching.

20. THE ASSUMPTION OF MOSES

More correctly (see Oxford edition, A.P., ii, 407) the Testament of Moses, is an Apocalyptic piece, containing in the form of predictions, by Moses just before his death, an account of the subsequent history of the Jewish people down to the writer's own time, i.e. about the beginning of the Christian era. He was certainly a Jew. He probably agreed with some of the views of the Pharisees, but he certainly was not one himself, for reasons which have already been explained and need not be repeated. He was merely one of the unnamed types of the Judaism of his time. As his interest was Apocalyptic his ethics are only implied, not stated; what there is in his book that is ethical is only common stock.

s

21. THE SECRETS OF ENOCH (2 ENOCH)

An Apocalyptic book whose existence was not known till 1892. It exists in two Slavonic versions, but the original work, or most of it, was probably written in Greek. The author was probably a Hellenistic Jew of Alexandria (see Introd. to Oxford Edition). For the most part this book follows the usual Apocalyptic lines, as they are found, e.g., in 1 Enoch. There are descriptions of journeys in heaven and of the sights which were there shown to Enoch. There are also passages explaining the motion of the sun and moon. The book is not a second version of 1 Enoch, and perhaps may be entirely independent of it, except so far as both books deal with the same main subject. But in one respect there is a marked difference between them. 2 Enoch contains a number of ethical sayings, some of them of great beauty, and such as are found in no other Apocalyptic work except Testaments. Thus: ' If ill requitals befall you, return them not either to neighbour or enemy; because the Lord will return them for you and be your avenger on the great day of judgment, that there be no avenging here among men ' (2 Enoch l. 4). ' Blessed is he who implants peace and love. Cursed is he who disturbs those that love their neighbours ' (*ib*. lii. 11-12). ' He who does injury to soul of man does injury to his own soul, and there is no cure for his flesh nor pardon for all time' (*ib*. lx. 1). There are several chapters in the immediate context of these passages which are mainly ethical, and in quality not unlike those quoted. They come as a sudden and pleasant surprise after the wearisome unrealities of commonplace Apocalyptic, as when a traveller in the desert finds a well of fresh water amid the barren sand. Why the author was moved to write these things we cannot tell. If he had not written them, no one could have said that they were wanting. As he has written them, one can only wish that he would have written many more of the same kind, even if he left out much of his fantastic imagery. It has been remarked before that the Apocalyptic spirit and the ethical spirit do not get on well together. 2 Enoch is mainly a proof of this. All the more beautiful are the scanty flowers which have managed to bloom in that unwholesome soil.

22. 2 BARUCH.   24. 4 EZRA

The special interest of 2 Baruch lies in the fact that it expresses the reaction of its author to the great disaster of the fall of Jerusalem in A.D. 70. In this respect it is closely akin to 4 Ezra, in which the same theme is dealt with even more forcibly. Both are Apocalyptic in form; and, in both, the ethical element finds little or no direct expression. The writers were concerned with other subjects of more pressing concern. The problem for both of them, but especially for the author of 4 Ezra, was to find an explanation of the terrible disaster which had befallen Israel in view of Israel's fidelity to the Torah and the God who had given it. 2 Baruch, which is a composite book, alternates between hope and despair; but the writer of 4 Ezra fairly faces the question whether the Torah is, after all, sufficient to meet the needs of the soul, especially in a time of such desperate trial. He makes Ezra put very searching questions to the angel who is his heaven-sent instructor; and no candid reader will easily admit that the angel gives satisfactory replies. Ezra, like Job before him, is overawed rather than convinced.

Both 2 Baruch and 4 Ezra represent views which must have been held by many Jews who were dismayed by the fall of Jerusalem, and whose faith in the fundamental tenet of Judaism was severely shaken. But the Pharisees, as Pharisees, never shared those views; and it is wholly incorrect to regard these two books as containing the Pharisaic reply to the lesson of the great disaster*. The Pharisees never wanted the war, and would have prevented it if they could. They were dragged into it by the wild fanatics of the Zealot party; and it is these, if any, smarting from their defeat and filled with despair, whose feelings find expression in the two books. This alone is enough to justify the assertion that they were not written by Pharisees, quite apart from the general considerations already stated and several times referred to.

All this lies entirely off the lines of ethical teaching, and is only mentioned because 4 Ezra at least is one of the great books of the non-canonical literature, by reason of the passionate emotion of the writer which breaks through in spite of the artificialities of the Apocalyptic form. It is indeed wonderful that a writer so desperately in earnest should still find in that form a means of expression at all adequate to his purpose. But

* See *Pharisees*, p. 191 *sq.*

neither 2 Baruch nor 4 Ezra have any direct contribution to make to the study of Jewish ethics, and are therefore not further noticed at present.

23. 3 BARUCH

An Apocalypse having some affinity with 2 Baruch and 2 Enoch. It is mainly taken up with the visits of Baruch to the seven heavens, one after the other, described with much detail of trivial invention, and with little trace of the lofty purpose which is the chief if not the only justification of Apocalypse as a literary form. A list of sins occurs in xiii. 4 which may help to give an ethical colour to the work.

25. THE PSALMS OF SOLOMON

These are a set of eighteen psalms written apparently in the middle of the first century B.C. The original language was almost certainly Hebrew, but the psalms are only known in Greek or in translations from the Greek. The earliest reference to them is as late as the fifth century A.D. They came to be known at all only through their occasional use by the Christian Church. They are nevertheless wholly Jewish in character, and they have much in common with some of the Canonical Psalms. Thus they have the familiar division of men with the righteous and the wicked, pious and sinners. They have also the ferocity of denunciation of the wicked which is to be found in some of the Canonical Psalms, though carried to an extent greatly exceeding that which the earlier Psalmists allowed themselves. The opposition which underlies all these Psalms seems to correspond very closely with that between the Pharisees and the Sadducees. A better case for Pharisaic authorship might be made out for the Psalms of Solomon than for any of the non-canonical books. Certainly the writer (or writers) showed strong signs of approval of the Pharisaic position; but this he might quite well do without being himself a Pharisee. It is still true that the Pharisees pursued a method of teaching with which the writing of books of any kind was quite out of keeping. The writing of psalms would be no less so. Also, if these had been written by a Pharisee, why should the Pharisees exclude them from the Canon? They certainly did not find a place in the Canon even of the Greek Old Testament, and there is no evidence that the Pharisees ever heard of them. They must have become known, through the medium of translation, in Alexandria, and it is quite conceivable that they were composed there. There is nothing to show that they were ever widely known.

Their ethical value, such as it is, consists in the description of the respective characters of the righteous and the wicked; but as the description in either case proceeds from a violent partisan, the ethical value is much reduced. Historically, rather than ethically, the Psalms of Solomon throw a good deal of light on the Judaism of the time.

26. 4 MACCABEES

A short piece in the form of a discourse by some Alexandrian Jew probably about the beginning of the Christian era. It is Jewish in matter, but quite un-Jewish in form. And even in matter it is largely Greek. That it was ever spoken in a synagogue is quite out of the question. Its ethics are such as a Greek would read into a Hebrew text, and only to that extent do they belong to Jewish ethical teaching. The book reads as if it were a sort of school essay on a given subject, and independent importance of any kind can hardly be claimed for it.

Chapter VIII

THE NON-RABBINICAL LITERATURE AND PHARISAISM

WE have now surveyed in some detail the two main developments of Judaism in the period with which we are concerned,
and are in a position to make the comparison of the one with
the other to which it has been the main object of this book to
lead up. There will remain still to be undertaken the survey of
the Jewish ethical teaching in the New Testament, especially
in the Gospels; but that survey will be made more easily and
with less need of repetition if we have already ascertained the
relation between the Rabbinical teaching and that which is
contained in the Apocrypha and Pseudepigrapha. And this is
all the more desirable because the literature which includes
these books was, on the whole, earlier in date than the New
Testament writings. That there were many points of contact
between the ethical teaching of Judaism and that contained
in the New Testament is beyond all question, and it will lead
to a better understanding of the nature of those contacts if
we have already learned in some degree the character of the
parent Judaism. Reserving therefore till the next main division
the study of the New Testament material, we proceed in the
present chapter to the comparison between the Rabbinical
and non-Rabbinical presentations of the Jewish ethical teaching, in the light of what has been shown in the earlier chapters
of this work.

The term ' comparison ' is used here to include unlikeness as
well as likeness between the two objects to be compared.
Likeness there certainly was, in so far as both assumed those
fundamental ethical concepts which have been referred to as
the common stock. It was this common stock which held them
both within the bounds of Judaism. In regard to the Rabbinical
development from the common stock, there is no question of its
ever having gone beyond those bounds. Rabbinism is concentrated and intensified Judaism. But the development from
the common stock along non-Rabbinical, and especially
Apocalyptic, lines led into regions of thought and speculation

where the connexion with Judaism would sometimes be hardly recognisable if it were not for the presence of the ethical element. And even that ethical element is in some cases by no means conspicuous, the primary interest of the respective writers being in fact not ethical at all. It is for this reason that many of the non-canonical books have been treated in the foregoing chapters with what may have seemed undue brevity. It would have been a very long task to follow up the various lines of speculation which branch out from some of these books, into regions of history, cosmogony, folk-lore, mythology, and others, all important more or less, but all leading away from Judaism into something which was not Judaism. There was no occasion, for the purpose of the present work, to engage in that long task. It is sufficient, as it is very important, to recognise that in all the books which make up this literature there was, in greater or less degree, a tendency away from Judaism. Their authors were Jews and wrote as Jews; but the horizon towards which they looked lay further away than the frontiers of Judaism.

The presence of the common stock in the ethical teaching, alike of the Rabbinical and the non-Rabbinical line, is of course the basis of the likeness between them, and can easily be recognised. But the profound difference between them is much less seldom recognised, if, indeed, it has ever been recognised by those scholars, mostly Christian, who have exalted the non-Rabbinical teaching at the expense of the Rabbinical.

The difference lies in the fact that the two bodies of thought are not, so to speak, on the same plane, have not the same purpose in view, and do not use the same methods by which to attain that purpose. Or, more accurately, while the Rabbinical teachers had a definite aim and a definite method, the non-Rabbinical writers had no common aim and no special method. Both the one and the other imparted ethical teaching; but the Rabbis were not satisfied with merely imparting such teaching. Their whole system was an ethical *discipline*, the practical application of what was taught in the doing of right actions and the refraining from wrong ones, the needful guidance being provided by the Torah, duly interpreted. Books, other than the Scriptures, were not needed for the end which they had in view, and books they did not use. If they had done so, they would have defeated their own purpose.

The non-Rabbinical teachers, on the contrary, were writers of books ; and were only teachers so far that their books were there for anyone to read and learn from, as he might have inclination and opportunity. No one was compelled to read them or to learn what was taught therein. The writers were not united by any common purpose; they were solitary individuals, each writing as he thought fit and whatever he chose, according to the circumstances of his time and the place where he lived. These writers appeared from time to time during a period of some three centuries, and it is only in that sense that they form a group at all.

Their books became known, in translations, to the Gentile world, and such popularity as they acquired was due to Gentile readers. Most of them owed their preservation to the action of members of the Christian Church, who found in them material congenial to their own ideas. That they, or any of them, were well known or widely read by Jews in Palestine there is no certain evidence ; the fact that in no case except that of Ben Sira has the original Hebrew text survived, makes it unlikely. The Rabbinical teachers show no sign of any acquaintance with them.

It was through these books, and others of like kind, if there were any others, that Gentiles had their only means of learning what Jews were thinking and what they had to say. And if Gentile readers supposed that in these books they learned all that Jews were thinking, and all that they had to say, they made a very natural mistake. They had no means of knowing what was being done by an organised body of teachers, who had for several centuries pursued a definite line, had built up a coherent system, and developed its principles by hard thinking and untiring patience. Of what was being done in the Beth ha-Midrash there was no written record which the Gentiles could read, nothing to show them that anything at all was being done. With the result that what was done there, by way of ethical teaching, did not directly influence Gentiles at all, and was not intended to do so.

The Rabbinical teachers concentrated on what they considered to be the essence of Judaism, and cultivated it intensively;

they did not make it their primary aim to bring it into contact
with the Gentile world, still less to accommodate it to Gentile
ways of thought. Whether they were right or wrong in following
this policy is not here the question; but the fact remains that
the type of Judaism which they developed by following that
policy was the one which finally survived and which shaped
the Judaism of all the succeeding centuries. It is in this type,
if anywhere, that the real essential Judaism is to be found, that
which had most vitality and which was most clearly conscious
of its own significance. The Judaism which found expression
in the non-Rabbinical literature did not survive, as Judaism.
What was of value in it, or what was thought to be of value,
was taken up into the service of other forms of religion,
especially Christianity; and it was able to be so made use of
precisely because it was not of the essence of Judaism, and
because, by being written and translated, it was put within the
reach of Gentiles and virtually offered to them.

Now modern Gentiles have, with much less excuse, fallen
into the same error as the Gentiles who first read the Apocrypha
and Pseudepigrapha. They have supposed that in reading these
books they were learning to understand the Judaism of the time
of those writers, as in its essence it really was. They have accordingly laid great stress upon the importance of these books for
the study of Judaism, and have blamed Jewish scholars for
neglecting or disparaging them, by comparison with the Rabbinical literature. The reason why Jewish scholars, notably
Jost and Grätz, have assigned a less important place to the
Apocryphal and cognate literature by the side of the Rabbinical
is simply that these scholars were able to compare the two,
out of a knowledge of Rabbinics to which no Christian scholar
can lay claim, and of which very few Christian scholars have
ever seen the necessity, or felt their own want. The modern
Gentile, following the lead of Charles, Bousset, and Schürer,
has studied with diligent care the Apocryphal literature, and
devoted to it an elaborate provision of critical apparatus and
editorial scholarship which would perhaps rather astonish the
original writers of some of the books in the great Oxford edition.
He has believed himself to have come into possession of an
ancient treasure of knowledge concerning the Judaism of that
time. And no doubt he has found something which he could

find hardly anywhere else, and which therefore he does well to study. But he does not know the Judaism of the Rabbis, the work of centuries of hard thinking and persistent teaching; if he did, he would realise the futility of setting up, as more important than the achievement of this long-continued effort of concentrated thought, the productions of some twenty or thirty individual writers, each uttering his own thoughts and with no driving power of a common purpose behind him. Also he would realise that it is a mere waste of time to argue that any of those writers were Pharisees, solely on the ground of some likeness between what they respectively taught.

Merely considered as the result of mental effort, and spiritual effort also, the colossal fabric reared by the Rabbinical teachers, when compared with the works of the non-Rabbinical writers is as a mountain to a number of mole-hills. But it may be urged that the mountain is barren, while the mole-hills are evidence of labour which has not been useless. Or, to drop metaphor, it is claimed that in the Apocryphal and Pseudepigraphical books, especially the Apocalyptic works, the free prophetic spirit found liberty of utterance, which was denied it by the ' tyranny of the Law' (Charles). It has been shown above (p. 182 f.) that there was never any kind of constraint which would have prevented anyone from writing (and publishing, if he could) whatever he liked. But even if there had been such a constraint, it is surely a rather curious expression of ' the free prophetic spirit ' when it seeks safety under an assumed name. Whatever else it may be, it is not ' free ' when it does so; and its claim to be ' prophetic ' rests on its appropriation of just those elements in the ancient prophecy which were of least spiritual worth and most easily imitated. It is not here contended that Apocalyptic was mere imitation, a literary device deliberately employed without a serious purpose behind it. There can be no doubt that the Apocalyptic writers were perfectly sincere and deeply in earnest, and that makes their effort only the more pathetic. For they were men who were greatly troubled by the calamities of their time and the failure of the promised golden age to which Israel had been taught to look forward. They tried to recapture the secret of the prophetic faith which had beheld that future; they succeeded in reproducing the forward gaze, and thought that with it they had recovered the ancient faith. But the

[267]

ancient faith was not to be rekindled by such means; and what really inspired Apocalyptic was not faith, but anxiety, a hope that was never far from despair, a courage that tended to falter, and that could only be whipped up by new visions and promises. This is why the Apocalyptic form was repeated over and over again, in spite of the disappointment of all previous hopes, and explains why even the author of 4 Ezra, by far the greatest writer of those who used the Apocalyptic form, nevertheless chose that form for what he had to say.

There was strong and deep faith in many Jewish hearts even in the darkest times, and by reason of that faith Judaism was enabled to survive; but it owed nothing of its strength and depth to Apocalyptic teaching, and whether by deliberate choice, or happy chance, or by divine guidance, it kept itself free from that dangerous influence. There were strong men who did not lose their heads in the storm of calamity, but the Apocalyptists were not amongst them.

The appeal of Apocalypse was to the weak mind and the unbalanced judgment, as it was in itself the product of weak minds and unbalanced judgment, of men who were at heart terrified and dismayed, and who tried to keep up their courage by brave words. Apocalyptic does not represent the real essential Judaism of its time, and it failed to do so just because it followed a line which led away from the central position into regions where the controlling power of that Judaism was less and less strongly felt. It was like seaweed growing on a rock, which is torn off by the wild waves while the rock remains. Apocalyptic is always mournful in spite of its glamour of promise. It is a witness to the violence of the storm, which has shattered hopes and left ruin; and the story which underlies the Apocalyptic literature is amongst the saddest of those which make up the history of the Jewish people.

The real strength of Judaism, the persistent vitality and unconquerable faith which enabled it to survive through all the storms which threatened to destroy it, was that which was fostered and strengthened by the teachers of the Rabbinical line, the Sopherim, the Pharisees, and the Rabbis.

Let the Gentile say what he will of their system, their theory, and their practice, out of the little that he usually knows about it ; but the fact remains, and all the subsequent history of

Judaism rests on that fact, that it was they and they alone who saved Judaism, the real essential Judaism, whose strength and whose splendour they had learned to know through centuries of loyalty and resolute faith.

Who they were, what they did and why they did it, has been shown at length in the earlier chapters of this book; and it has also been shown, in later chapters, who were the writers of the Apocryphal and cognate literature, and what they accomplished and wherein they failed. The two have been set side by side, as was promised at the outset; and the reader is left to draw his own conclusions and express his preference as he will.

THE NEW TESTAMENT AND PHILO

CHAPTER IX

THE TEACHING IN THE SYNOPTIC GOSPELS

To approach the Synoptic Gospels from any direction is to approach a subject upon which innumerable books have been written, which presents problems of the greatest intricacy, and which raises far more questions than have as yet been answered on lines of general agreement. There are few, if any, signs that the battle of the critics is dying down, though the point of keenest strife may shift from time to time. Of course, a great deal of what is involved in the Synoptic problem (using that term in the widest sense) does not concern the object of the present work; but even on the limited field which will here have to be explored, occasions will not be wanting on which controversy might easily arise. No one can write about the Synoptic Gospels from any point of view without bringing in Jesus; and to write of the Jewish ethical teaching in those Gospels is to open the way for controversy over questions of comparison, priority, originality, as between the teaching of Jesus and the Jewish teaching which most closely resembles his. It would be comparatively easy to deal with such questions if there were not behind them the rivalry of two great religions, one of which claims Jesus as its founder, a rivalry, moreover, which has lasted from his time down to the present day. For Judaism has never been superseded, either *de jure* or *de facto*, and is a living religion for all purposes, as truly now as it was in the age of the Old Testament, and no less in the age of the Talmud. Christianity, whatever its leaders may have thought and said about Judaism, has always been confronted by a rival who refused to admit its claims.

The differences between Judaism and Christianity are fundamental, not merely in theological doctrine, but in ground principle; but yet in some of their features there is a strong likeness between them, and the fact remains that Christianity had its origin in Judaism, however the manner of that origin may be explained. Jesus and his immediate followers were Jews, and it does not appear that he, at all events, ever supposed that he was anything else. It is obvious, and admitted by all, that the earliest records of his life and work show him as one who spoke as a Jew to Jews, whose immediate surroundings, material and mental, were wholly Jewish, and the drama of whose life was set on a Jewish stage and played mainly by Jewish actors. With the drama of his life we have no present concern; but the teaching which is ascribed to him is to a large extent so markedly Jewish in form that the question of its relation to other known Jewish teaching cannot be avoided. It is this question which will form the subject of the present inquiry. The reader will observe that this inquiry does not extend to a general survey of the ethical teaching of Jesus, whether that which was original to him or that which was ascribed to him. Such a survey could, of course, be made, but to make it is not the object of this book. The particular inquiry before us is a necessary sequel to the study which has been made in the earlier chapters, of Jewish ethical teaching in two representative literatures; and it is necessary, because, in the Synoptic Gospels, we are met by a third body of teaching whose likeness to what has been already ascertained is too close to be accidental, and whose nearness in point of time makes comparison unavoidable. In other words, the teaching of Jesus is only relevant to the present inquiry so far as it is, in form or substance or both, in line with other Jewish teaching. By far the larger part of his recorded teaching comes under this description, and even that which does not takes its point of departure from what was essentially Jewish.

There does not seem to be any need to try to distinguish critically between sayings which were genuine utterances of Jesus and others which were, or may have been, attributed to him at various stages in the process of compiling and editing the Gospel records. Such an attempt, though well-nigh every critic makes one, is beset with great difficulties and liable to serious objection. It suffers from the want of any decisive criterion by which the critical judgment can be guided, and is therefore largely influenced by subjective considerations. In the case of any given saying it is seldom possible to prove definitely either that Jesus did say it or that he did not. At the most there is some general probability one way or the other, supported by plausible or even strong arguments, with a liberal resort to interpolations and re-arrangement of the text. The fact that a given saying is found in one Gospel only, or two, or three, is not decisive as to its authenticity; neither is its presence in or absence from Q, nor would it be even if all critics were agreed as to the exact contents of Q. The whole structure of Gospel criticism rests upon a foundation which can never be secure till the element of probability is replaced by certain fact and assured knowledge; and that this will at last be accomplished does not at present seem to be very likely. That Jesus said some of the words recorded in the Gospels can hardly be questioned, except by those who deny that there ever was a historical Jesus at all. But to determine exactly which he did say and which he did not say is seldom if ever possible. That he uttered a considerable number, even the greater part, of the sayings recorded in his name cannot indeed be strictly proved, but is by no means improbable, much more probable than that he did not. To decide exactly between the genuine and the unauthentic sayings of Jesus might be compared to the process of defining the exact limits of a shadow, e.g. on the moon. The more delicate and powerful the instruments employed, the more difficult it is to determine the precise line between the light and the darkness; while the ordinary observer, using no instrument other than his eye, can see well enough for all practical purposes where the shadow falls and where it does not fall. So in the case of the teaching of Jesus, precise and exact knowledge of the genuine as distinguished from the unauthentic has so far not been attained, and is the less likely to be attained in proportion to the delicacy of the methods employed; while the ordinary reader can see well enough that on the whole the teaching of Jesus was of such and such a character. But neither in the one case nor in the other can so great a certainty be attained as would form a secure basis for a further argument, as being safe from challenge. A reasonable probability is the most that seems attainable.

Now, in regard to the teaching ascribed to Jesus in the Synoptic Gospels, it is not of crucial importance for the purpose of the present inquiry to decide between the authentic and the unauthentic sayings, nor is the inquiry made vain by the

T   [273]

impossibility of doing so. The Gospels contain, amongst other things, a body of teaching, associated rightly or wrongly with Jesus, and accepted as his by those, whoever they were, who gave to the Gospels their final form as they have been transmitted and are now read. It is this body of teaching as a whole which we have to examine; and the line of distinction to be drawn is not that between the authentic and the non-authentic, but that between the Jewish and the non-Jewish in the form of its expression.

For whatever reason, the Gospel of Matthew contains the greatest amount of the ethical teaching of Jesus; and though important features are to be found in Mark and Luke, it would be possible to gain a fair knowledge of his teaching from Matthew alone. That Gospel contains the Sermon on the Mount as a whole, the other Gospels contain much, but not all, of the same material scattered over a number of different contexts. The fact of its being arranged in Matthew as a connected discourse shows that whoever so arranged it regarded it as a sort of compendium of the ethical teaching of Jesus. The reader is reminded that the term 'ethical' is used here, as throughout this book, in the sense explained at the outset (see above, p. 2), viz.: teaching in regard to the conduct of life as man's service of God. It does not imply any distinction between ethics and religion; on the contrary it marks them as inseparable. For a Jew there could be no religion which was not ethical, and no ethics which was not religious. A Jew, therefore, would regard nearly all the teaching recorded in the Synoptic Gospels as ethical, while a Christian would not; but only because the Christian is accustomed to distinguish as two what the Jew regards as one. Both would agree that the teaching in the Gospels has for its object the conduct of life as man's service of God.

The keynote of that teaching is found in the saying (Matt. vii. 21): 'Not every one that saith unto me Lord, Lord, shall enter the kingdom of heaven, but he that doeth the will of my Father which is in heaven', with which compare (Matt. xii. 50): 'For whosoever shall do the will of my Father which is in heaven he is my brother and sister and mother'. And one of the petitions in the Lord's Prayer is: 'Thy will be done, as in heaven so on earth'. It is in close accordance with this that practically the whole of the teaching recorded in the Gospels consists of injunctions to do this or that. The whole stress is laid on doing; and it is everywhere implied, though not everywhere expressly stated, that what is to be done is the will of God. This is entirely in accordance with the Rabbinical teaching as shown above (pp. 51-2); for their whole system rests on the axiom that the doing of the will of God must come before everything else. That is the one essential, whatever else there may be. For Jesus also the same axiom was fundamental; and his main quarrel with the Pharisees was that he rejected the halachah, which they regarded as the exact and only right way of doing the will of God, at all events in those cases on which a halachah had been or could be defined. And it was just because he regarded the doing of the will of God as the one essential that he rejected the halachah, for, in his view, that was not and could not be the only right way of doing the divine will. It will be observed that on nearly all the occasions of controversy between him and the Pharisees, according to the record, the point at issue was a question of halachah.

The fundamental axiom, then, of the teaching of Jesus was fundamental also in the Rabbinical teaching; for him and for them the doing of the will of God was the one essential that took precedence of everything else. The motive for doing the divine will was, for the Rabbinical teachers, simply the love of God. Every act done by way of serving him was a fulfilment of the precept: ‘Thou shalt love the Lord thy God with all thy heart,’ etc., and the reaction of the man who so served God was joy, ‘the joy of the commandment’ (see above, p. 134). The act commanded must be done for its own sake, *lishmah* (p. 133), and not for reward. Jesus named the commandment: ‘Thou shalt love the Lord thy God,’ etc., as the greatest in the Torah; and though he did not explicitly give this as the motive for doing the divine will, he cannot be supposed to have given any lower motive. It is indeed the only motive admissible in either his teaching or that of the Rabbis. And because his teaching and theirs started from the axiom that the doing of the will of God is the one essential, it follows naturally that both made use of the concept of Reward. What the Rabbis meant by Reward has been shown above (pp. 135-6). Reward denoted the better condition in which a man found himself who did the will of God as compared with a man who failed or neglected to do it. The expectation of reward was never regarded as the motive for doing the action. Jesus used the term 'reward' in several instances, thus (Matt. v. 12): 'Great is your reward in heaven'. Again (*ib*. v. 46): 'For if ye love them that love you, what reward have ye?' Again (*ib*. vi. 1): 'Else ye have no reward with your Father which is in heaven'. Compare also the phrase: 'Thy Father which seeth in secret shall recompense thee' (*ib*. vi. 4, 13). There is nothing to show that Jesus meant by reward anything different from what the Rabbis meant by it. For them and for him it rested on the belief that to God, being holy and just, it could not be indifferent whether a man did his will or not; and that in some way the man who did his will was in a better condition, by reason of the divine approval, than the man who did not.

The kingdom of God (heaven) formed the central idea of all the teaching of Jesus. Everything turned on that or had some bearing on it. Whatever he meant by it, Jesus from first to last preached the kingdom of God. And, whatever it was taken to mean by those who used the term, the concept of the kingdom of God was wholly Jewish. It had its origin far back in the older Scriptures, and is found in the Apocryphal and cognate literature; but it is nowhere found in non-Jewish literature except where it has been consciously borrowed, as by Christian writers. The term was used in more than one sense, and it is not always possible to decide in a given passage the particular meaning of the term in that instance. But the point at present is simply this, that in speaking of the kingdom of God, Jesus was using a purely Jewish term, and using it just as it had been used for centuries before his time. It has not been shown that he added any new feature to the meaning which it had for the common understanding of those who heard him.

So also the term Messiah (Christ) was a purely Jewish term, and, like the term 'the kingdom of God,' it had several meanings. But those meanings were all interpretations of a Jewish idea, and were wholly contained within the limits of Judaism. If Jesus understood the term Messiah in a sense different from any which it bore in the usual Jewish acceptance, then he was *ipso facto* not the Messiah, though he may have been something greater than that name would indicate. He used the term, and apparently no one ever challenged his use of it; and that is all that matters for the present purpose. Whether he ever applied it to himself is quite another question.

Concepts like those of the kingdom of God and the Messiah are more properly parts of the framework of his teaching than of its actual contents; but they are of importance for the present inquiry because they show how Jesus made use of Jewish concepts, which were familiar to all who heard him, as the means by which to convey his own teaching. He used them, indeed, not as something alien which he adopted, but as being the natural and obvious terms to use, he being a Jew speaking to Jews. And it was the same with the word Torah, which we read in our New Testament as Law. It is true that Jesus did not regard the Torah in the same light as that in which the Pharisees regarded it, and he repudiated their system of interpretation of the Torah which led to the halachah. He, on occasion, criticised the Torah, as when he declared (Matt. xix. 8) that what the Torah enjoined concerning divorce was a concession made by Moses to human hardness of heart, and not, as the Pharisees held, a divine revelation. But he is recorded as saying (perhaps at the beginning of his ministry): ' Think not that I came to destroy the Torah or the prophets; I came not to destroy but to fulfil ' (Matt. v. 17). And evidently he regarded the Torah as being in truth divine teaching, though not the only divine teaching, nor, in the last resort, the most authoritative. He quoted from it in argument, as in the instance just given and elsewhere; and he accepted as perfectly natural the challenge to say which was the greatest commandment in the Torah (Matt. xxii. 36). In other words, he habitually spoke of the Torah as of something which was perfectly familiar to his hearers as to himself, one of the elementary concepts of Judaism alike for him and for them. In the passage just referred to (Matt. xxii. 36), the two commandments which he quoted are both from the Torah (Deut. vi. 5 and Lev. xix. 18), and he gave them obviously as being in themselves the greatest, and not merely as the greatest in the Torah. He did not add ' But I say unto you ', and then give some higher and more inclusive precepts. It has already been shown (above, p. 239 f.) that the combination of these two commandments had already been made a century before his time, and that the text from Leviticus did not need any expansion on his part to make 'neighbour' equivalent to 'fellow man' (above, pp. 144-149). Jesus was not introducing anything new in his reference to these commandments. The Scribe (Mark xii. 32) highly approved of what Jesus had said, as he certainly would not have done if there had been anything new in it; the answer of Jesus was such as any teacher of Torah would naturally give if he were asked.

It has been stated above that one of the leading ideas in the Rabbinical teaching was that of the Imitatio Dei (see above, p. 129 f.). Man was created in the likeness of God, and the supreme end and object of his life was to realise that likeness so far as he could by doing such things as God did, and by being holy as God is holy. The two terms in which the Imitatio Dei is summed up are Kedushah and Hasiduth (*ibid.*), the former being further developed into the idea of Kiddush ha-Shem and its opposite Hillul ha-Shem. This connected group of ideas was evidently known to Jesus, but he did not make them so prominent in his teaching as the Rabbis did. The 'hallowing of the name' is the object of the second clause of the Lord's Prayer, but does not seem to occur elsewhere. Nor is any use made of the terms Kedushah and Hasiduth, holiness and saintliness. But when Jesus said (Matt. v. 48): 'Ye therefore shall be perfect as your heavenly Father is perfect,' it would seem likely that he had before his mind the text, which was fundamental in Judaism (Lev. xix. 2): 'Ye shall be holy for I the Lord your God am holy'. Whether he intentionally changed the word of the text from 'holy' to 'perfect' is a question which would be more easily answered if we knew exactly what he meant by 'perfect'. But the idea of Imitatio Dei is clearly expressed, and a variant occurs in (Luke vi. 36): 'Be ye merciful even as your Father is merciful,' which is almost exactly on the lines of the Rabbinic teaching (above, p. 130).

If the Sermon on the Mount is rightly regarded as a compendium of the teaching of Jesus, then it is clear that his teaching dealt entirely with Jewish ideas, even in those passages in which he substituted his own precepts for those give to 'them of old' (Matt. v. 21-48): 'Ye have heard that it was said . . ., but I say unto you . . .,' etc. His hearers would know perfectly well what he was referring to, his contrasts being based on passages from the Torah, and even from the

Decalogue*. So far as he intended his own precepts to supersede those of the Torah, and not merely to extend and intensify their meaning, his teaching was obviously his own and cannot be brought into line with that of the Rabbis. Yet it is not recorded that any objection was made to him on the ground that he was setting aside the Torah as it was certainly made on other occasions. It seems more likely that what he intended was to imply that the teaching of the Torah was good so far as it went, but that it really meant a great deal more than it said. Thus the commandment, ' Thou shalt not kill,' really forbade anything in the nature of anger or even contempt, and not murder alone. The commandment, ' Thou shalt not commit adultery,' really extended to the unclean thought, and not alone to the sinful act. This extension of meaning in regard to this form of sin was well known to the Rabbis. Jesus indeed was only doing, in regard to the precepts of the Torah, what the Rabbis did, i.e. he amplified and extended them by the light of his own ethical sense, though he reached the same result by a different way. Some of these extensions of the original scope of ancient precepts go beyond anything which could be paralleled in Rabbinic sources. ' Love your enemies ' has always been felt by Jewish critics as an impossible demand. To refrain from anger, to take no vengeance, to do good to the enemy if the opportunity presented itself, all this was possible and often insisted on in Jewish ethics; but to love him, in any real sense, was beyond human power. From the Christian side it is urged that this was a heroic paradox, an ideal with all the impossibility of an ideal. We are not here concerned with the explanation of the saying, but only with the fact that here, at all events, Jesus went beyond the limits of any Jewish teaching known in his time or since. The same objection is made to other precepts in the same context, ' Resist not evil '; ' Whosoever shall smite thee on thy right cheek turn to him the other also'; ' If any man would go to law with thee and take away thy coat, let him have thy cloak also '; ' Whosoever shall compel thee to go one mile,

---

* But in the case of ' Thou shalt love thy neighbour and hate thine enemy', the quotation is not accurate. There is, as everyone knows, no text in the Old Testament which says 'Thou shalt hate thine enemy'. Neither is there a text in these words in the Rabbinical literature. It would be interesting to know if anyone who heard Jesus pointed this out to him.

go with him twain'. No Jewish ethics has ever admitted that these precepts were justified, or that they could be acted on without causing wrong in their turn. Yet it is possible to see a way by which Jesus may have arrived at these paradoxes along a Jewish line. It has been shown above (p. 140) that the Rabbinical ethics counted it for a virtue that a man should not insist on his legal rights, but should, for the sake of promoting harmony and brotherly love, accept something less; the name for this principle was *liphnim mishurath ha-din*. It is at least conceivable that Jesus had in mind this principle (whether he knew the formula or not) and that he intended his precepts as illustrations of the kind of conduct implied in it. The precepts remain heroic paradoxes as before, or ' interim ethics ' if that be preferred; but they are paradoxes such as might naturally arise in a Jewish mind working on Jewish ideas.

Without going through the Sermon on the Mount, let alone the three Gospels, verse by verse, we may compare the teaching of Jesus with that of the Rabbis in regard to some specific virtues; and first of all we will take love to father and mother. This is one of the cardinal virtues in Judaism, being contained in the Decalogue. What the Rabbis taught concerning it has already been shown (see above, pp. 161-3). Jesus included it amongst those which he told the young man to observe (Matt. xix. 19); and he did not in so many words disown it. But it should be remembered that he is recorded to have said words which certainly would tend to weaken the obligation. Thus (Matt. xii. 46-50, and parallels) when he was told that his mother and his brethren stood without, desiring to speak to him, he replied: ' Who is my mother? and who are my brethren? and he stretched forth his hand toward his disciples and said " Behold my mother and my brethren"'. Again (Matt. x. 37) he said, ' He that loveth father or mother more than me is not worthy of me '. And in Luke xiv. 26 his recorded words are: ' If any man cometh unto me and hateth not his own father and mother . . . he cannot be my disciple '. The point at present is not what he meant by these words, assuming that he said them; it is simply that by saying them he certainly appeared to diminish the force of the original commandment. To this extent his teaching was off the line of the usual teaching on the subject.

Next, we will take the virtue of Forgiveness. Jesus adds to the Lord's Prayer the saying (Matt. vi. 14, 15): 'For if ye forgive men their trespasses, your heavenly Father will also forgive you; but if ye forgive not men their trespasses, neither will your Father forgive your trespasses'. This is exactly paralleled in the Rabbinical teaching, 'Let this be a sign in thy hand; so long as thou hast mercy on thy fellow, the All-present [*Makom*] hath mercy on thee, and if thou art not merciful, the All-present is not merciful to thee' (j. B. Kam. 6*c*; the first clause also in Pesik. R., p. 165*a*). These passages are later than Jesus; but the question of priority and dependence as between his teaching and that of the Rabbis will be discussed in the next chapter. It has already been shown (p. 157 f.) how great was the stress which the Rabbis laid upon forgiveness as between man and man; and, in dealing with the Testaments of the XII Patriarchs, we have noticed the very remarkable teaching on that subject (p. 241), than which nothing more lofty is to be found in either Jewish or Christian literature, on that particular subject. It is clear that Jesus was substantially in agreement with the current teaching of his time in regard to forgiveness; though it may be noted that he did not work out the subject in reference to the injurer as fully as the Rabbis did. His general teaching was on the same lines and to the same effect as theirs; and they raised no objection to it except in regard to his claim, as they took it to be, that he had authority to forgive sins (Matt. ix. 2, and parallels). This, however, is a theological question, and does not affect his ethical teaching. We are concerned here not with who he was, but with what he taught. So far as forgiveness between man and man is concerned, there is no appreciable difference between what he taught and what the Rabbis taught; and in regard to God's forgiveness of man the same is true, though there is one apparent exception. In Mark iii. 29 and parallels there is the famous saying about the Unpardonable Sin: 'Whosoever shall blaspheme against the Holy Spirit hath never forgiveness, but is guilty of an eternal sin'. The words 'hath never forgiveness' (*en lo mehilah olamith*) occur in the Rabbinical literature (j. B. Kam. 6*c*, and elsewhere), and the word *olamith* is found in quite trivial connexions; which shows that neither the whole phrase nor the particular word carried any such tremendous meaning as Christian theologians

[281]

have read into the Gospel text. It implied severe condemnation, as of a sin which was above all others hard to forgive; but it certainly did not imply eternal reprobation on the part of God. The Rabbis had no such idea, neither had Jesus; and, if those who were responsible for rendering his words into Greek had known more of his native language, they would not have made such an unfortunate and disastrous blunder. Jesus ought not to be held responsible for a theological monstrosity.

He used the words in reference to slander, because the Pharisees had said of him: ' By the prince of the devils casteth he out devils'. And it was precisely in reference to slander, though not this particular slander, that the words ' hath not forgiveness forever' were used in the passage (j. B. Kamma 6c) quoted above. Slander, or any other form of word or act by which a man was put to public shame, was severely condemned in the Rabbinical teaching; and when Jesus denounced (Matt. v. 22) the man who should say to his brother *Raka*, or 'Thou fool', he was taking exactly the same line.

So also his teaching about veracity, honesty, sincerity, and truthfulness was on the same lines as that of the Rabbis, even though he chose to brand the Pharisees as hypocrites. Why he did so is most readily explained* by the fact that he did not know the halachah except as a practice which he condemned, and had no understanding of what it meant to those who taught it and made it their rule of life. He was not more severe than they were in denouncing hypocrisy and every form of insincerity and falsehood. What they said about these things has already been shown (see above, p. 153 f.); what he thought about them may be gathered from his sayings in Matt. vi. 1-18 about almsgiving, prayer, and fasting, because the point in all these passages is the need for an inward sincerity which does not depend on, and ought to avoid, any signs of outward approval. He did not tell his hearers not to give alms, not to pray, or not to fast. The last is worth noting, because it would not have been surprising if he had released his disciples from the obligation to fast, and, in fact, it is remarked (Matt. ix. 14) that his disciples did not fast. Almsgiving, prayer, and fasting were among the most usual, and in a sense necessary, expressions of

* See my *Pharisees*, p. 116 *sq.* Jesus is merely a particular instance of those who know halachah only by observation, not by practice.

the Jewish religion. Judaism would be almost unthinkable without them. Jesus no doubt condemned the way in which these religious duties were, or seemed to him to be, performed by those whom he called the hypocrites. In regard to almsgiving, if anyone ever did literally 'sound a trumpet before him' (Matt. vi. 2) when he gave alms, he would be deserving of contempt; but there is no evidence that anyone, certainly not any Jew, let alone any Pharisee, ever did such a thing, or dreamed of doing it. But Jesus knew that there were in the Temple thirteen boxes for the reception of gifts, amongst other things for alms. These boxes were called 'Trumpets', from their shape. He knew also that there was in the Temple a room called ' The Chamber of the Silent', where those who wished could make their gifts in secret, and where those who received charity could do so without being known. I repeat the suggestion made elsewhere* that Jesus said in effect: ' Do not put your alms into the " Trumpets ", but put them in " The Chamber of the Silent "'. The mistaken reference to the synagogues and the streets may have crept in from v. 5.

The injunctions in respect of almsgiving, prayer, and fasting are followed by the warning not to lay up treasures upon the earth (Matt. vi. 19, 59), which leads into the more general thought of not being anxious for the morrow. The whole drift of the passage is on Jewish lines. The phrase, ' lay not up treasures upon earth,' is found in substance, though not verbally, in T. Peah. iv. 18, and variants occur elsewhere. The injunction ' Be not anxious for the morrow ' is made the subject of a haggadah (Mechilta, Beshall., p. 47*b*) based on Exod. v. 13; literally, 'the thing of a day on its day'. There is not an exact parallel, but the thought is the same. And the closing words, ' Sufficient unto the day is the evil thereof,' are found almost exactly in b. Ber. 9*b*, where Moses addresses them to God. The meaning, as there explained by Rashi, is the same as in the Gospel text. The words may well have been a proverbial saying in common use. In like manner the saying 'with what measure ye mete it shall be measured unto you ' (Matt. vii. 2) occurs in the Mishnah (Sotah i. 7), and the principle of ' measure for measure ' was well known to the Rabbis. This also may well have been a proverbial saying, which any teacher might

* See my *Judaism in the New Testament Period*, pp. 150-1.

[283]

naturally use. The figure of the mote and the beam (Matt. vii. 3) is found in b. Erach 16*b*, where it is used by R. Tarphon, early second century A.D.; but again looks like a proverbial saying. ' Physician, heal thyself ' (Luke iv. 23) is there said to be a proverb (parable, *mashal*), and it is not likely to be the only proverb which Jesus made use of. ' Knock and it shall be opened unto you ' is found in another connexion (Pesik. R. C., p. 176*a*), and may be a proverb, as may also ' Ask, and it shall be given you ', ' Seek, and ye shall find '. Whether original to Jesus or not, there is nothing un-Jewish about these sayings. Indeed, the whole passage from the beginning of Matt. vii. seems to be mainly made up of references to well-known sayings, and is fitly concluded by the Golden Rule: ' All things there- fore whatsoever ye would that men should do unto you, even so do ye unto them'. The saying, in positive or negative form, and usually shorter than here, is found in several places, the earliest being Tobit iv. 15 (see above, p. 250, and reference there to Abrahams, *Studies*, i, p. 20 *sq.*). Hillel, in b. Shabb. 31*a*, gives the negative form of the saying, and adds: ' This is the whole Torah '. It is significant that Jesus said ' This is the Torah *and the prophets* '. Jesus may have heard Hillel's remark quoted by someone, and enlarged it. If he knew nothing about it, the likeness is certainly remarkable.

If Jesus, as the above examples show, made use of proverbial phrases current in common speech, he also made use of the parable form. Here, too, he was working on Jewish lines, for the parable was an ancient, perhaps a very ancient, means of conveying instruction. There are parables in the Old Testa- ment, and they occur by hundreds in the Rabbinical literature. There is a close relation between the parable and the symbolic visions of the Apocalyptic writers, though the advantage is all on the side of the parable. But if Jesus took up the form of the parable, he made the substance of it unlike anything that had ever been seen before. Some of the parables, indeed, such as those in Matt. xiii. 44-50, are quite short, being no more than a mere comparison, where a single action forms the basis of the likeness. Parables on this small scale are quite common in the Rabbinical literature. They are usually intro- duced by the formula, ' To what is the thing like? To . . . so and so,' and then follows the parable. But the great parables

in the Gospels are worked out on a scale and with an elaboration of detail for which, so far as I know, there is no parallel
in the Rabbinical literature. It is, however, only a matter of
degree. The parable form was in use by Jewish teachers, and
had been for a long time. Some were more skilful than others,
and Jesus, as it would seem, was the most skilful of all.

Enough has been brought forward in this chapter to show that
the ethical teaching of Jesus covered a very large part of the
ground taken in the Rabbinical teaching. On some points it
did not, but went outside that ground; as e.g. in the great
declaration about clean and unclean (Mark vii. 15, and, in
particular, v. 19). Also the ' heroic paradoxes ' noted above. It
is by no means contended here that Jesus was a mere echo of
the Pharisaic teachers. It is contended that, having something
of his own to say, he naturally used many, very many, of the
usual terms in which to express those of his thoughts where no
controversy was involved. And it is this considerable element
alone which is the subject of the present inquiry. The position
here taken is that there was a large amount of ethical teaching
common to all in that age who gave such teaching at all; and
that what is recorded in the Synoptic Gospels, to the extent
indicated above, shows how this common material appeared
quite naturally in the teaching of Jesus, whatever else his
teaching might contain. With the latter we are not here concerned; not because it is not extremely important in itself, but
because this whole book is a study of *Jewish* ethical teaching,
and does not extend its survey to teaching which was not
Jewish. Jesus is here considered not as a religious leader on his
own account, exerting an influence of immeasurable importance, but as a teacher whose recorded sayings form a particular
case of a general fact of his time.

There is, however, one element in his recorded sayings which
has close affinity with those aspects of Judaism represented in
the Apocryphal and especially the Apocalyptic literature. In
all three of the Synoptic Gospels are to be found passages of an
Apocalyptic character, ostensibly spoken by Jesus. These are
not indeed ethical in the sense in which that word has been
used throughout this book, and they do not belong to the
common ground because, as has been shown at length, the
Rabbinical teachers did not include Apocalyptic in their

subject-matter. None the less Jesus, or whoever gave to his words the final form in which they are now read, may have shared in the Apocalyptic element in Judaism though the Rabbis did not. The material common to the Gospel record and the Apocalyptic literature is as unmistakable in its way as the material common to the Gospel record and the Rabbinical teaching. In any case, the Apocalyptic matter in the Gospels cannot be passed over without notice. Only very brief notice, however; for, as has been pointed out more than once, the Apocalyptic teaching is not, strictly speaking, ethical at all; and, in the literature which chiefly contains it, the amount of Apocalyptic matter on the whole varies inversely as the amount of ethical matter. So it is also in the Gospel record, where the Apocalyptic matter is not apparently very large in amount. In the most conspicuous passage (Mark xiii and parallels) much of what is said appears to refer to the war period which ended with the capture of Jerusalem A.D. 70. If this is so, then the main contents of the passage are later than the time of Jesus and cannot have been spoken by him. They are in style and matter much like other Apocalyptic writings such as have already been examined; and it can hardly be denied that whoever put the Gospel Apocalyptic passages into their present form was acquainted with one or more written works of that kind. ' Let him that readeth understand ' (Matt. xxiv. 15) is a clear intimation to the reader of the Gospel that he will find the answer he needs in some Apocalyptic work. There is thus a close affinity between the Gospel record and the Apocalyptic literature already studied; and there may have been— indeed, there almost certainly was—some acquaintance with that literature on the part of at least the final editors of the several Gospels. Whether Jesus himself had any such an acquaintance is quite another question; and, in accordance with what has been said above (p. 272 f.), I do not offer any positive answer to it. I only suggest that a sufficient point of attachment of Apocalyptic matter to the teaching of Jesus is provided by the fact of his preaching the kingdom of God. This he constantly did; and, whatever he meant by it, a Messianic and Apocalyptic meaning could be, and certainly was by many of his hearers, put upon the term. This would make it possible to include in the record of his words all the

Apocalyptic material now found in the Gospels; and to do so in all good faith, even though Jesus may never have spoken it. If there be indeed such a fundamental incongruity between ethical and Apocalyptic teaching, as has been maintained above, then the student may fairly ask himself whether Jesus, whose insistence on the ethical side was so strong as his recorded teaching shows it to have been, was likely to have attached so much importance to the Apocalyptic side. Those who were responsible for the final form of the Gospel record may, and probably did, attribute to him sayings which he did not utter. If they did this in regard to ethical sayings, it is equally likely that they did so with regard to Apocalyptic sayings; with only this difference, that the Apocalyptic matter which they incorporated was of a kind for which they could easily find examples in writings of that description, while the ethical teaching they could not easily find still less imitate.

These are mere suggestions of a method of regarding the Apocalyptic matter in the Gospel record. That is only subsidiary to the main subject of this book, because, like the similar matter in the Apocryphal and cognate literature, it represents a divergence from the main stem of Judaism, which was intensely ethical. And possibly the presence of Apocalyptic matter in the Gospels marks, as it does in the older literature, a tendency away from Judaism, and is one of the signs which point to the final breach with Judaism on the part of Christianity. So far as the Gospel record is concerned, all that is taught, Apocalyptic or ethical, is taught in Jewish terms, and forms a twofold common ground with the older Judaism. On the ethical side it has close affinity with the teaching of the Rabbinical line. On the Apocalyptic side it has close affinity with the literature of that class. All of it is attributed to Jesus in the Gospels as they are now read, and much of it, at all events of the ethical teaching, is probably authentic. The question must next be considered: How did it come about that there was so large an extent of common ground between the teaching of Jesus and the other bodies of teaching already examined? To this question the next chapter will be devoted.

Chapter X

THE REASON FOR THE COMMON GROUND

The fact that there was, between the ethical teaching of Jesus and that of the Rabbis, a likeness so close and so far-reaching, as has been shown in the foregoing chapter, cannot be regarded as a mere coincidence. If it were, it would be a case of a whole series of coincidences, not of one only. Coincidence may be at once ruled out. The alternatives which remain are either borrowing on one side or the other, or dependence on a common source. The argument concerns only so much, a very large portion certainly, of the teaching of Jesus as was, in form or substance, similar to that of the Rabbis. In regard to what was not such, his originality is not called in question.

But even in regard to what was common to both it has often been claimed that the originality belonged to him, not to the Rabbis; as on the other hand it has been maintained that the originality belonged to the Rabbis and not to him. It seems to be assumed by scholars on both sides that there must have been borrowing, in order to account for the likeness. But if it can be shown that borrowing on either side was extremely improbable, and that another explanation will fit the facts more completely, it will not be necessary to spend much time on the theory of borrowing.

When a man borrows, he does so in order to obtain something which he does not already possess. In the case before us, if Jesus borrowed from the Rabbis, it must have been because he thought that they had what he had not, viz.: Ethical ideas expressed in positive teaching of a kind superior to any which he had, or such as he had not been able to arrive at for himself. If the Rabbis borrowed from him it must have been for the same reason. If not, why borrow? Now the amount of the common ground is very considerable, as has been shown in the previous chapter; and it is the contents of the common ground which form the subject of the borrowing, if borrowing there were. Is it to be supposed that either Jesus on the one side or the Rabbis on the other were so entirely destitute of ideas on the subjects included in the common ground that he or they must make up the deficiency from elsewhere? Yet so it must necessarily have been, on the ' borrowing ' theory. If all the matter of the common ground were cut out from the recorded teaching of Jesus, an immense gap would be left, and the remainder would be by no means enough to account for the influence which Jesus produced by his teaching. In like manner, if the common ground were cut out of the teaching of the Rabbis a similar gap would be left, and that too in the teaching of a body of men who had been engaged since the time of Ezra in developing the interpretation of the Torah along ethical lines, both as halachah and haggadah, and not along ritual and ceremonial lines except so far as these also were ethical. Considering that all their work was based on the Scriptures in general and the Torah in particular, it is inconceivable that on the subjects included in the common ground they should have had nothing of their own to say, and must wait till Jesus came and supplied the want. Merely to state what is implied in the ' borrowing ' theory is enough to show that it is untenable. And, if this were not enough, it may be added that whatever Jesus thought of the Rabbis, and his words to them were sharp and severe, they on their side were entirely hostile to him. The allusions to him in the Talmud and Midrash* make it quite impossible to believe that the Rabbis would ever have knowingly taken over anything which he had taught; and they could not have done it unknowingly. Of course it might be said that the alleged borrowing took place at a time when the controversy between them had not yet become acute, or when it had not yet begun to show itself; but even in that case the difficulty would remain, that there would then be, on the one side or the other, the huge deficiency of ethical ideas which could only be met by borrowing. The attempt to account for the common ground by borrowing, on the one side or the other, is a hopeless failure.

That the key to the right solution of the problem is to be found in the Synagogue will appear from a consideration of the facts in regard to ethical teaching in the time of Jesus. Leaving him for the moment out of account, and considering the period

* See my *Christianity in Talmud and Midrash*, where all the passages are collected and form the first half of the book. See especially the story of Eliezer b. Horkenos, *ib.*, pp. 137-145.

immediately before his public appearance, we find that the Pharisees were the only religious body to make a point of giving such teaching at all, and that they did it by means of the Synagogue, an institution which was entirely under their direction and expressed their ideas. The Sadducees never troubled about the religious training of the people, apart from answers which might be given by priests in the Temple to persons who sought direction upon doubtful points. It was the practice from of old to seek Torah from the priest (Jer. xviii. 18); and, although in the period with which we are concerned the Pharisaic teachers of Torah had been long established, it is conceivable that the ancient practice of consulting the priests was not wholly extinct. But this would only concern individual persons who took the trouble to go to the Temple for the purpose. The Sadducees did nothing outside the Temple for the religious instruction of the people. There were no Sadducean synagogues. The Essenes lived, for the most part, in isolated communities; and, though presumably they instructed their own members, they had as Essenes no appreciable influence upon the Jewish people as a whole. The Zealots were busy with other things than religious instruction, except so far as revolution could be brought under that head. The Pharisees were the only ones who provided religious instruction definitely and of set purpose, and on as large a scale as they could. The Synagogue which was their means of doing this was linked up with the Beth ha-Midrash and the Great Beth Din, in the manner described in an earlier chapter (see above, pp. 96-108). What is there explained at length cannot, of course, be repeated here; but the reader should bear it carefully in mind, if he would understand the condition of things in regard to religious instruction in the period with which we are at present concerned.

The Synagogue was the place where the Torah, as divine teaching, was brought to bear upon the lives of the people, of those at all events who attended there. And, as there were by this time synagogues in nearly every town and village in the country, they must have influenced a considerable proportion of the population. Not everyone went to Synagogue; and, of those who did so, not everyone conformed to the full demand of the Pharisaic discipline. But all who were present would necessarily hear the teaching that was given and the prayers that were recited. Both the teaching and the prayers were the result of the deliberations of the Teachers of Torah in the Beth ha-Midrash; and, so far as halachah was declared for the guidance of the people, it was what had been authorised by the Great Beth Din. All this had been going on for centuries, as the Sopherim and the Pharisees had gradually developed their system; and all this was in full operation at the time at present under consideration.

What the nature of the teaching was which was given in the Synagogue has been shown in two previous chapters (see above, pp. 109-126, 126-169); and, if the arguments put forward in those chapters are sound, we are justified in saying that the main stream of ethical teaching flowed continuously, from its source in the Torah and the Scriptures generally to the time when it was collected and arranged in the various Midrashim, substantially without a break and without a change of direction. It is not here contended that everything recorded in a later Midrash, Pesikta Rabbathi for instance, was actually said in the Ezra-Hillel period. It is contended that the general lines of ethical thought were unchanged, the general view taken of the main virtues and vices remained the same, so that the same or similar things could be said about them, and that where there was variation it was in the working out of details not in the statement of main principles. This applies mainly to the Haggadah; in the case of the Halachah there was change, and it is correct to distinguish between the older Halachah and the later Halachah; though this is done sometimes by those who have no close acquaintance with the subject of their remarks. But in regard to the Halachah the modifications made from time to time were for the purpose of greater ethical efficiency (see above, p. 112 f.).

Such was the ethical teaching given through the agency of the Synagogue, the same in its main features, different only according to the ability of the teacher who set it forth, the needs of the occasion and so on. All, teachers and to a large extent hearers also, were associated in a common work, whose object was to realise in their actual life the implications of the Torah as the supreme revelation of God.

So far as is known, the whole life of Jesus was spent in such a way as would bring him under the influence of the Synagogue and of the teaching which was given there. Even when he had begun his public career, he went to Synagogue 'as his custom was' (Luke iv. 16) on the Sabbath day. It was never remarked of him that he had had at any time broken that custom, that it was something strange for him to be seen in a synagogue; nor is it recorded of him that he ever said a word against the Synagogue as an institution or against the practice of going there. For him, as for most of his countrymen, the Synagogue was part of the regular order of things, and to go there on the Sabbath a custom which raised no question.

If, then, Jesus had been accustomed, from early childhood and through youth up to manhood, to go to Synagogue on the Sabbath, he would hear from week to week, or as often as a discourse was given, such teaching as has been described above and designated as the 'common ground'. And he would begin to hear it long before he was of an age to form his own ideas about it, or to criticise it if he were inclined to criticise it. What he heard would be teaching having for its object the right conduct of life; and the terms in which that teaching was given were necessarily the current phrases and ideas appropriate to that teaching. There were no others to use, or no others which could by any remote possibility be heard in a village synagogue. He grew up therefore accustomed to hear these phrases or to use them himself, and to cast his thoughts upon religion into these forms, unless for any reason he found them unsuitable for his purpose. The extent of what has been called the common ground marks the extent to which he accepted without challenge the words and ideas of the religious teaching with which he had grown up. They were what came naturally, perhaps even unconsciously, into his mind when he would himself think and speak of religion, as a teacher. If they conveyed what he wished to say, why should he seek for other means of expression? If they did not convey what he wished to say, why should he use them? He did use them, to the extent indicated by the common ground. Moreover, he used them to express and to mean what they always had expressed and meant, as in the current usage of the time they were always understood. No one ever challenged his use of them, or remarked that he was putting a new meaning into the old words. If, as has often been alleged, he took the old words and gave them a more spiritual sense his hearers were quite unaware of his doing so, and accepted what he said without question, obviously because it was what they had themselves been accustomed to teach and to hear. They showed themselves ready enough to challenge him when he disputed the validity of the halachah; and if they could have found a flaw in his ethical teaching they would hardly have passed it over. In regard to the common ground, and just because it was common, they had no reason to challenge him. What he said was what they said, taken for granted on both sides without question.

In regard, therefore, to the matter of the common ground, the case of Jesus is simply an instance of how the general ethical teaching as it had been developed and variously expressed up till his time appeared in him, and appeared naturally and, in a sense, necessarily. We have found it in the Rabbinical teaching, in Ben Sira, and in varying degree in the Apocryphal and cognate literature. Even the Apocalyptic writings, so far as their teaching is ethical at all, are, on the whole, in accord with the general teaching of the time. Which means that all in that time who concerned themselves with ethical teaching started, so to speak, from a common base, and that what originality they showed appeared when in one direction or another they struck out lines of their own. To study that originality, whether in the case of Jesus or any other, is obviously not within the purpose of this book.

It has been argued that Jesus arrived at the ideas and phrases which appear in his teaching by way of his own independent study of the Scriptures; so that he owed nothing to the influence of the Synagogue on which so much stress has been laid in this chapter. That he did study the Scriptures no one would deny for a moment; probably he knew them very well, for he could always quote the right passage when he wanted it. And it has already been shown, in examining the various examples of ethical teaching in previous chapters, that such teaching was derived from the Scriptures, and, on the whole, was what they taught only carried in some cases to a higher level, and developed in greater detail. But it does not follow, and is very unlikely, that an independent thinker setting out to study the Scriptures for himself should arrive at conclusions which, over so wide a field as that of the common ground, coincided so closely with those of the teachers of whom, *ex hypothesi*, he had been independent. Also, however much Jesus studied the Scriptures for himself, the fact remains, until the contrary has been shown, that he did come under the influence of the Synagogue in the manner described during practically the whole of his life; and presumably it had the effect upon him which has been suggested. With that the question of the common ground of the ethical teaching may be left to the judgment of the reader.

The presence of Apocalyptic matter in the Gospel record has already (p. 285 f.) been referred to as forming a secondary common ground as between the Gospels and the Apocalyptic writings. A word may be said on this point before leaving the subject of the common ground. The Apocalyptic matter in the Gospel record is ascribed to Jesus, along with all the other sayings. The period which elapsed between the death of Jesus and the time when the earliest Gospel, Mark, received the form in which it is now read, was quite long enough to allow of Apocalyptic matter being introduced into the record even if it were not authentic. It is closely akin, both in matter and style, to the usual type of Apocalyptic; indeed, if it occurred in some other work, most of it would not suggest any connexion with the Gospel. Whoever wrote it (or spoke it) in its present form knew very well what Apocalyptic writing was like.

Now that Jesus himself ever read an Apocalyptic book rests on no evidence except the passages now in question, and to conclude on that evidence that he did is to beg the question. The reader is reminded of what was said above (p. 188 f.) about the state of things in regard to the reading and circulation of books in Palestine in the period with which we are concerned. If what is there put forward is well founded, it is in the highest degree unlikely that Jesus ever had an Apocalyptic book in his possession, or any other book except the Scriptures. Scholars have written about ' Books which may have influenced our Lord '; but it remains to be shown that they ever did influence him, except so far as he may have heard something in a general way of their contents. ' If Jesus and his immediate disciples had any acquaintance with notions such as we find in the Apocalypses, say Enoch 45-58, it may be taken for certain that they did not get them by reading the books, but by hearsay, perhaps remote hearsay. In the same way they had their knowledge of the teaching of the Scribes from the homilies of the Synagogue and other religious discourses. With our Gospels the case is antecedently somewhat different. One or more of the writers may have looked up things in books, as they undoubtedly looked up Bible texts and brought in more scripture. But that even they drew immediately on Apocalyptic writings is not demonstrable' (Moore, *Judaism*, i, p. 131). Those are the weighty words of a great scholar in the particular field with which this book is concerned; and though they shatter a good many theories which have been put forward, they will hold good until, if ever, some greater scholar refutes them.

The extent and nature of the common ground mark the degree in which Jesus, whatever he may have been in himself and whatever else he may have taught, was in regard to his ethical teaching in line with the other teachers of his time and country. And the Apocalyptic matter in the Gospel record, whether spoken by him or not, shows no originality, and is all of a piece with that contained in contemporary writings of the kind. With this conclusion we may leave the subject of the common ground.

CHAPTER XI

THE PASSAGE OF THE JEWISH ETHICAL TEACHING INTO CHRISTIANITY

THE fact that there is so close a likeness between the ethical teaching of the Rabbis and that of Jesus, as has been shown and explained in the two preceding chapters, a likeness, moreover, so wide in its range of subjects, can be stated in another way by saying that the Jewish ethical teaching passed over into Christianity, and did so by the bridge of the teaching of Jesus. It is beyond question that in the Christian ethical teaching, not merely that recorded in the Synoptic Gospels but that contained in the New Testament generally, there is a great deal which is Jewish in form and substance; but it is also true that in such teaching, at all events outside the Synoptic Gospels, there is a difference which clearly marks it as in some way un-Jewish. That difference does not appear so clearly in the teaching of Jesus himself as it does in that of his followers, but it is not wholly absent even from his. A Jew reading the New Testament would probably find himself inclined to admit that a good deal of the ethical teaching was very like what he was accustomed to, but that yet it did not sound quite the same. If the melody was the same, it was played on a different instrument. It is well worth while to ascertain, if possible, why there was this difference and exactly in what it consisted. Even if it were the case that Jesus himself simply took over from the Jewish teaching just what commended itself to him, it is certain that this was not what his followers did. What they took they took from him, apart from such knowledge of the Scriptures, and, in some cases, of the Synagogue teaching as they might have already acquired. He was the bridge by which the Jewish teaching passed into Christianity; and when it had passed over the bridge it found itself in a territory which was not Jewish, and its own character underwent a certain modification. This transition is what has to be explained. And it is not explained by saying that the difference between the Jewish and the Christian teaching, especially the teaching of Jesus himself,

[297]

is that the latter is more spiritual than the former, more lofty, more universal and the like. It is quite impossible to establish by any proof such alleged difference of quality; and merely to assert it without proof is to beg the question. That was not the difference between Jewish and Christian ethical teaching, even in the case of Jesus himself; and still less is it so in the case of the New Testament writers. To seek for differences of spiritual quality as between the one side and the other is to go off on a false scent, and to make comparisons which are not merely invidious but also futile. The problem must be approached from a quite different direction.

The transition from Judaism to Christianity, at all events in regard to the ethical teaching with which alone we are concerned in this book, was made when the place hitherto occupied by the Torah was taken by Christ. I use the name Christ rather than Jesus in this connexion because, in the New Testament, which expresses the completed transition from the one religion to the other, Christ is the name mainly used in referring to the source of the revelation from which the new religion drew its inspiration. In one sentence, what the Torah was (and is) for Judaism Christ is for Christianity.

The process of change from one to the other was made in two stages. The first was that in which the passage was made from the Torah, as the supreme authority and chief source of divine revelation, to Jesus who was his own authority, who at least acknowledged no other authority as overriding his own reason and conscience. He did not repudiate the Torah, he recognised its great importance partly on its own account and partly from its age-long sanctity; but he did not allow it to have the final word, if that meant surrendering his own intuitions of right and truth. This is the meaning of what was said (Matt. vii. 29): ' He taught them as one having authority and not as their scribes'. The point of this comparison is not in the custom of the Scribes to guarantee their own teaching by that of some earlier teacher, but in the fact that their authority was the Torah while his authority was himself. We are not concerned with the question why he claimed and exercised that authority, we are simply noting the fact that he did claim and exercise it; which is a fact, whatever the explanation may be.

The second stage in the process of change was that in which

[298]

Christ became to his followers the supreme authority and chief source of divine revelation. We leave on one side all other aspects of the person and work of Christ, as they were variously apprehended and defined by his followers. In the matter of the ethical teaching he came to be regarded by his followers as the one above all who could and did reveal the way of the perfect life, the life which men as children of God ought to live, the things they ought to do and those they ought not to do, and the spirit, temper, or frame of mind by which their life ought to be inspired. What he taught came to them with an authority than which none was higher. When the Christian would know what his duty was, how he was to order his life in such a way as to be most pleasing to God, he turned to Christ either for precept or example, or for the illumination of soul which would enable him to see what he was looking for. This is precisely what the Jew did, and does, in regard to the Torah; and the crucial difference between the two forms of religion is that the one is centred on an Idea and the other on a Person. The transition from Torah to Christ as the seat of authority was the transition from a non-personal to a personal expression of revelation; but, on the one side as on the other, the revelation was there and was owned to be divine, invested with supreme authority. The ethical teaching, alike Jewish and Christian, was founded on that revelation, in the one case through the interpretation of the Torah, in the other by the direct words of Christ. Therefore, the contents of that teaching could and did pass over into Christianity with little appreciable change; but the motive for doing what the teaching enjoined was necessarily different on the Christian side from what it had been on the Jewish side.

The ethical teaching which passed over into Christianity was of two kinds, closely related to each other. There was, first, the body of teaching which has been described as the common ground, and which Jesus may be said to have acquired by inheritance—or, rather, which expressed his own ethical ideas in the customary phrases and concepts of the time. This body of teaching, as it is recorded in the Gospels, must have been in existence, if only as oral tradition, before the Gospels were written, though it may not have been gathered into any orderly form. Whatever it was, and however it was remembered and repeated, it was remembered and repeated as being his. There would be no other reason why it should be remembered and repeated. It was of no interest to any one that what was thus remembered and repeated was to a large extent what had been taught in the Synagogue, and what some, at all events, of his earliest followers had heard there. For all alike who followed him the teaching was his, and they received it only because it was his. It was nothing to them that it had its source in a distant past, whence it had come down alike to him and to them.

The second body of ethical teaching which passed over into Christianity was that which was contained in the Scriptures. This was the ultimate source of all Jewish ethical teaching, and it continued to be so, to a considerable extent, in Christianity. For the Scriptures as a whole were taken over as the sacred books of the new religion; indeed, not taken over but immediately and instinctively used as the credentials and divine warrant of the Christian movement.

The Scriptures, read as they were read constantly by the converts to Christianity, would exercise upon them the same influence in the ethical direction which they always have exercised upon their readers. No doubt the ethical was not the chief motive, still less the only motive, with which the early Christian ' searched the Scriptures '. But it was one of the motives, and with the other motives we are not here concerned. Thus, the Christian Church found itself at the very outset in possession of a body of ethical teaching which was of divine authority, either because it was contained in the express words of Christ or because it was written in the Scriptures. And this is what is meant by what was said just now, that the contents of the teaching passed over into Christianity with little appreciable change.

But the motive for doing and being what was enjoined by the teaching was not the same for the Christian as it had been for the Jew. In the last resort, indeed, the motive was the same for both, but not in the immediate statement of the motive. For the Jew the motive was loyalty to the Torah, the precepts of which were to be obeyed for the sake of the Torah, *lishmah* (see above, p. 133 f.). For the Christian the motive was loyalty to Christ, and his precepts were to be obeyed for his sake and as a sign of discipleship. The Christian in the New Testament is

[300]

constantly called the servant of Christ, and his first duty is to obey his master. The contrast between the attitude of the Jew to the Torah and that of the Christian to Christ is apparently very great; and it is emphasised by no one more than Paul, who, indeed, had experience of both. It is mainly from him that the Christian has learned to set over against each other the ' bondage under the Law ' and the ' freedom wherewith Christ has made him free '. The contrast is hardly more than superficial. There was a certain difference in the attitude of mind as between Jew and Christian; but it was not of the kind suggested in the contrast drawn by Paul, and was very much less than he, to judge by his general conception of Judaism, would be in a position to recognise.

It is the general assumption that the Jew is bound by the ' Law ' in such a way as to leave him no freedom of choice in regard to his religious and moral duties, while the Christian is free to follow the dictates of his conscience, and is bidden to do so. Whatever truth there may be in this statement, it is by no means the whole truth, and as it stands it is not true at all. The problem is more subtle than such a rough-and-ready solution would seem to indicate. A nearer approach to the truth can be made by the help of a careful analysis of the Jewish and of the Christian positions respectively in regard to this matter of freedom and bondage; and one result of that analysis will be to disclose the ultimate difference, already referred to, between the ethical teaching as it was in Judaism and the same ethical teaching as it was after it had passed over into Christianity.

Let us consider first the case of a Jew trained in the ethical teaching of the Rabbis, as set forth in earlier chapters of this book. What are the several factors which in his case combine to produce the resulting action? There is first of all God, whose will he desires to do. Next, there is the Torah, the written record of the revelation which God has made of what his will is. The motive by which he desires to do the divine will is his love towards God. He feels the obligation to show that love by doing what God would have him do. In order to learn what that is, he turns to the Torah, and he finds there expressions of the divine will in the form of precepts, *mitzvoth*, some of which are wide in their scope, like ' thou shalt love the Lord thy God ' and ' thou shalt love thy neighbour as thyself ', and others which

are restricted in range, like ' thou shalt not sow thy field with
two kinds of seed ', and others of every degree of extended
reference. As he may have occasion to do one or other of these,
he will find his directions in the Torah, but the obligation
to do them is what he owes to God, and he owns that obligation
as being himself a free agent able to choose whether he will
obey or disobey. Now in regard to some of the mitzvoth, he
has more detailed guidance, as to the manner of doing them,
in the halachah, which is the definition given by the wisest
teachers of what the right way is of doing the divine will in a
given case. Halachah is itself Torah, being one of its precepts
set forth in more exact detail and with greater clearness; much
as some part of an object seen under a microscope is part of the
object although seen in fuller detail. And being Torah it is a
revelation of the divine will, more closely defined, and therefore to be done from the same motive, viz.: the love of God.
In regard to other mitzvoth there is no halachah, but there is
still the obligation, and this is pre-eminently the case with
'Thou shalt love the Lord thy God'. That includes everything
else, and no halachah could ever define it. How it should be
obeyed was left to the conscience, ' committed to the heart '
(see above, p. 137 f.); and the meaning of that is that the
obligation involved in love to God and consequent duty towards
him was always present, and that the halachah, where there was
a halachah, only defined the precept of the Torah at this point
or at that. The whole ethical life of a man was within the range
of love to God and consequent desire to do his will. With such
motive, and the guidance of the halachah if there was a halachah known to him, and by the prompting of his own conscience
if there was not, the Jew regulated his action in any given case.
  Now let us consider the case of a Christian, by a similar
analysis. What are the several factors which in his case combine
to produce the resulting action? There is first of all God, whose
will he desires to do. Next, there is Christ in whom, or through
whom, comes to him the revelation which God has made of
what his will is. The motive by which he desires to do the
divine will is his love towards God. He feels the obligation to
show that love by doing what God would have him do. He
turns to Christ, either for a distinct precept or for illumination
of his conscience by contemplating the source of revelation.

[302]

But in his case there is no halachah. If there be a precept in the words of Christ, it remains in his words as he gave it; and there is no one who has authority to define its meaning in greater detail. If there is no precept, then the Christian fulfils his obligation by following the dictates of his own conscience.

Comparing these two cases, we find that they correspond step by step except at one point, indicated by the presence or absence of the halachah; and in each case the final action is that of a free moral agent, able to choose whether he will obey or disobey the divine will. Assuming that in each case there is a given amount of energy of will directed towards the same objective, viz.: the doing of the will of God, the difference is only in the way in which the energy of the mind reaches its object, and that way is different mainly because the medium of revelation is in the one case an Idea and in the other case a Person. Halachah was possible and even natural in the one case, because an idea can be developed, and halachah was the development of Torah at the point defined. But a person cannot be developed; and the fuller understanding of the revelation made in or through that person can only be attained by study of his own words and still more by contemplation of himself, whereby the disciple hopes to become, and in some degree does become, ' as his master'.

Further, we have to inquire into the nature of the obligation felt in each of these two cases. It is usually said that the Jew is under the constraint of an external authority, while the Christian is free from such constraint. What precisely is the authority in each case? and in what sense, if any, is it external? The ultimate authority, alike for Jew and Christian, is of course God. The obligation to do his will is owned by both. Is that an external constraint or not? It is a constraint, though not a compulsion, because it gives a lead to the will so that it may act in the right direction. Without that lead action would have no moral quality. And the constraint is external because it is not imposed by a man on himself. It originates with God, and is only so far internal that it is discerned and owned in the conscience. But if it is said that the Torah is an external authority, and that there is no such authority for the Christian, the contrast becomes on examination less evident than it appears at first sight. The Torah is *ex hypothesi* divine revelation, recorded in a book developed by competent interpretation. Apart from the fact of its being divine revelation, it has, and can have, no authority. That which it has belongs to it as the expression of the mind and will of God. The halachah is only a part of Torah and carries the same authority for the same reason. Therefore, the externality of the Torah does not affect, still less create, its authority. And if the man who owns that authority were not a free moral agent, he could not recognise that authority or feel the obligation which it imposes. Christ also is, *ex hypothesi*, divine revelation, or better, the medium of divine revelation. And, whether that revelation be expressed through his spoken words or by his personal character as apprehended by the disciple, his authority, so far as the revelation is concerned, is the authority of God whose mind and will are therein revealed, and not his own.

Further, when it is said that a Jew is not free to go against the Torah, it may be asked: Is the Christian free to go against Christ? What the one can do the other can do, and neither would willingly do it. If the Christian regards Christ as the revealer of God's will, then either he will feel himself bound by the precepts of Christ or he will not. If he feels himself bound by those precepts then he is as much under external authority as the Jew with his Torah. And if he does not feel himself bound by those precepts, in what way do those precepts convey the revelation of the divine will? As before, the only point of difference between the two cases is the presence or absence of halachah; and the halachah was the basis of a discipline to which the Jew, if he accepted the Rabbinic system, voluntarily submitted, because to do so helped him to live his life as a service of God. The discipline imposed certain consequences upon disobedience, encouraged obedience and so on, as has already been shown in the earlier chapters of this book. But that discipline did not set up the obligation involved in doing the will of God; it was simply a means towards fulfilling that obligation, and an effective reminder of it. If the Christian had no halachah, and dispensed with the discipline which went with it, so be it; he was left with the original obligation as before, and his own resources for meeting it. These ought to be sufficient, and no doubt often are sufficient; but it is not, on the face of it, evident why the taking of careful thought for the fulfilment of an obligation and the provision of a constant reminder of it should be considered the mark of an inferior mind and a lower type of morality.

Having now to the best of my ability set forth the modification which the Jewish ethical teaching underwent in its passage into Christianity, I proceed to the last notable exposition of that teaching in the period with which are we concerned, viz., the writings of Philo. He lies in a different region than that of the New Testament and will be the subject of a separate chapter.

CHAPTER XII

PHILO

PHILO, the Jewish philosopher of Alexandria, is in some respects unique. If he was not the first, he was beyond question the greatest of those who have attempted the fusion of Judaism with Hellenism. That he himself was a Jew, not merely by birth but by conviction, is plain to every reader of his works. That the general system and body of thought which he worked out could in any true sense be called Judaism is extremely doubtful. It has never been recognised as such by those who have been qualified to represent Judaism. Certainly, if it was Judaism, it differs so widely from those other forms of Judaism which have been already examined that its affinity with them is scarcely to be recognised. We have seen, in the case of Christianity, that a considerable body of Jewish ethical teaching passed over from the older to the younger religion, and did so by means of the bridge provided by the teaching of Jesus. But in the case of Philo the change which took place was of a different kind, and was concerned with a different subject. That which was by Philo blended with Hellenism was not especially the Jewish ethical teaching. Such teaching of that kind as is to be found in his works is much more Greek than Jewish, certainly Greek in form and probably Greek in the manner of its derivation from main principles. Moreover, the ethical teaching in Philo does not take by any means so prominent a place as it does in the Rabbinical sources, or even in the Apocrypha and cognate literature. So much is this the case that for the purpose of this book Philo is really of but small importance.

Yet he cannot be left out, because he affords a second example, along with Christianity, of the transformation of Jewish teaching into something else. Whether or not his own system of thought can still be called Judaism, it marked a wide departure from such Judaism as was known in his time; and Philo's influence upon later theology and philosophy was not exerted towards the furtherance of Jewish ideas or the attainment of Jewish objects. He himself was as consciously a Jew as Jesus was; but he, no less than Jesus, opened the way for a departure from Judaism into something which did not profess to be, and certainly was not, Judaism. It is therefore necessary, in order to complete and round off the subject of this book, to consider this second departure from the main Jewish stock. This might have been done, and, if chronology alone were to be considered, might have been better done before dealing with the New Testament; for Philo (born about 20 B.C., died perhaps after A.D. 50) was earlier than the writers of the New Testament, though contemporary with Jesus. But the rise of Christianity, and in this connexion the transformation of the Jewish ethical teaching into the Christian, were of far greater importance, both in themselves and their results, than the speculations of the Alexandrian philosopher. He is accordingly here relegated to the second place.

The main links which connected Philo's philosophy with Judaism were two, viz.: Belief in God, as personal and as one; and belief in the Torah, as the divine revelation made through Moses. These beliefs are not so much connecting links between Judaism and Philo's philosophy as rather fundamental Jewish beliefs which he retained in full force, and with which he combined his Greek ideas. It is in virtue of these two fundamental beliefs that he is entitled to be regarded as a Jew, but at the same time as a Jew of a very unusual type. He does not fall within any of the usual classifications of Judaism; and he serves to prove by one more example the complexity of Judaism in the period with which we are concerned. To call him a Hellenistic Jew is to say very little, because there were probably as many types of Hellenistic Judaism as there were of Palestinian. With any known type of the latter Judaism he certainly cannot be identified.

We have seen, in connexion with the writers of the Apocryphal and cognate literature, that their bond of union with the main stock of Judaism was the ethical teaching, which formed a basis substantially the same for them all. They, and especially the Apocalyptic writers, diverged from the main stock in this direction or in that; but they never left their base in the fundamental ethical teaching, and no question could ever arise as to whether or not they were Jews. In the case of Philo, how-

ever, the same could not be said. The ethical teaching which
was fundamental in the older Judaism was not the base of his
Judaism, nor even a marked feature of it. Of course, his
philosophical system included ethics and he had much to say
about virtue and vice; but his teaching was not ethical in the
sense which has been given to that word throughout this book,
viz.: teaching directed to the right conduct of life as man's
service of God. Virtue and vice had their place in human life,
doubtless; but Philo's explanation of how they came to be there
was very different from that of any of the older teachers. It was
Greek, not Jewish; and thus it appears that, in regard to the
particular subject of this book, Philo is almost a minus quantity.
Yet even this negative result calls for explanation, since it is
highly remarkable that the blend of Judaism with Hellenism
effected by Philo should involve the loss of an element so
characteristic of the older Judaism. To offer an explanation of
this negative result will be the subject and the main justification
of the present chapter.

For a full account of Philo's system the reader is referred to
the extensive literature which has gathered round his writings.
No attempt will be made here to give such an account, because
it would be entirely irrelevant to the purpose of this book, and,
even if it were necessary, would only be satisfactorily done by
someone with a thorough and expert knowledge of Philo's
works. The purpose in hand can be attained by the help of a
much less comprehensive knowledge. We have to consider the
two fundamental elements of Judaism to which Philo, no less
than his predecessors, steadfastly clung, viz.: First, the belief
in God as Personal and as One; and, second, the belief in the
Torah as the divine revelation made through Moses. His
treatment of the Torah will account for the almost complete
disappearance of the ethical teaching as it had appeared in the
older sources.

Philo's belief in God was substantially that of all his Jewish
predecessors, in that for him God was personal, the supreme
mind, self-conscious and self-directing, the creator who had
made all things, and made them because he chose to do so.
He made them so and not otherwise because he was perfectly
wise, and he made them at all because he was good. Creation is
the act of love. As Creator he had also made man, out of the

dust of the earth, matter, as regarded his body, by imparting of his own spirit as regarded his soul. Philo was true to Judaism in recognising that God and man were different, there could never be such a union that the identity of either would be merged in the other. Harmony there might be, but harmony could only exist between two. Man could strive to attain to the knowledge of God, and to do so was the highest end of life; but always such knowledge was of a divine object other than man himself. Philo, in blending Judaism with Hellenism, adopted much from the Stoics; but he never compromised his Theism with the Greek Pantheism. He was thus able to retain the personal relation between God and man, so that for him the terms father and child, as expressing that relation, included much more than the mere fact of origin of one from the other or the common nature shared by both. Man was the object of God's love, since God had given him all that he enjoyed, and had done so out of his free grace. Man, therefore, owed to God gratitude as to a benefactor; and his highest object in life was, or ought to be, to come to an ever fuller knowledge of God. Philo's belief in God would include all of the best in the Old Testament on that subject, but yet with a difference. For him, God was the God of all men, not of Israel in any exclusive sense. All his teaching was applicable to man as man, so far as he was capable of receiving it, and had no special reference to Israel. No doubt God had given the Torah to Moses, and through him to Israel; but the Torah in its true meaning was intended for all mankind. The particular precepts, and other teaching contained in it, when rightly explained, did not refer to Israel alone but contained lessons of divine truth and wisdom for all men. And, so far as Israel had any special function, it was to act as the medium through which this divine revelation was to be made available for the whole human race. Thus Philo stands for unqualified Universalism; and, though indications are not wanting in the Old Testament and in the Rabbinical and Apocryphal literature of a wider outlook than the merely national, Philo abandoned practically all national limitations in his conception of the relation between God and Man.

Of the Unity of God Philo had no more doubt than any Jew. Not that he laid any stress on the numerical one-ness of God, but that for him there was no question of number at all, there

was simply God, the supreme Reality on whom depended all
and everything in heaven and earth and in the mind of man.
It is true that he does hint at a threefold apprehension of God,
but it is only of three aspects of the one supreme and only God;
and Philo never felt that he was in danger of infringing the
Divine Unity, the corner stone of Judaism for him as for all
Jews.

Philo's second main Jewish belief was in the Torah, as the
highest divine revelation. This was in a sense the foundation of
his whole system, for almost all his arguments are supported
by texts from the Torah. Yet his use of it was very different
from that of any of his predecessors, and calls for careful
examination.

It has been shown above that the Maccabean Revolt had for
one of its main results the establishment of the Torah as the
supreme authority in Jewish religion, an authority acknowledged by everyone openly challenged by no one. And it was
pointed out at the same time that there were wide differences
of opinion, amongst Jews, as to what the Torah really was,
and what was the proper way of dealing with it.

Sadducees and Pharisees took diametrically opposite views on
these questions; but alike for them and all who stood midway
between them, the Torah was owned as the supreme revelation.
Therefore it did not follow that because some writer had much
to say of the Torah he was on that account a Pharisee. The
justice of that remark is seen in the case of Philo, for he treated
the Torah as practically the only divine revelation, at all
events the only written record of such revelation, while it would
be absurd to call him a Pharisee.

Philo's use of the Torah is remarkable. For him it not only
took precedence of all the other Scriptures, as it did for Jews
generally, but it almost eclipsed them in his thought and
attention. His references to Canonical books other than the
Torah are comparatively very few, though it can hardly be
supposed that he did not know the whole of the Scriptures or
the greater part of them. One would have thought that he
would find much that was congenial in the writings of the great
prophets, especially in the universalism of the Second Isaiah,
or in the hymns of the Psalmists. If he did, he has not given any
clear indication of the fact. And perhaps the reason why he

[311]

concentrated on the Torah to the exclusion of the rest of the Scriptures was that he set out to show how the wisdom of the Greeks was already contained in the revelation given to Israel, and that he desired to convince Greeks that such was the fact. For that purpose the Torah was especially fitted, because it was in Philo's view a self-contained body of legislation, precept, and instruction, all delivered to Moses by God himself in the most direct and solemn manner. To no other, prophet, psalmist or sage, had such a tremendous gift been entrusted, so great a commission been assigned. No other, therefore, could serve so well to carry conviction to the Greek readers of Philo whom he was trying to persuade. Moses is for him the great law-giver, the chief prophet, the wisest teacher amongst men, since his words contained only divine wisdom and truth.

It has often been remarked as strange that Philo should have made all his citations from the LXX, when it would be expected that so learned a Jew would read the Scriptures in Hebrew. Yet, if his purpose was to convince Greeks of the excellence of the Scriptures, and to expound to them the hidden wisdom they contained, his arguments would carry more weight if he could appeal for his proofs to words which Greeks could read for themselves. If at the same time he did not himself read Hebrew easily, perhaps not at all, this method would have still greater advantages.

Philo would have yielded to no Rabbi in his veneration for the Torah, but he would have followed no Rabbi in the way in which he regarded it and the use to which he put it. To both, Philo and the Rabbis, it was the supreme divine revelation; but to the Rabbis it was the revelation of the will of God and of his ways, teaching of all that it concerned man to know for the living of his life in the service of God. Moreover, it referred in the first instance to Israel, and only through Israel to mankind at large. The object of the Torah, at all events on its preceptive side, was that those to whom it was given should do what was commanded and refrain from what was forbidden. Hence, for the Rabbis, the interpretation of Torah along the lines of Halachah and Haggadah, in which they summed up their answer to the question: How shall a man best serve God by the life he lives?

Philo looked at the Torah from a very different point of view.

For him, the main purpose of life at its highest was to be found not in the *doing* of right actions, not in the doing even of the will of God as such; it was to be found in seeking to know God. That gives the clue to the meaning of the whole system of Philo; in the last resort, everything turns on that. He sets forth his views on the nature of God and of man, of the relation between them, and the ways by which it is possible for man to rise ever higher towards fuller (though never complete) knowledge of the ultimate divine Reality. Philo's writings cover a wide range of subjects, and deal with most of the great problems of the higher life; and through all can be traced the longing desire for more perfect knowledge of God, nearer approach to him. Philo is a mystic as well as a philosopher, and perhaps mystic is his highest title to fame.

It is evident that there could be no place in his system of thought for any such results as the Rabbis drew from their study of Torah. There could be neither Halachah nor Haggadah in Philo's exposition; for since the *doing* of the actions commanded by God was not in his view the main end of life, there was no point in defining exactly the right way of doing those actions. Haggadah was not intrinsically impossible; but Haggadah such as the Rabbis knew it does not appear in Philo. What does appear is highly characteristic of him, and that is Allegory. His object, in expounding the Torah, was to find there not directions for conduct but statements of truth, disclosures of wisdom, all that could throw light on the mental and spiritual nature of man, and on the mystery of God. Allegory was the only way, it would seem, in which he could obtain the desired result. To use the Rabbinical method was out of the question. The Apocalyptic method might have been made to serve the purpose, but would have been cumbrous and far less direct. The method of Allegory might be said to have the advantages of Apocalyptic without its drawbacks; for Allegory was, in a sense, Apocalypse without the vision, so that the reader was told at once the hidden meaning instead of having it suggested to him in some fantastic contrivance of imagination. If Philo had wished to take the Apocalyptic line, he had many examples to follow on the Jewish side. He learned Allegory from the Greek side; and, by the use he made of it, found a home for Greek ideas in a Jewish medium, to which they were in themselves entirely uncongenial. Allegory is as much a *tour de force* as Apocalypse; both are exempt from verification or control, both are at the mercy of the pious imagination, and it is hard to say which of the two is the more destructive of all sense of contact with reality in the dull and tedious results to which they lead.

It follows from Philo's definition of the highest aim in life as the knowledge of God, that ethical teaching, in the sense so often assigned to the term in this book, could have no direct importance for him and could occupy but a small place in his system. For him, virtue was a condition of soul which God helped man to acquire, or even developed in him, in proportion to his ascent in the scale of wisdom and goodness towards more perfect knowledge of God. The virtues and vices are by Philo arranged and treated on Greek not Jewish lines; and, while in their contents they largely coincide with the corresponding Jewish virtues and vices, the motives which inspire them and the means by which they are acquired, so far as they are acquired, are entirely different. Philo knows nothing of the *simhah-shel mitzvah* (see above, p. 134), nor of *lishmah* (p. 133), and takes but small interest in performing the mitzvoth at all. The whole of what is set forth in the earlier chapters of this book in regard to the ethical teaching of the Rabbis would have little or no attraction for him. He had his own way of arriving at the same, or, as he would no doubt consider, better results. He followed that way; but in so far as he did so, he journeyed into a region where according to Jewish ideas he was a stranger. He took with him his belief in God and in the Torah as the divine revelation. But the ethical teaching, which for so many, perhaps all, of his Jewish predecessors constituted the chief meaning of the revelation made by God in the Torah, he could not carry with him, and it withered away in the new home where his spirit was henceforth to dwell. And with him ends the second attempt to carry over the Jewish ethical teaching into foreign surroundings, and the last presentation to be made, in this book, of the Jewish ethical teaching in the early centuries. Indirectly, it continued in its Christian form to exercise an influence upon the spiritual development of the human race which will last while Christianity lasts. But the direct line of the Jewish teaching must be traced in the Talmud and the

Midrash, and in the long succession of ethical books reaching down through the Middle Ages to the present time. The Apocrypha and Pseudepigrapha fell by the wayside; the Apocalyptic cries of triumph and despair died away in silence; only the true and authentic voice of Israel, speaking through her sages and her saints and sounding ever the note of the Torah given from God, is heard through the centuries, even unto this day.

INDEX I

SUBJECTS AND NAMES

ECCLESIASTES (Koheleth), book of, 24-27; why included in the Canon, 24; epilogue to, 25-7; possibly not Jewish, 27

Eliezer b. Horkenos, 135, 203, 290*n.*

1 Enoch, book of, a compendium of Apocalyptic, 211, 215; ethical teaching in, 218-20; hatred and vengeance in, 219; no appeal to individual responsibility, 220

Enoch, Secrets of (2 Enoch), 258; ethical beauty in, 258

Erub., 121

1 Esdras, book of, 246

Essential, the, of religion in Rabbinical Judaism, 53, 124, 141, 265 f.

Esther, additions to the Canonical, 254

Ethical teaching, defined, 2, 10; in the various types of Judaism, 3; in the Torah, differences, 10; Rabbinical, expressed as Halachah and Haggadah, 53; based on Scripture, 53; given orally, 56 f.; popular effect of, 56, 81; how differed from non-Rabbinical, 63; a discipline, 167 f., 191, 264, 304; during Ezra-Hillel period, evidence for, 110, 166-7; standard of, 179; common ground, with non-Rabbinical, 179, 206-7; and that of Jesus, ' spiritual quality ', 294, 297 f.

Ethical motive changed in passage to Christianity, 300

Ethical obligation of the Jew under Torah, 134 f., 301 f.; of the Christian under the Gospel, 302 f.

' Evasions of the Law ', alleged, 121, 154

Exile, the, 13

' External books ', the, 195-6; constraint, 303

Ezra, 13, 117; -Hillel period, 31, 110; -Hillel period, importance for ethical teaching, 31; a real person, 32; Rabbinical view of, 33; main object of, 33-4, 38; makes the Torah supreme, 36 f.; opposition to, 40; institutes exposition of the Torah, 41; ordinances attributed to 33, 57; why omitted from Ben Sira's list of worthies, 202

4 Ezra, book of, 258 f.; not written by a Pharisee, 259

FATHER AND MOTHER, honour to, 161-3, 280

Forgiveness, 157-161, 281; and the duty of the injurer, 161

Gemiluth hasadim, 134, 142

Genibuth daah, 156

Ger, 146

Gezeroth, 69

God, unity of, not merely numerical, 151; idea of remoteness of, derived from Apocalyptic, 218; Kingdom of, 276, 286; doctrine of, in Philo, 309 f.

Golden Rule, the, 148-9, 250, 284

Good deeds, 141 f.

HAGGADAH, 50, 53-4; how differs from Halachah, 53; no system of, 127; only found in Rabbinical literature, 192

Hagiographa, no definite formation of Canon of, 7, 15-16; want of unity amongst, 15; not all collected at once, 16

Halachah, 50, 55; how differs from Haggadah, 54; ethical development of, 109-126; need for, 111; could be modified, 112; relation of, to text of Torah, 113; why defined at all, 123-6; as law, 139; absent from Apocryphal and Pseudepigraphic literature, 192; absent from Christian ethics, 303; absent from Philo, 313

Ha-sha‘ah tzerichah lecach, 117

Hasidim, 83, 92

Hasiduth, 130

Hasmoneans, Beth Din of the, 89, 97, 116

Hatred, occasional expressions of, in Rabbinical literature, 150

Hellenism described, 75 f., 86; effect of, on Jews, 78

Hillel, 116, 148

Hillul ha Shem, 132 f., 153

Homeros, 195 and *n.*

Honesty, 155-7, 282

Hughes, Maldwyn, 142*n.*, 172*n.*

Hypocrisy, 153, 282 f.

Hyrkanus, John, 89, 94, 99

IMITATIO DEI, 129-133, 148, 237, 278

Isaiah, martyrdom of, book, 256

Index II

A. RABBINICAL PASSAGES CITED

1. Mishnah
Peah ii. 6, 65, 95
Pesaḥ x. 5, 113n.
Hagg. ii. 2, 94, 95
Sotah i. 7, 283; viii. 1, 2, 48-9; ix. 15, 203
B. Kam. viii. 1, 73, 119; 7, 160
Sanh. x.(xi.), 1, 195
Edu. viii. 4, 67
Aboth i. 1, 59, 102, 118; 2, 44, 46, 60, 142; 3, 135; 3-12, 65, 94, 147; 4, 21; 10, 133; 18, 152; iii. 15, 141; iv. 13, 141
Jad. iii. 5, 7, 197; iv. 6, 195n.

2. Tosephta
Peah iv. 18, 19, 143, 283
Shabb. xiii. 5, 159
Joma v. 12, 153
Gitt. v. 4, 5, 144
Sanh. vii. 1, 101
Jad. ii. 13, 196 and n.

3. Palestinian Talmud
Ber. 14b, 135
Meg. 75a, 33
Ned. 41c, 147
Kidd. 61b, 161
B. Kam. 6c, 281, 282
Sanh. 28a, 195

4. Babylonian Talmud
Ber. 9b, 283; 12b, 160; 28a, 153; 33a, 106
Shabb. 13a, 118; 13b, 197; 14b, 65, 96; 31a, 148, 284; 55a, 153
Erub. 13b, 72
Pes. 113a, 153
Joma 35b, 101, 116; 84b, 115; 85b, 117
Succ. 20a, 33
Bez. 30a, 121
Jebam. 79a, 143; 90b, 114
Gitt. 61a, 144
Sot. 14a, 143; 42a, 153

Kidd. 31a, b, 162; 40b, 142
B. Kam. 82b, 33, 57
B. Mez. 58b, 54, 137, 156n.; 82a, b, 57; 99b, 140
B. Bath. 12a, 72, 114; 14b, 23; 60b, 120
Sanh. 21b, 33; 82a, 89, 97; 92a, 153; 100b, 203
Shebu 39a, 157
A. Zar. 19a, 135; 36b, 89, 97
Hull 44b, 118
Erach. 16b, 284
Kallah 51a, 157

5. Midrashim
Mechilta 37a, 130; 47b, 283; 59b, 140; 89b, 156; 103b, 117
Siphra 86c, 131; 88d, 137; 89a, 147; 99d, 133
Siphrē ii. 84b, 135; 85a, 130; 107b, 114; 140a, 154
Aboth R. N. 26, 148
Ber. R. xxiv. 7, 148
Koh. R. on xii. 12, 195
Pesik. R. C. 152a, 73; 176a, 284
Pesik. R. 165a, 281
Tanhuma 87b, 44
Midr. ha-Gadol 549, 131

B. OLD TESTAMENT PASSAGES CITED

Gen. i. 27, 130; iii. 21, 143; v. 1, 148; xi. 3, 145; xv. 10, 145; xviii. 1, 143; 19, 143; xxv. 11, 143; xxv. 19, 24, 151
Exod. v. 13, 283; xi. 2, 145; xv. 2, 130; xviii. 20, 140; xx. 10, 111, 115; xxi. 24-25, 73, 118; xxiv. 3, 86; 7, 156; xxxiv. 6, 7, 130
Lev. xix. 2, 11, 130, 131, 278; 14, 137; 18, 144-8, 239, 240, 277; 33, 34, 146; xxii. 32, 133; xxv. 14, 17, 155
Num. xv. 24, 97
Deut. iv. 2, 113; 24, 143; v. 33, 136; 29, 156; vi. 4-7, 11, 239; 18, 140; vii. 3, 38; xiii. 5, 143; xv. 1-3, 119;

C. APOCRYPHAL AND PSEUDEPI-GRAPHICAL PASSAGES CITED

D. NEW TESTAMENT PASSAGES CITED

ABBREVIATIONS

RABBINICAL TITLES USED IN THIS BOOK

A. Zar.	Abodah Zarah
A. d. R. N.	Aboth de Rabbi Nathan
Ber.	Berachoth
Ber. R.	Bereshith Rabbah
Bez. .. ∴	Bezah
B. Kam.	Baba Kamma
B. Mez.	Baba Mezia
B. Bath.	Baba Bathra
Edu.	Eduioth
Erach	Erachin
Erub.	Erubin
Gitt.	Gittin
Hagg.	Haggigah
Hull.	Hullin
Jad.	Jadaim
Jeb.	Jebamoth
Jom.	Joma
Kidd.	Kiddushin
Koh. R.	Koheleth Rabbah
Mech.	Mechilta
Ned.	Nedarim
Pes.	Pesahim
Pesik. R.	Pesikta Rabbathi
Pesik. R. C.	Pesikta de Rab Cahana
Sanh.	Sanhedrin
Shabb.	Shabbath
Sot.	Sotah
Succ.	Succah
M. (before a title)	Mishnah
T. („ „)	Tosephta
b. („ „)	Babylonian Talmud
j. („ „)	Palestinian (Jerusalem) Talmud

Titles of books in Old and New Testaments and Apocrypha, etc., are abbreviated as in ordinary usage.